STAINED GLASS

THE NEW JERUSALEM

HEIDI RABE

ISBN: 099721211X
ISBN-13: 978-0-9972121-1-2

Photography by Heidi Rabe

The photo of Heidi Rabe has been provided by Tickle Photography at jordantickle.com.

I love You, Lord.
Thank You for a precious journey.

CONTENTS

1

BUTTON TREE PHOTOGRAPHY

It was a couple of weeks before Christmas when I said to my husband, "You know, I think I'm ready for a camera." Little did I know that he had already purchased one for me. It was a good beginner camera. In the months to come I graduated from the auto setting and began to experiment with all the bells and whistles. I even took two classes at the local art center where I learned about composition, light, and the value of a tripod.

Funny enough, I like to take pictures of buttons. I know that sounds strange, but please allow me tell you how it all began. When I was little, my grandparents had a closet in their basement in Richfield, Minnesota. Each shelf held exciting things like old dishes, shoes, scraps of material, and a box of buttons. In addition to the woods out back, the buttons became some of my favorite things. When my grandparents moved from their home in Richfield to a condominium in a neighboring city, my grandma gave me that box of buttons. Through the years some of the buttons decorated clothing, others rolled away, and many new ones became a part of the collection.

In recent years I've experienced many losses including both my grandmas, my mom, two aunts, and my cats. I like to think that God has used photography to help me see life with fresh eyes. Each time I take a picture of a button, I am reminded of the women who taught me how to sew. I call it "button tree photography." On the third anniversary of my mom's passing, I took the picture below. It, of course, reminds me of her.

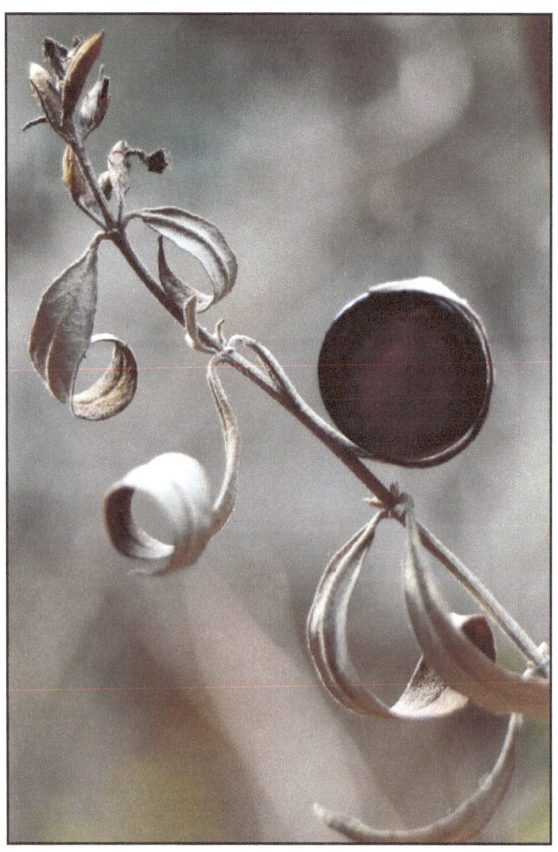

White

The Book of Revelation has more verses about the color white than any other book in the Bible. Throughout my testimony we will be sure to take a look at several passages from Revelation as well as Ezekiel.

The beloved disciple, John, describes a vision he had of the Lord while he was on the island of Patmos. He says, "The hair on his head was white like wool, as white as snow, and his eyes were like blazing fire" (Revelation 1:14). White hair often symbolizes wisdom. As we grow older, it is normal to sprout a few gray or white hairs. So, who else could be wiser than the First? In verse 17, Jesus describes Himself as the "First and the Last."

White can also symbolize righteousness, purity, holiness, dedication to God, and even joy.

Out of all my buttons, I would have to say that the white ones are my favorites. They go along beautifully with the small circles of light often captured in photos. I call them "buttons of light," although I'm sure they have a more technical name.

Day

I prefer natural light in photography. My teacher said that it is better to take pictures in the morning or the evening. Direct sunlight in the afternoon may provide too much light for most photographs. You may notice, however, that

I took a couple of my button pictures in the heat of the day. I am still learning, but it seems that with the right camera settings, it is possible to capture a button that has been lit up by the sunshine.

So, let's take a moment to go all the way back to the beginning of creation. When God first created the heavens and the earth, darkness was over the surface of the deep (Genesis 1:1-2). Then, in verse 3, we see the first words spoken from the mouth of God in Scripture. He said, "Let there be light." And at that very moment creation was given the beauty and goodness of light, which God called "day" (v. 5). And then He called the darkness "night." This all took place on the first day.

The Hebrew word for "light" in the first verses of Genesis speaks of illumination in every sense, including happiness. Yes, God's light brings happiness! I grew up in Minnesota where we experienced long winter days. When the sun decided to peek its face through an overcast sky, it made me happy. There is another sunshine, which I will call our "Son-shine." It is the light of the Lord Jesus. In John 8:12, He says, "I am the light of the world. Whoever follows me…will have the light of life." According to the Strong's Concordance, the Greek word for "light" in this verse means "to shine or make manifest, especially by rays." When I happen to catch a ray of sunshine in a picture, it reminds me of God's light, how it touches each one of us whether we realize it or not. Just as the sun lights the earth and the sky, so the Son of God lights our lives with His

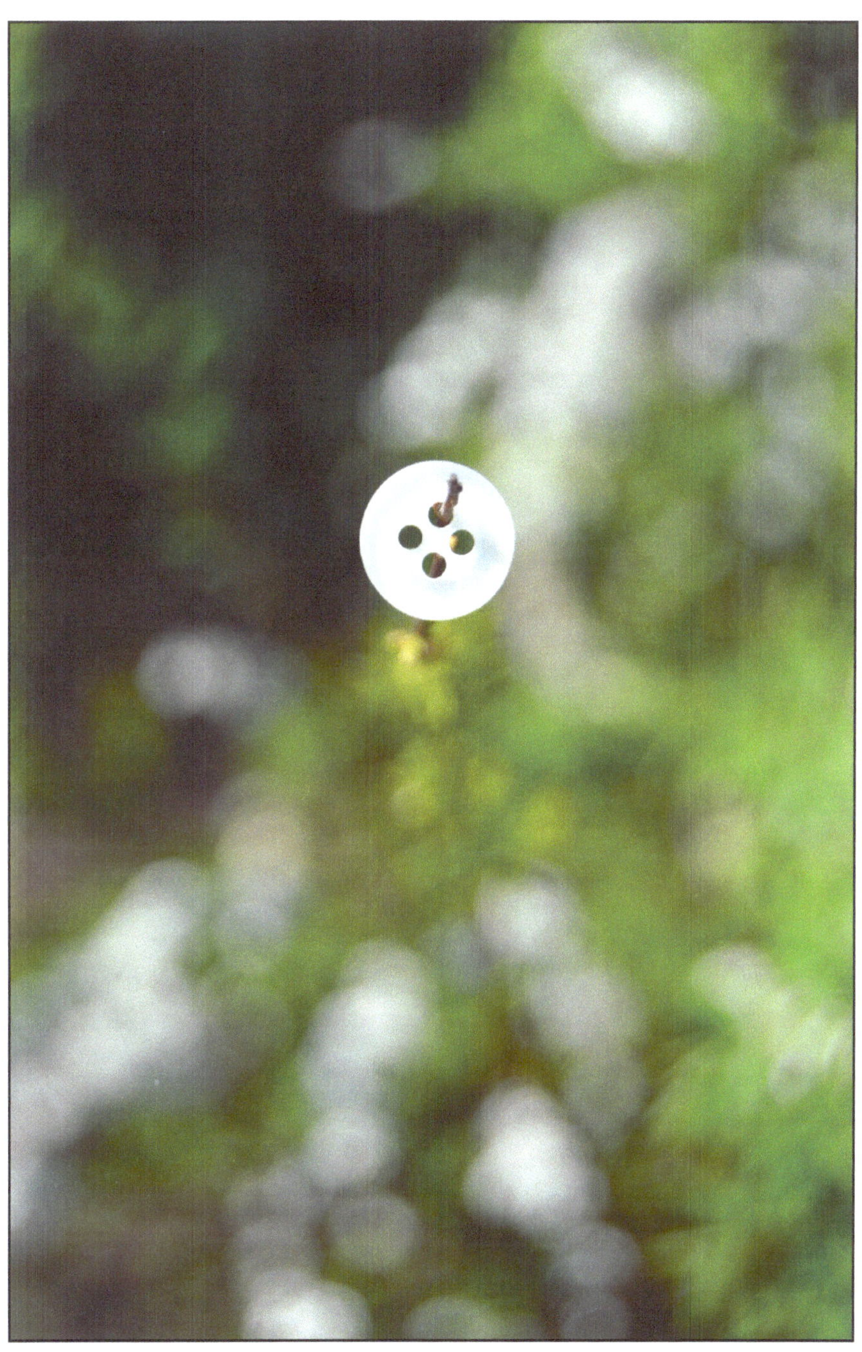

goodness and love. In fact, Psalm 23:6 says, "Surely your goodness and love will follow me all the days of my life...."

Night

A little over five years ago my husband, Kirk, and I went to the local animal shelter in search of a cat. We found a middle-aged tuxedo named Katarina, and she just happened to have special needs. They described her as "cute as a button," which really is an understatement. We brought Katarina Buttons home and fell in love with her snuggles and hugs.

Three years later, we decided Katarina needed a buddy. That's when we found Princess at the local mall. She was a year younger than Katty, and she had all black fur. I immediately said, "She looks like a Leila." We soon discovered that "Leila" means "night" in Hebrew. It also means "dark-haired beauty." I felt in my heart that Princess Leila was the right addition for our home. We quickly realized that she sits for food (just like Katarina), takes treats from our hands, nibbles crunchy pellets on her plate in straight lines, and walks around the edges of the rug. We call her a very proper panther.

The main reason I wanted a camera was to take pictures of Katarina and Leila. Black fur, much like nighttime photography, is a challenge to capture at times, but I think I'm finally getting the hang of it. I couldn't ask for better girls.

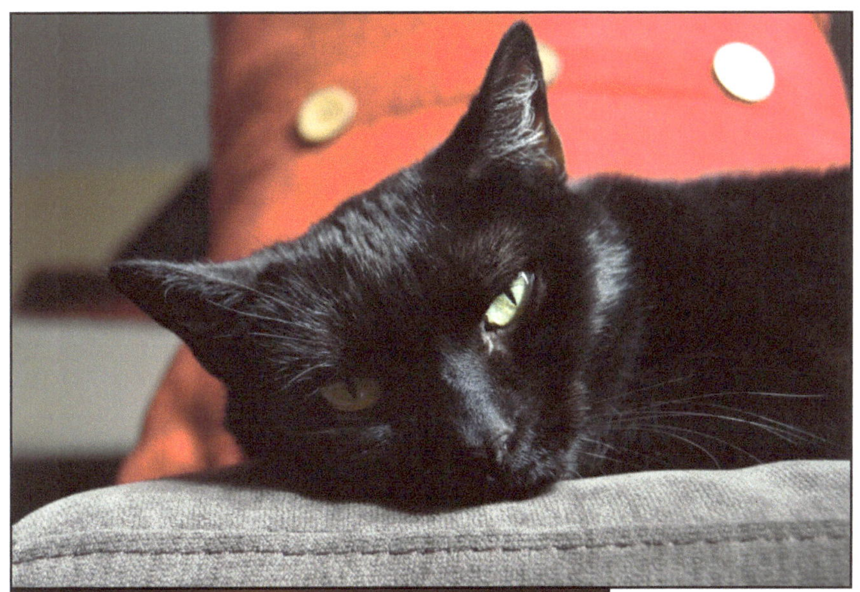

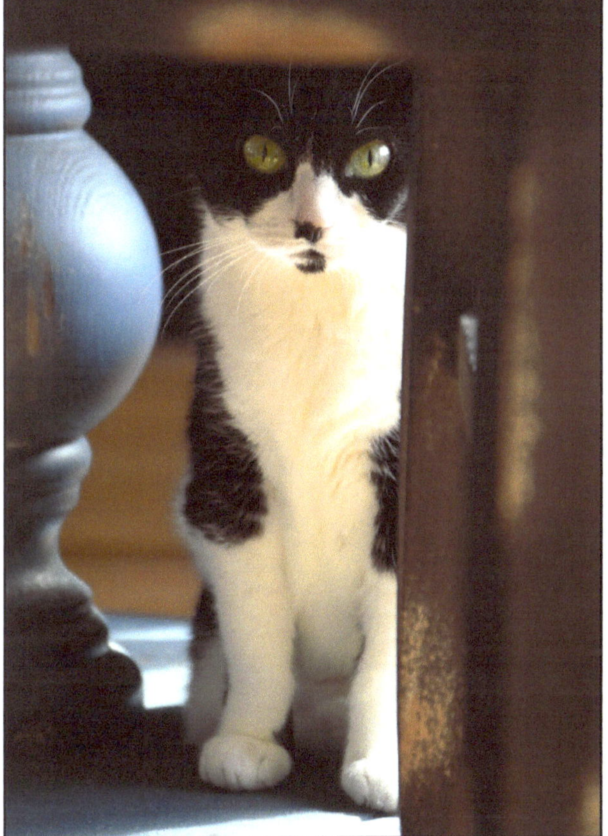

Leila
&
Katarina

Red is perhaps the most visible of all colors. It stands out like a sore thumb much like some of our personal sins. In Isaiah 1:18, the Lord likens our sins to scarlet, as red as crimson. White, however, is often described as the absence of color. In verse 18, the Lord tells us that our sins will be white as snow.

Jesus, of course, died on the cross for our sins. Ephesians 1:7 says, "In him we have redemption through his blood, the forgiveness of sins, in accordance with the riches of God's grace that he lavished on us." God's forgiveness cannot be earned (Ephesians 2:9). There are not enough good things we could ever do to erase our sins. It is only through the work of the cross. The blood of Jesus has been shed for our sins. He alone is perfect. He was the Lamb without blemish or defect (1 Peter 1:18-19). We have been redeemed by the precious blood of Christ. Our sins, though red as crimson, have been made as white as snow. Thank You, Lord!

Next we have the color orange, which reminds me of fire. The Greek word *phos* can translate to either "light" or "fire," depending on the context. A more common word for fire, however, is the Greek word *pur.* Generally speaking, fire often relates to a manifestation of God. For example, the angel of the Lord appears to Moses in some flames of fire within a bush (Exodus 3:2-6). Also, as already noted, John describes Jesus as having eyes like blazing fire.

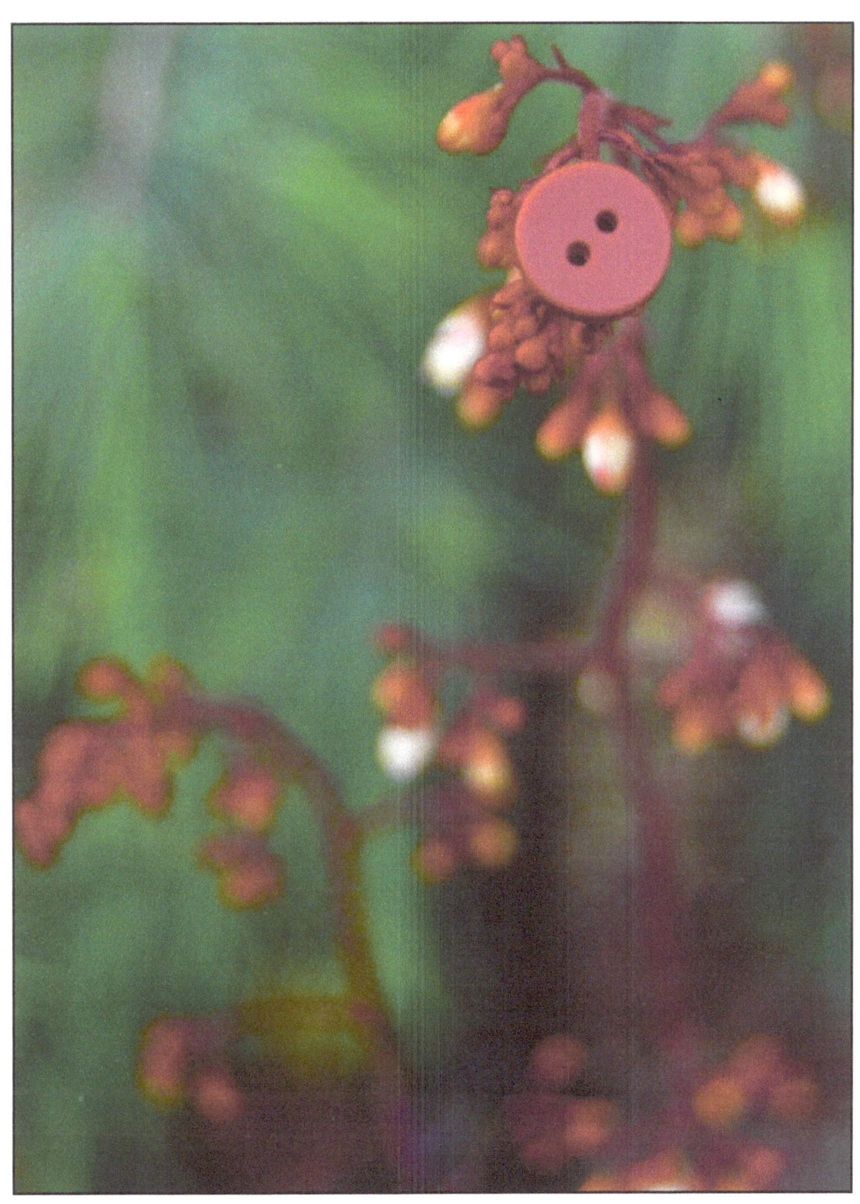

The Christmas story is one of my favorites in the Bible. When the Magi saw Jesus with His mother, Mary, they bowed down and worshiped Him (Matthew 2:11). Then they gave Him gifts of gold, frankincense, and myrrh.

Isaiah 60:6 tells us that people will come to the City of the Lord, "bearing gold and incense and proclaiming the praise of the Lord." Nations will draw close to God's light and radiance (vv. 3, 5). The very first verse in this chapter says, "Arise, shine, for your light has come, and the glory of the Lord rises upon you."

The color yellow represents many things in Scripture. It reminds us of God's light, glory, eternal life, and even the gifts of gold for our precious King.

The next color is green, which reminds me of gardens filled with flowers and trees. On the third day of creation, God said, "Let the land produce vegetation: seed-bearing plants and trees on the land that bear fruit with seed in it, according to their various kinds" (Genesis 1:11).

God's people are even compared to trees in the Bible. The prophet Jeremiah tells us, "Blessed is the one who trusts in the Lord, whose confidence is in him. They will be like a tree planted by the water that sends out its roots by the stream. It does not fear when heat comes; its leaves are always green. It has no worries in a year of drought and never fails to bear fruit" (Jeremiah 17:7-8).

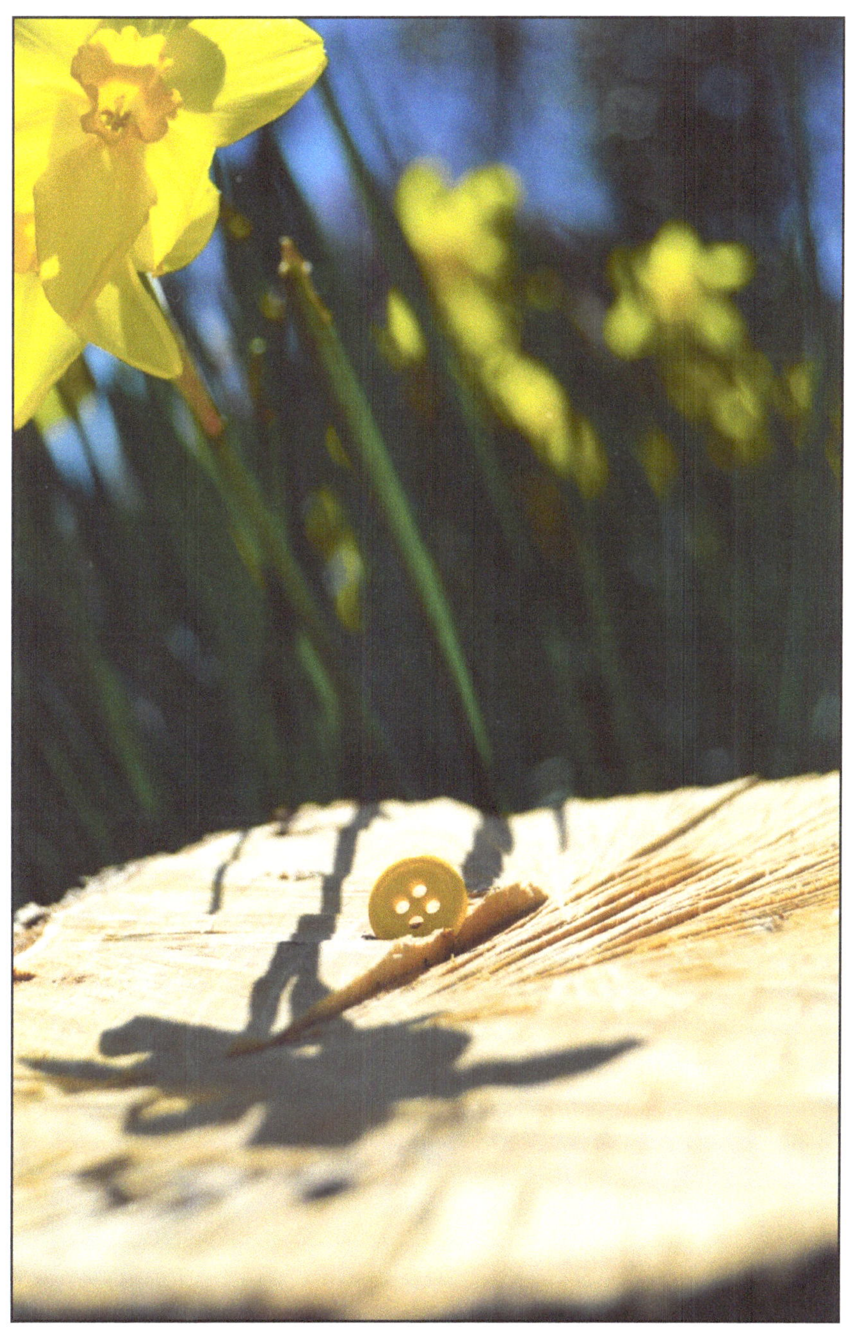

There is nothing like being outside on a clear day with a blue sky overhead. Ever since I was little, blue has been my favorite color. The thought of God and Heaven have been close to my heart for as long as I can remember.

The Hebrew word for "blue" is *tekeleth.* The color apparently comes from the shell of a cerulean mussel. The Strong's Concordance describes it as "violet" or "blue." As I think about a rainbow, I am reminded of the last three colors, which are blue, indigo, and violet. As we continue with our study, it will be helpful to keep these three colors in mind.

Blue often represents God, Heaven, royalty, and holy living. And purple maintains the royal message as it points to majesty, high officials, and wealth.

Perhaps the most well-known person associated with purple in the Bible (aside from Jesus, of course) is Lydia. She was a "seller of purple." Some translations add the word "cloth." Purple was an especially expensive dye at the time since it was difficult to extract. Therefore, only wealthy people could afford it.

When Paul ministered to Lydia, the Lord opened her heart to respond to the message (Acts 16:14). It is amazing to think that the King of kings, Jesus, became the focus for Lydia that day by the river. She would never have a more royal visitor.

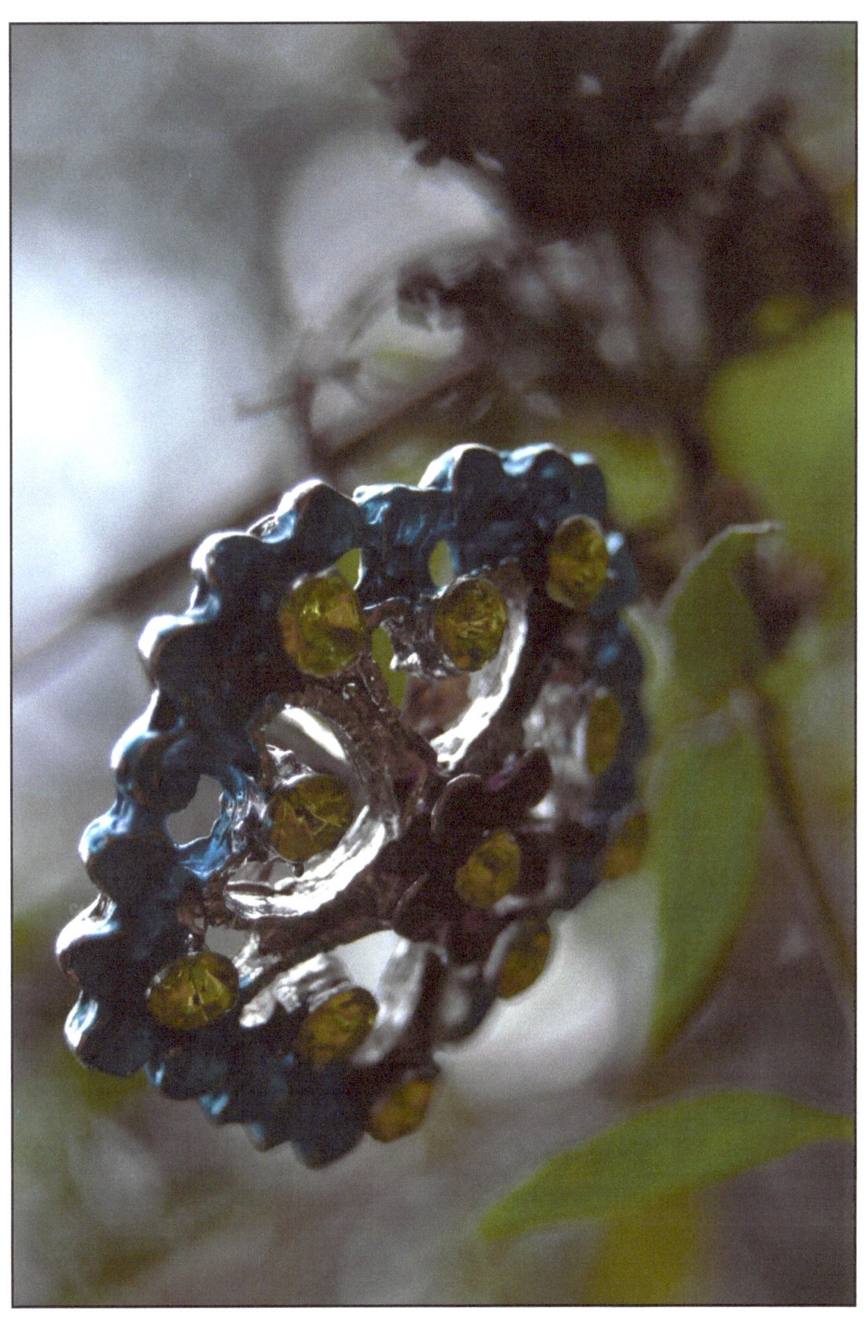

There are five references to crystal in the Bible: one in Job, one in Ezekiel, and three in Revelation. I hadn't planned on quoting Job, but his insight is noteworthy. In man's search for precious things, Job wonders where wisdom is found. He says, "Where does understanding dwell?" (Job 28:12). People mine for silver (v. 1). Lapis lazuli comes from rocks (v. 6). There is a constant search for hidden treasures, and yet people don't seem to comprehend the worth of wisdom (v. 13). Job says that "neither gold nor crystal can compare with it" (v. 17). The Strong's Concordance describes "crystal" as "glass" or "crystal." In Ezekiel, it resembles "rock crystal," "frost," or "ice." Then, in Revelation, it is "clear as crystal."

One thing suddenly comes to mind: I would never want anyone to compare my button pictures to a crystal ball. The miracle button, which I will introduce in chapter two, is what I call a "biblical button." The prophecy has already been laid out in Scripture. The picture within the button simply illustrates the story.

So, then, why did God give me this interesting button? According to Job, we can find wisdom and understanding with God (v. 23). So, in my pursuit of knowledge, I look to God for wisdom in His Word. I seek Him through prayer. Job's final verse tells us that the fear of the Lord is wisdom. May our greatest pursuit be to look to God, to fear Him, to know Him, to obey Him, and, of course, to love Him.

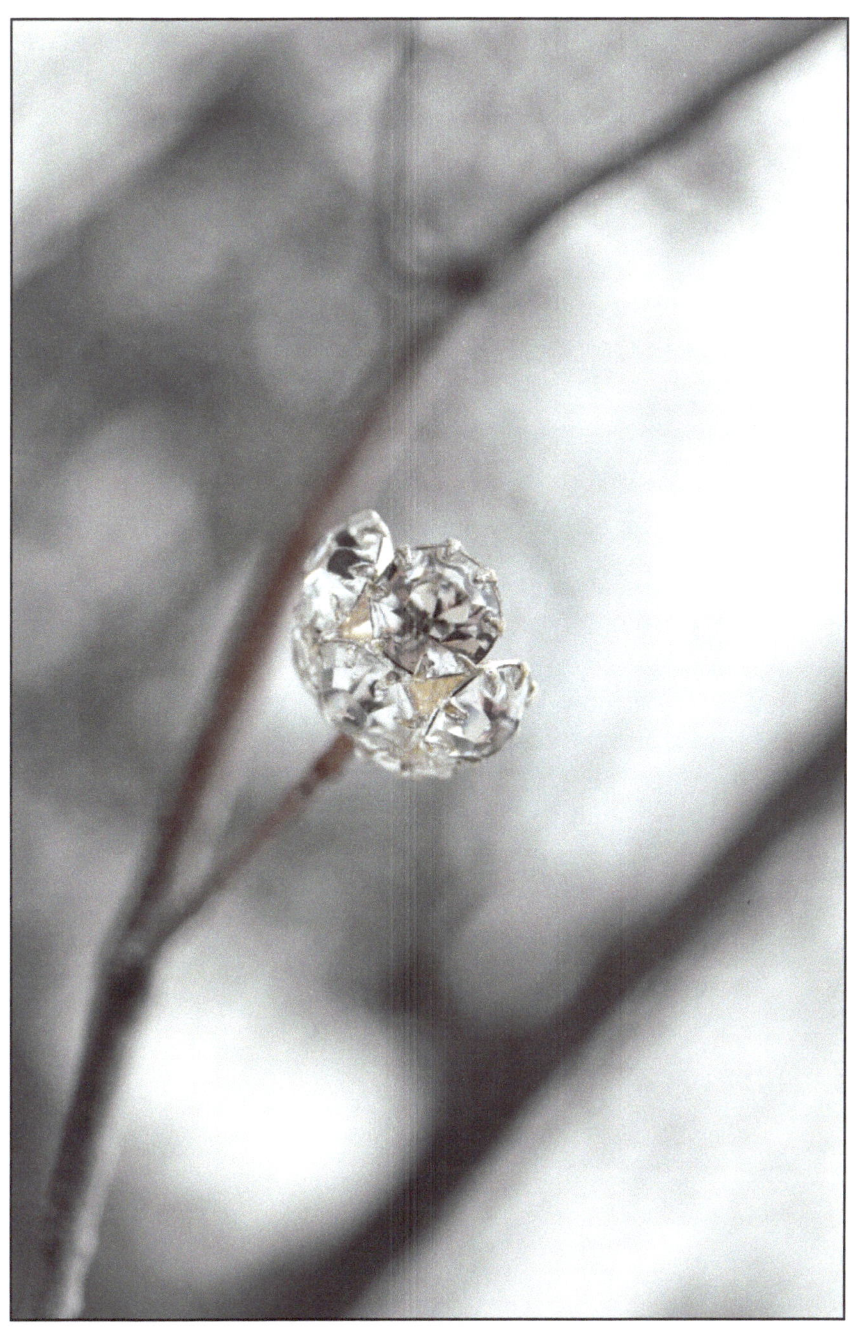

God's creation continues to amaze me. Each week a family of crows brings me gifts in exchange for food. The most interesting thing they ever left me was a small figurine of the Great Carpenter. They even found a button I had lost in the yard when I was taking pictures. Ten days later, I discovered it on my front step. It had a small scratch on its surface, probably from a beak.

As wonderful as I find life on earth right now, there is a place that God is preparing for us. Abraham even looked forward to "the city with foundations, whose architect and builder is God" (Hebrews 11:10). One day God will bring Heaven to the New Earth. Until that day arrives, we will continue to dream about the Holy City.

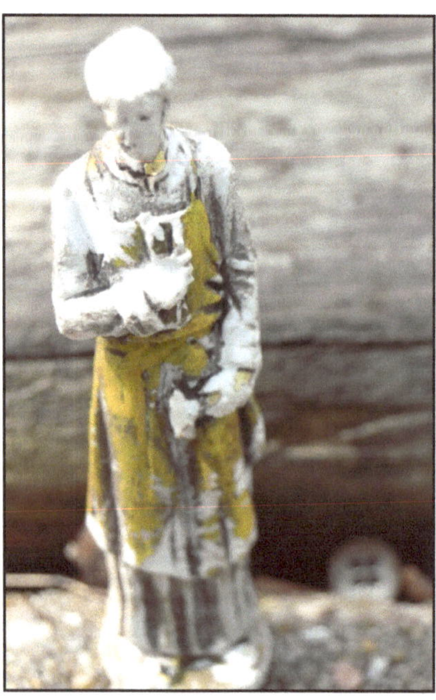

2

PRECIOUS GEM

It was the week of my birthday. Kirk and I made a trip to the local fabric store in search of some buttons. I had never photographed clear or sparkly buttons before, so I was very excited. As I mentioned earlier, I received a camera for Christmas and then started a photography class in March. It was now July, so I had about four months of button pictures under my belt. When we returned home from shopping that evening, the sun had nearly set. I rushed around the yard, hoping to snap a few pictures, but it was already getting dark.

The next morning couldn't arrive too soon. I finished some of my daily tasks so nothing would get in my way. It was around noon when I finally found a little time to go outside to my favorite butterfly bushes. Since the branches are thinner than most, they offer a perfect place to thread a tiny button.

It was about 95 degrees that afternoon and very humid. I had probably taken about fifty pictures when I began to feel beads of sweat forming on my forehead. Thankfully, the front door was only a few steps away. I headed inside to cool off and, of course, to take a look at the photos. Overall I thought they were nice, but then I noticed a small bubble inside one of the buttons. I didn't want to have to touch-up anything. I'm not very skilled in that area. Plus, it requires a great deal of patience and time. I thought it would be better to brave the heat and try again.

I grabbed a handful of buttons and placed them in my front pocket. I chose different ones this time. One was a small pink button with tiny facets like a diamond. I placed it on a branch and then proceeded to take several pictures in a row. Sometimes things just seem to fall into place. During those 15-20 seconds it seemed as if everything clicked. The way I took the pictures was different from anything I had ever experienced. I even tried to repeat the process in the months to come, but I couldn't figure it out. It may have been a once in a lifetime opportunity.

When I went inside to look at the pictures, I noticed a white cloud in the last three photos. There was nothing white around the butterfly bushes, so I figured condensation may have formed on the camera lens. It also could have come from the direct sunlight that day.

I immediately deleted any blurry pictures. Then I began to analyze the remaining ones. A good half an hour must have passed before I noticed something unusual. There was a

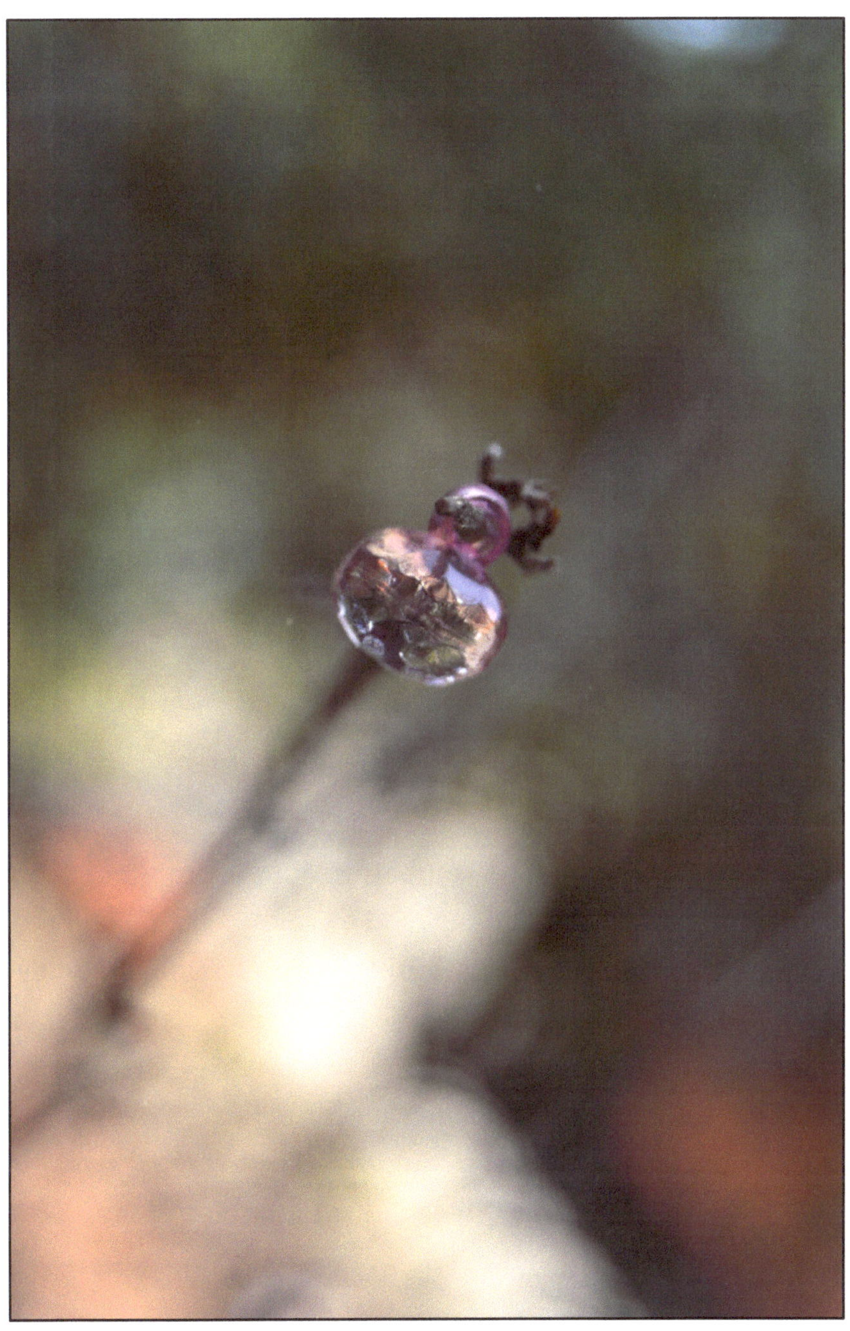

scene within one of the buttons. It looked like mountains and a river. I zoomed in to get a closer look. Right away I recognized it as the New Jerusalem! I quickly opened my Bible to Revelation and read the following: "I saw the Holy City, the new Jerusalem, coming down out of heaven from God…" (21:2). Then, in verse 10, John explains, "And he [the angel] carried me away in the Spirit to a mountain great and high, and showed me the Holy City, Jerusalem, coming down out of heaven from God. It shone with the glory of God, and its brilliance was like that of a very precious jewel, like a jasper, clear as crystal" (vv. 10-11). Finally, I read verse 18, which says, "The wall was made of jasper, and the city of pure gold, as pure as glass." I couldn't believe it! There it was in Scripture. And there it was inside of a tiny button. I couldn't wait for Kirk to get home from work, to show him this truly amazing birthday gift from the Lord.

Funny enough, try to guess the very first thing I did with the picture. It's almost too embarrassing to admit, but it certainly shows how humans tend to think. Okay, I will tell you. I actually covered up a couple of spots that I thought were imperfect. One was a bubble in the river. The other was the white spot in between the two golden buildings. That spot was surprisingly difficult to fill. There was a bright light around it that I couldn't seem to cover. As we take a closer look at the photo and what it represents, you will see what a mistake I made that day.

At this point in time, and in my heart, I knew the Lord had

given me these photos. Two of them seemed extraordinary. Unfortunately, I had deleted a couple of the pictures, but thankfully I recovered them months later.

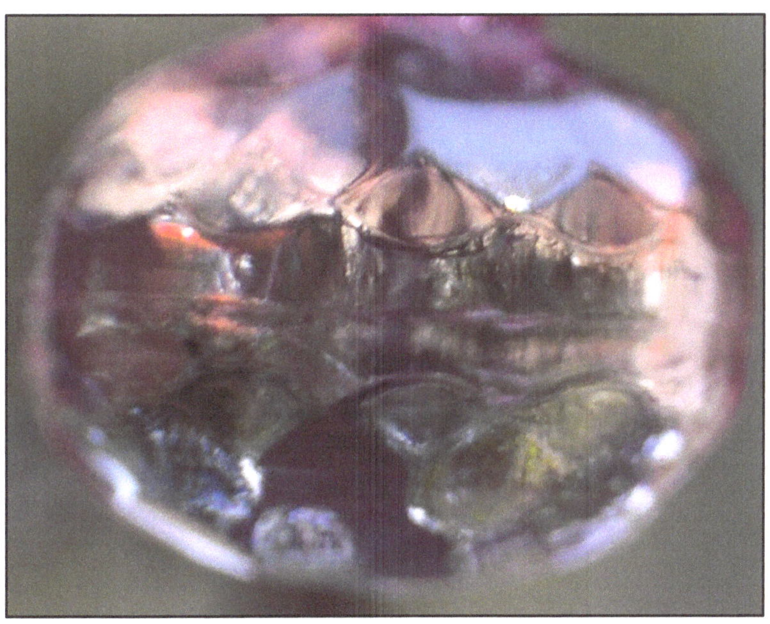

So, to me it seemed strange to say that God had given me photos. I was new at photography, so I didn't want to sound prideful. I have come to realize, however, that pride would take credit for this work of art. Sure, I picked out the button and placed it on the branch. I even snapped the photos. But there's no way I could have placed that *painting* inside of the button. I am below average when it comes to art, and I'm only a beginner photographer. But I guess the Lord likes to use the foolish things, doesn't He?

As I examined the "precious gem" of a picture, I tried to make sense of the colors. Red mulch covered the ground beneath the bush. There were also green leaves and purple flowers all around. When the flowers die, they take on a bronze or copper color. We also had a blue sky that day as well as a lot of sunlight. When combined with reflection and refraction, it is possible that God used a palette of available colors to create a picture of His heavenly home.

For six months I treasured two of the photos. I hadn't noticed anything significant about the other ones yet. Since it was a busy time in our lives, I rarely even looked at the two. But it was the last day of January, and Kirk was finishing an important project for work. While he kept busy upstairs, I sat in the office downstairs and began to look at the miracle photos more carefully. That's when I noticed a face above the red wall. I also saw an ox. I have cropped the first picture for better viewing.

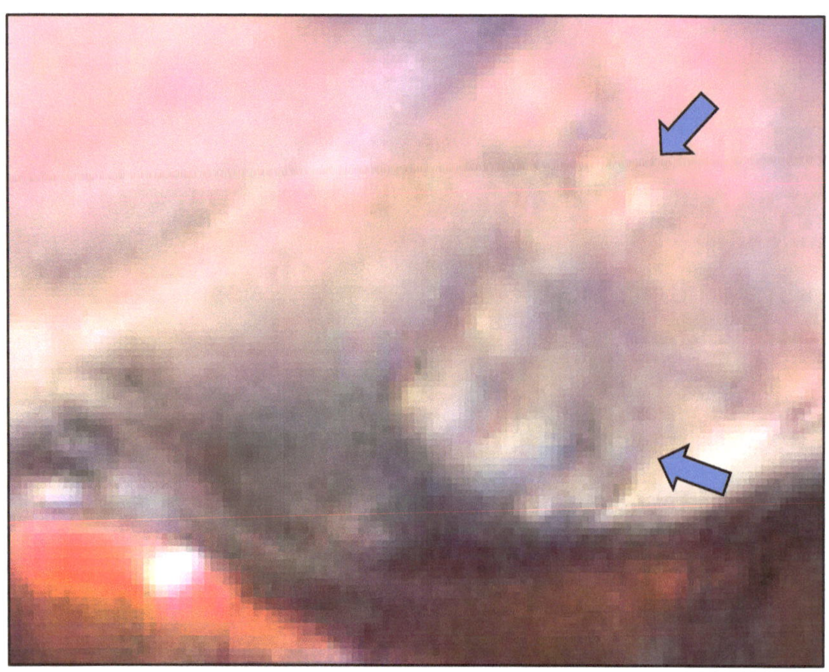

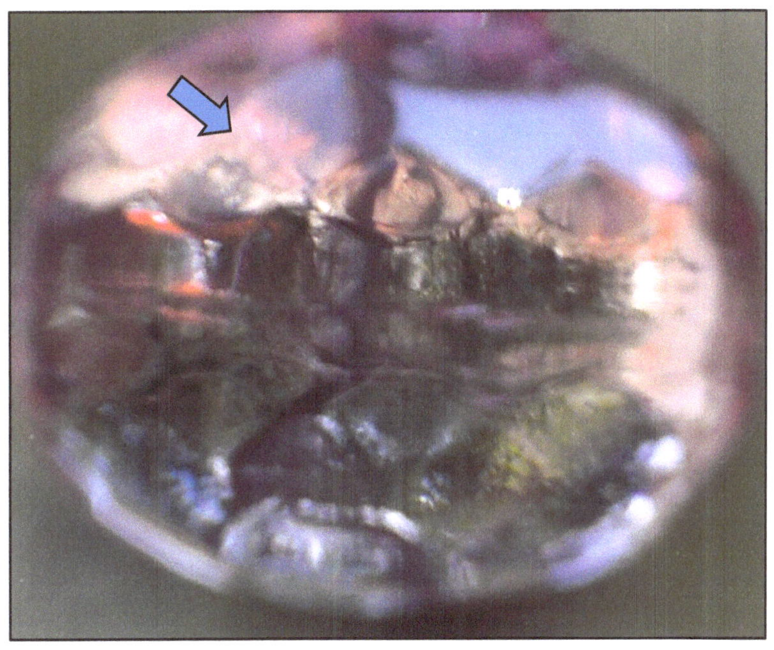

In the second picture, you can see a very clear image of a young ox or calf.

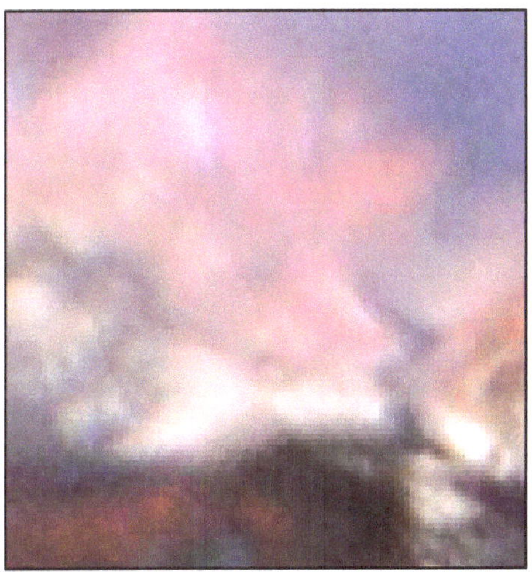

The Lord brought me to the Book of Ezekiel in October, so I was familiar with the four living creatures. In Ezekiel 1:10, the prophet tells us that "each of the four had the face of a human being, and on the right side each had the face of a lion, and on the left the face of an ox; each also had the face of an eagle." (Be sure to interpret this verse from the creatures' point of view.)

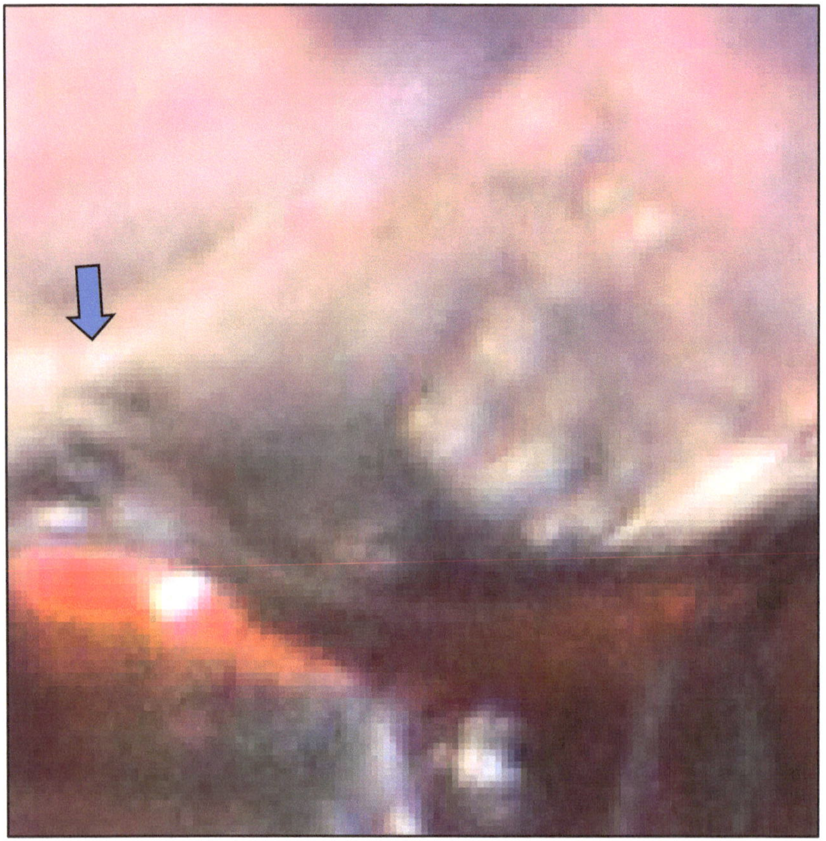

So, as I looked at the picture once again, I could see the eagle. It didn't have a point on its beak since, I'm guessing, it isn't necessary. Heaven and the New Earth won't have any death or killing (Revelation 21:4).

So then, according to Scripture, I knew exactly where the lion needed to be. As I zoomed in, I said, "Oh, there you are." He was in the right place, and he had a young face like the ox and eagle. Perhaps you can see him better in black and white.

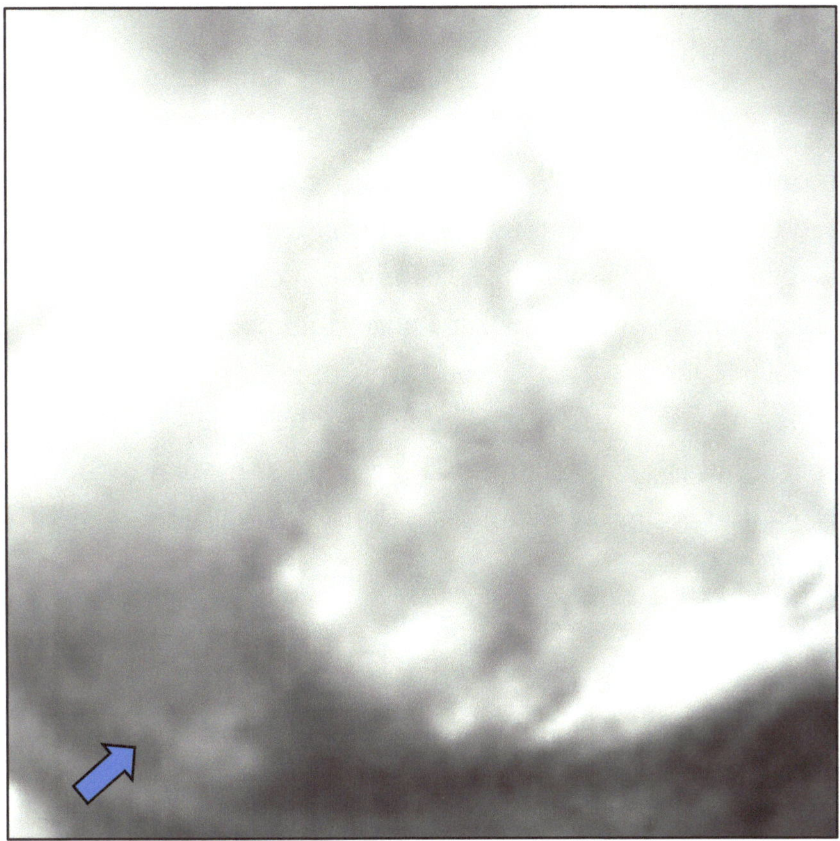

This was a new level of discovery for me. It really made my head go tilt. It was one thing to see the wall, the city, and the river. It was quite another thing to look at an image of one of God's heavenly creatures. For two days I tried to process what I had seen. This was more than I ever expected.

I've often said that God is the "God of the big picture" as well as "God of the details." There is nothing too big or too small for Him to handle. We can certainly see His great skill as an artist, as the Artist, when we look at the tiny details within the button.

In order to appreciate His craftsmanship, we should take a moment to look at the button's dimensions. The length of each side is .375 of an inch. That is equal to 6/16 or 3/8. The height is .25, which is 4/16 or 1/4 of an inch. We are talking about a very small space, and it keeps getting smaller. One facet on the button is only 1/16 of an inch! When we look at the four living creatures, they are in a space that is 1/16 of an inch long and 1/16 of an inch high. Now that is tiny! It is a miracle that we can see them at all.

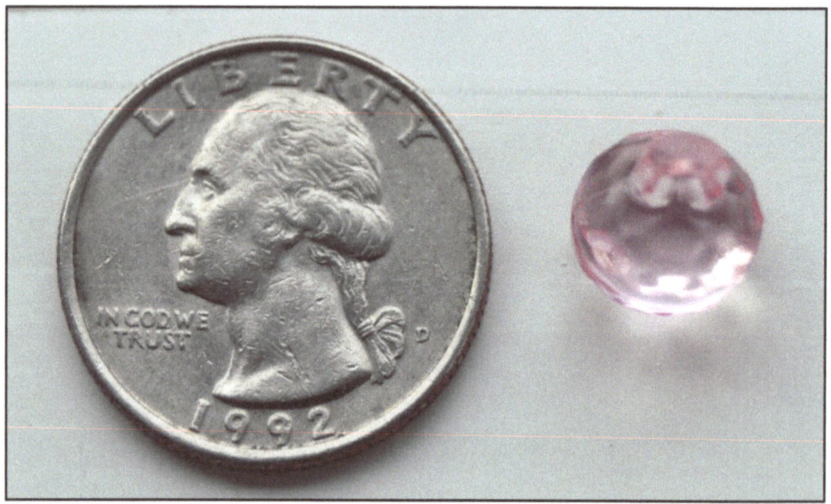

I have set the button next to a quarter in order to shed some light on its size.

Impressions

Stained glass windows are fascinating, don't you think? Vibrant colors get pieced together to create scenes from the Bible. I like to think of the windows as impressions of stories. Much like impressionistic paintings, we do not get to see every detail. There are plenty of things, however, to help us understand what the artist is trying to convey. When we look at *The Water Lily Pond* by Claude Monet, we know that we're looking at a pond underneath a bridge even though it isn't an exact representation. As we interpret the stained glass button, please keep an impressionistic view in mind. It is not necessarily an exact representation of Heaven and the New Jerusalem, but we can recognize enough details from Scripture to give us an idea of our eternal home.

When the angel measured the Holy City with a rod of gold, it came out to 12,000 stadia in length (Revelation 21:15-16). That is equal to about 1400 miles, which means God squeezed all of those miles into 3/8 of an inch! That is certainly a lot to fit into a tiny space. If someone tried to paint a picture of half of the United States in 3/8 of an inch, what do you suppose it would look like?

Study

This has been one of the most interesting journeys I've ever taken through Scripture. I find the pictures helpful in my studies. I hope you enjoy them too. So, let's get started!

"Study to shew thyself approved unto God,
a workman that needeth not to be ashamed,
rightly dividing the word of truth."

2 Timothy 2:15 (KJV)

3

FOUNDATIONS

Thank you for joining me on a walk through the Word of God (with the help of visual aids, of course). Throughout our study we will refer to the tabernacle of Moses, Solomon's temple, Herod's temple, and the millennial temple. According to Hebrews 8:5, the priests "serve at a sanctuary that is a copy and shadow of what is in heaven." So, what is in Heaven now? Well, we know that the New Jerusalem is in Heaven. And one day it will come down to the New Earth where God will live with His people forever (Revelation 21:2-3). When this happens, we will actually get to experience Heaven on Earth!

As we get a glimpse of the New Jerusalem in Scripture, let's take a moment to research three of the foundations. Please keep a heavenly perspective as we look at the photographs in light of God's Word.

I have reached the conclusion that the picture below represents the east side of the temple. When the man brought Ezekiel to the temple's entrance (probably the millennial temple), he saw water coming out from under the threshold and it was flowing toward the east (Ezekiel 47:1).

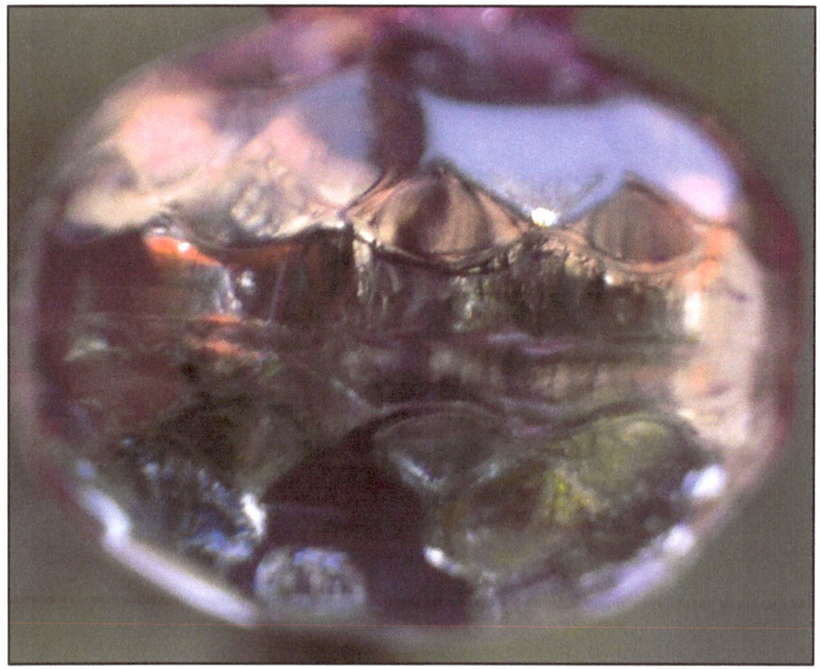

Kirk and I got blessed with a trip to Israel two years ago. After an extremely hot day in Masada, we were able to visit the Dead Sea. I have never seen so many people from all over the world having so much fun! We were like children, laughing and floating. It was a wonderful time.

Interestingly enough, the river that will come out from underneath the temple's threshold will flow east all the way to the Dead Sea (Ezekiel 47:8). At that time, the salty water will become fresh. Verse 9 tells us that "swarms of living creatures will live wherever the river flows."

As we look at the button picture, we can see the water flowing over steps or plateaus. The green banks on either side of the river, I believe, represent marshlands and trees. Therefore, I don't think the green on the ground represents a foundation.

The first three foundations of the New Jerusalem listed in Revelation are jasper, sapphire, and agate (21:19). Verse 18 tells us that the wall was also made of jasper. So, what color is jasper? Stones from ancient times do not necessarily go by the same names as what we have today. Therefore, we need to make an educated guess. One person said that red was the most common color of jasper, although it could also be found in yellow, brown, or green. The wall in this picture appears to have red, brown, green, and perhaps even a hint of yellow. It is possible, therefore, that the jasper wall has a variety of the jasper stone colors.

When John saw the Holy City, he described it as a very precious jewel, like a jasper, clear as crystal (v. 11). Some of the edges of the button could represent a transparent red jasper.

When the angel showed John the city, they began with the three gates on the east (v. 13). Therefore, I think the east side corresponds with the first three foundations in the list. We find the gates listed in the following way: east, north, south, and west. That means they would have started on the left side of the picture (our left) with the red stone and moved across to the right. As they turned the right corner, they would have arrived on the north side.

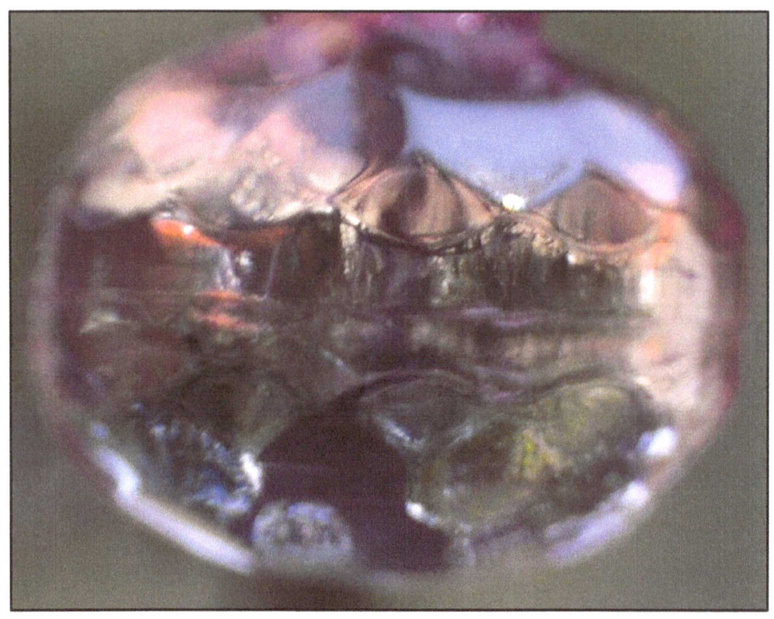

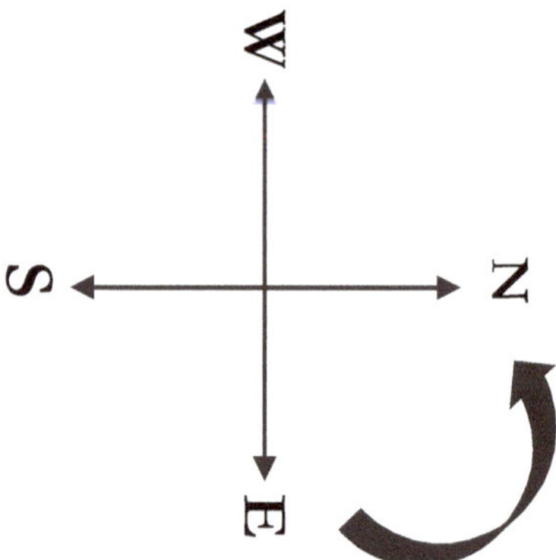

One day it occurred to me that the bright red stone on the ground could be the Lord's way of pointing out the first foundation, which is jasper. The next color we see lit up on the ground is light purple. Remember the last three colors of the rainbow? They are blue, indigo, and violet. When I first read that the second foundation was sapphire, I automatically thought of blue. The Strong's Concordance describes the stone as "a gem, perhaps used for scratching other substances." It says that it is probably the sapphire. Since the color is not clear in this explanation, I started to think that the stone could be different from what I originally imagined.

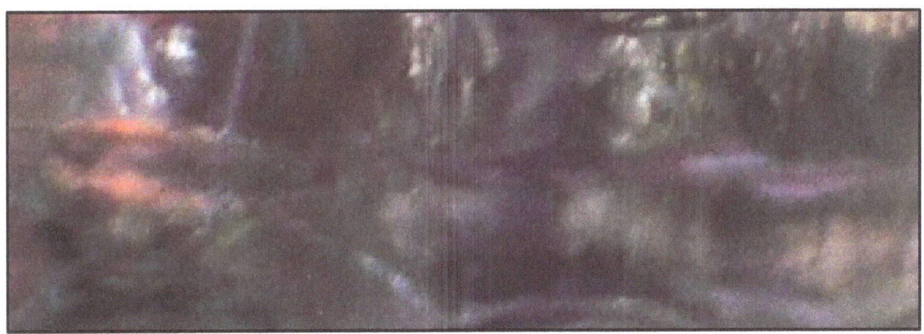

Since the sky in the picture on the left has a lavender tint (probably from the pink button), it is possible that the foundation contains more blue than what is pictured. In actuality, I believe the sapphire stone could be violet-blue.

Pliny the Elder lived around the time that the Book of Revelation was written. In his writing, he described "sappir" as "being like the night sky, spangled with stars." This points to the lapis lazuli stone, which can also have a violet-blue color.

A very interesting story in the Bible is when Moses, Aaron, Nadab, Abihu, and the seventy elders went up the mountain to see God (Exodus 24:9). "Under his feet was something like a pavement made of lapis lazuli, as bright blue as the sky" (v. 10). Please note how the violet in the center of the stone is like the sky in this picture.

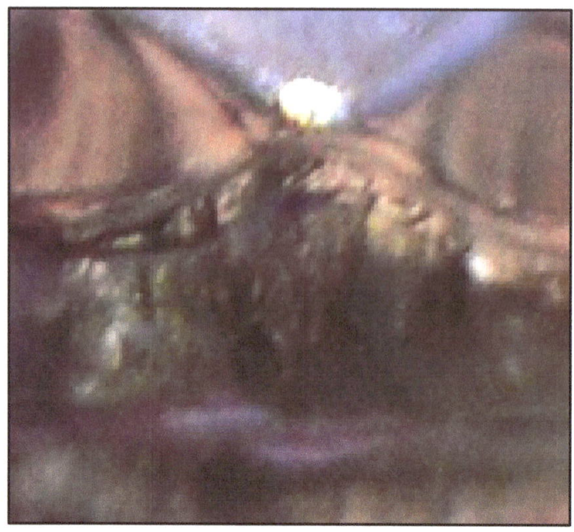

Finally, we arrive at the third foundation of the east wall. It is agate, which is also known as chalcedony. The Strong's Concordance describes it as "copper-like." On the right side of the picture, we can see the copper color just beginning to surface below the sapphire. If the foundations are in layers, they may look something like this.

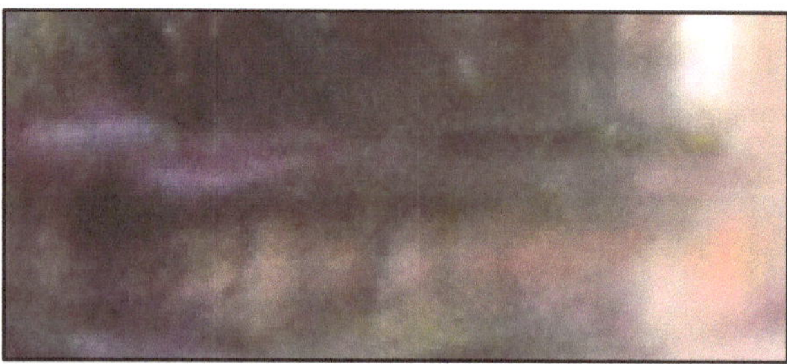

I tend to think that only one foundation represents one section of the city's wall. It is possible, however, that layers may exist where the foundations meet. This, of course, is only a theory.

Many years ago I had a dream about the New Jerusalem. This was before I knew anything about it. In my dream, Kirk and I were traveling through the mountains, which were gigantic red stones. It was similar to the red jasper in the picture. We met a man on the road who was making furniture out of the stone. It was all hand-carved with a garden filled with animals on each piece. I learned that he was making the furniture for our home, specifically for me. Like the Lord says, He has gone to prepare a place for us (John 14:2-3).

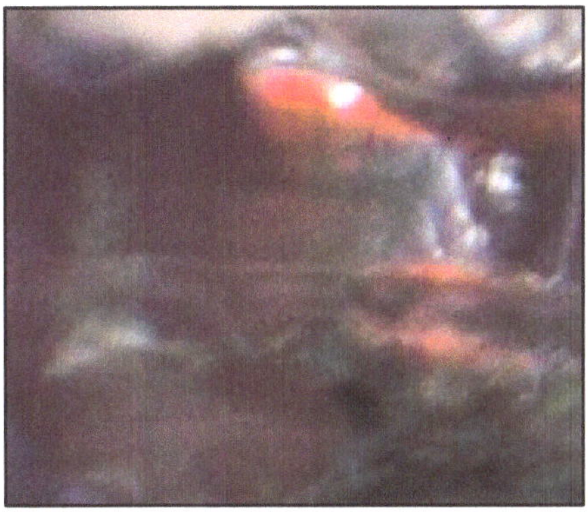

As we will see throughout our study, everything in Heaven and in the New Jerusalem points to Jesus. Without a strong foundation in Christ, our lives would crumble. Jesus told His disciples that "everyone who hears these words of mine and puts them into practice is like a wise man who built his house on the rock" (Matthew 7:24). There is no foundation more secure than our Rock, the chief cornerstone, Jesus (Matthew 21:42; Romans 9:33). In fact, the names of the twelve apostles of the Lamb are written on the twelve foundations (Revelation 21:14). These men shared the Good News of Jesus and, as a result, laid the foundation for the church.

"Enter his gates with thanksgiving and his courts with praise; give thanks to him and praise his name."

Psalm 100:4

4

GATES

God gave Moses precise instructions for the tabernacle as well as everything in it. Even Aaron's breastplate needed to have a specific design. There were twelve stones, one for each of the names of the sons of Israel (Exodus 28:21). The name of the tribe was engraved on the stone.

We find a similar situation in the New Jerusalem where the twelve gates will have the names of the twelve tribes (Revelation 21:12). Although they aren't listed in this verse, there is a reference to the millennial temple in Ezekiel. On the east side there will be three gates: the gate of Joseph, the gate of Benjamin, and the gate of Dan (Ezekiel 48:32). Ezekiel lists the gates from the north side to the east. Therefore, he would have started on the right side of the picture and moved across to the left side.

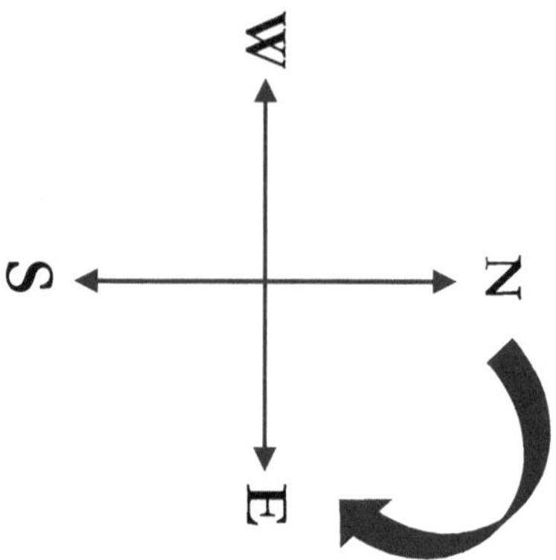

According to Ezekiel 48:32, here are the three tribes on the east side of the millennial temple in their proper order. (Remember to go from right to left.)

Dan **Benjamin** **Joseph**

Pearl

Let's begin with the gate in the middle. Perhaps the most common thing we know about Heaven is a pearly gate. John tells us that "the twelve gates were twelve pearls, each gate made of a single pearl" (Revelation 21:21). I have seen movies where they depict the gates like an entrance into a million dollar mansion, so that's how I imagined them until now. If my photos are correct, the gates actually resemble an igloo.

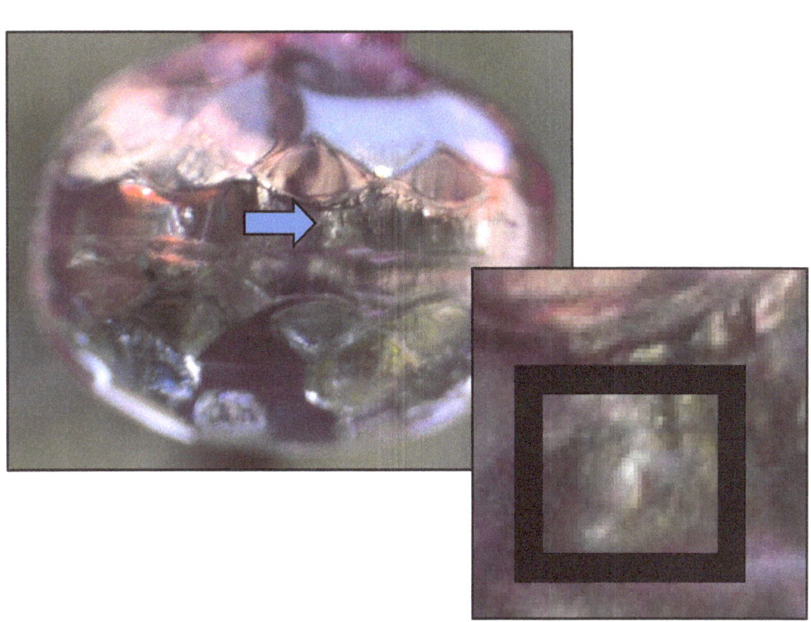

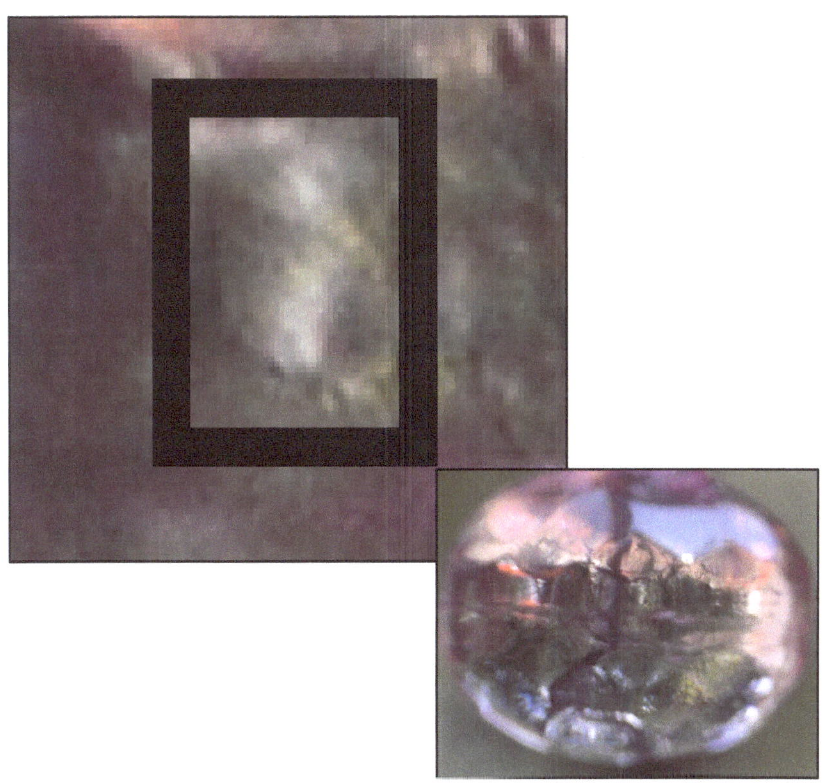

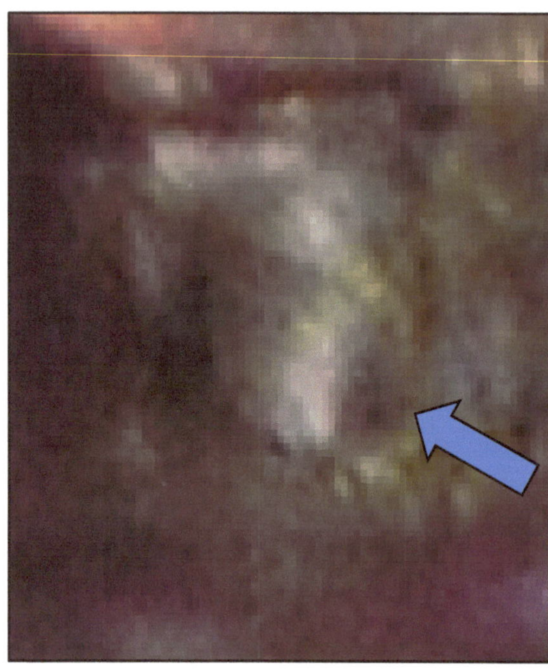

Entrance of a gate made of a single pearl

Jesus says that the Kingdom of Heaven is like a merchant looking for fine pearls (Matthew 13:45). When the man found one of great value, he sold everything he had and bought it (v. 46). There are some things in life that we may have to give up to follow the Lord. He is worth more than whatever we choose to leave behind. In John 14:6, Jesus tells Thomas, "I am the way and the truth and the life. No one comes to the Father except through me." Jesus is the door. He is the gate to Heaven (John 10:9). As we pass through a gate made of an enormous pearl one day, may we remember the great price that Jesus paid for salvation. May we praise His Name as we remember the words of Isaiah: "You will call your walls Salvation and your gates Praise" (Isaiah 60:18).

I grew up on the east side of Richfield, Minnesota. Some of the kids from the other side of town used to say, "East is least and west is best." In the Kingdom of Heaven, however, the east side has great value.

The East Gate is also known as the "Golden Gate." Since it was open on the day of the triumphal entry, some people believe Jesus entered the city through this gate.

Zechariah 9:9 tells us, "Rejoice greatly, Daughter Zion! Shout, Daughter Jerusalem! See, your king comes to you, righteous and victorious, lowly and riding on a donkey, on a colt, the foal of a donkey." The fulfillment of this prophecy is recorded in all four gospels. It is one of my favorite stories in the Bible, perhaps my very favorite!

There is an image of a donkey on the building above the East Gate in the second picture. It could be a memorial for the Lord to remember His triumphal entry into the Holy City. Please note that the donkey is lying down. Perhaps it is a symbol that he is resting from the finished work of the Lord.

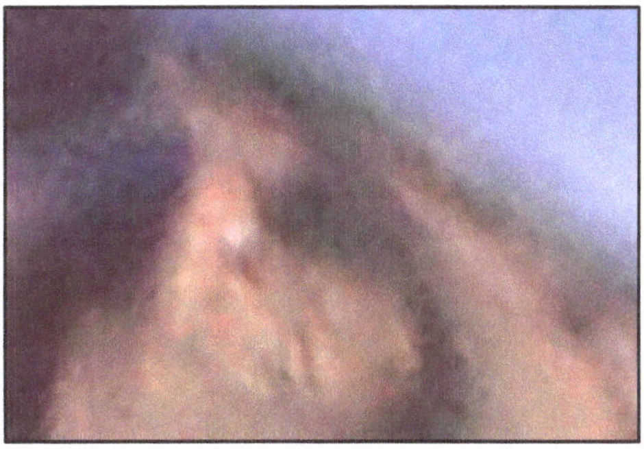

Donkey above the East Gate

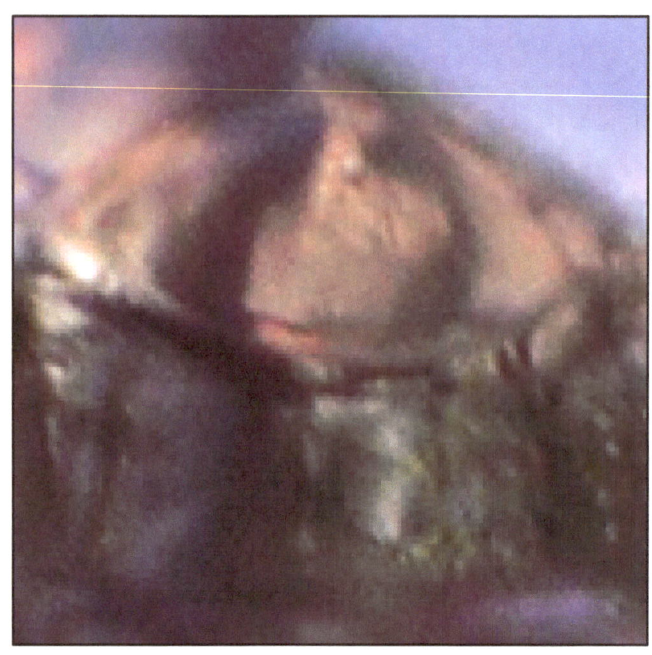

Glory in the East

The glory of the Lord led the Israelites out of Egypt. "By day the Lord went ahead of them in a pillar of cloud to guide them on their way and by night in a pillar of fire to give them light…" (Exodus 13:21). The glory of the Lord also appeared to Moses in flames of fire from within a bush (3:2).

The people built Solomon's temple to house the glory of God. First Kings 8:10 tells us that when the priests withdrew from the holy place, the cloud filled the temple. Unfortunately, God's presence eventually left Solomon's temple because of the people's sins. Ezekiel 10:18 explains that "the glory of the Lord departed from over the threshold of the temple and stopped above the cherubim." In verse 19 we learn that the cherubim stopped at the entrance of the East Gate. Ezekiel cries out to the Lord, and God shows him a vision of Israel's future restoration. Ezekiel tells us, "Then the man brought me to the gate facing east, and I saw the glory of the God of Israel coming from the east. His voice was like the roar of rushing waters, and the land was radiant with his glory" (43:1-2). This is an important verse for our study. I believe the photo below represents the return of God's glory. The land is certainly radiant! I have never seen a *painting* quite like it.

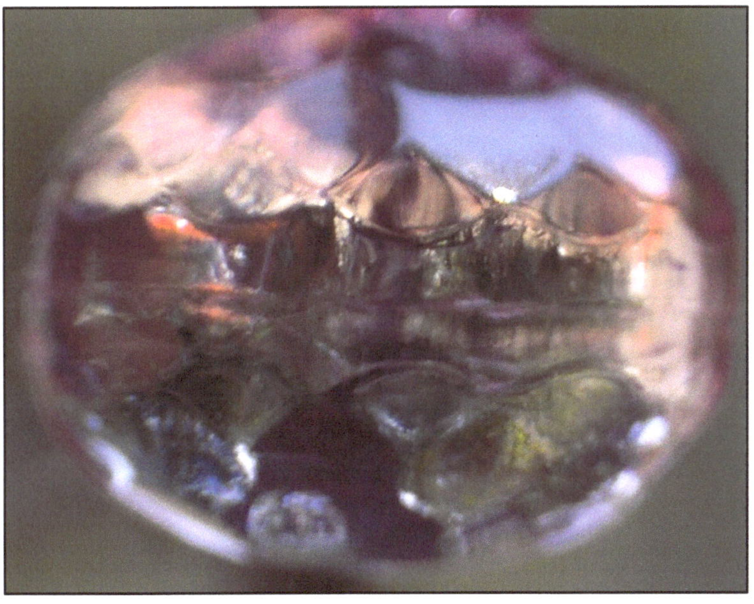

Benjamin

It is possible that the tribe of Benjamin's name has a spot on the East Gate in the New Jerusalem. I thought that

Joseph, Judah, or Levi would have had this place of honor, but instead God may have chosen the youngest of Jacob's sons and the smallest of the tribes.

As I researched Benjamin, I began to see why God may have chosen him. He was the second dearest son after Joseph. Before Moses died, he blessed the Israelites. This is what he had to say about Benjamin: "Let the beloved of the Lord rest secure in him, for he shields him all day long, and the one the Lord loves rests between his shoulders" (Deuteronomy 33:12).

The tribe of Benjamin received a very important piece of land. It included the cities of Jericho, Bethel, Gibeon, Ramah, Mizpah, and Jerusalem (Joshua 18:21-28). As we already know, Jerusalem is the city that God loves. He has chosen it for His dwelling place.

The tribe of Benjamin was also strong in battle. When Jacob gathered his sons together, he told each one what would happen in the days to come. This is what he said about his youngest son: "Benjamin is a ravenous wolf; in the morning he devours the prey, in the evening he divides the plunder" (Genesis 49:27). I was pleasantly surprised to find the face of a wolf above the East Gate in the first picture.

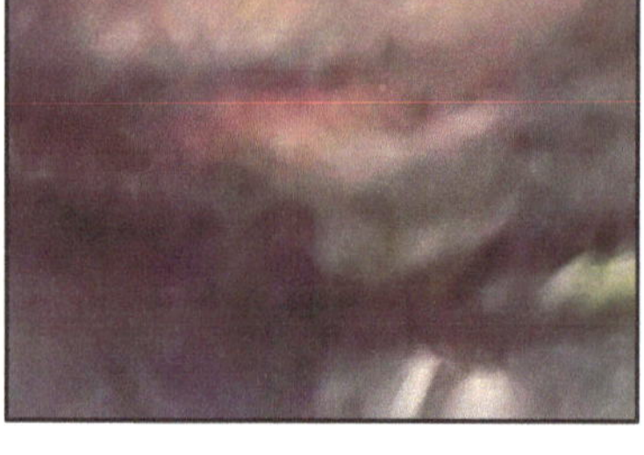

Horse Gate (Dan)

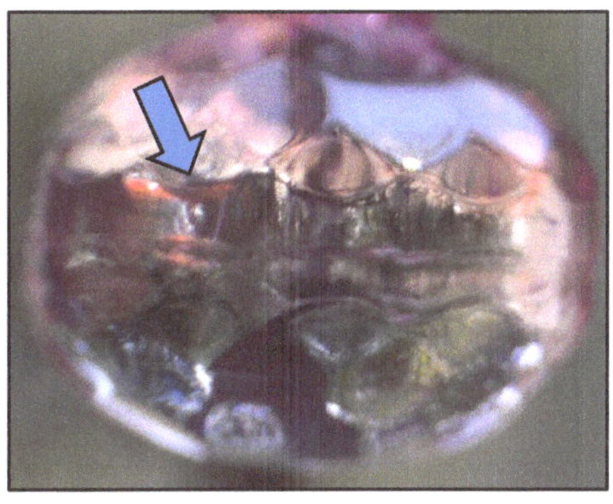

Next, we arrive at the Horse Gate, which is on our left side. If you look carefully at the picture below, you can see part of the pearl in the lower left-hand corner. There is also a tunnel that leads to the city. John tells us that the wall is 144 cubits thick (Revelation 21:17). That comes out to about 216 feet long!

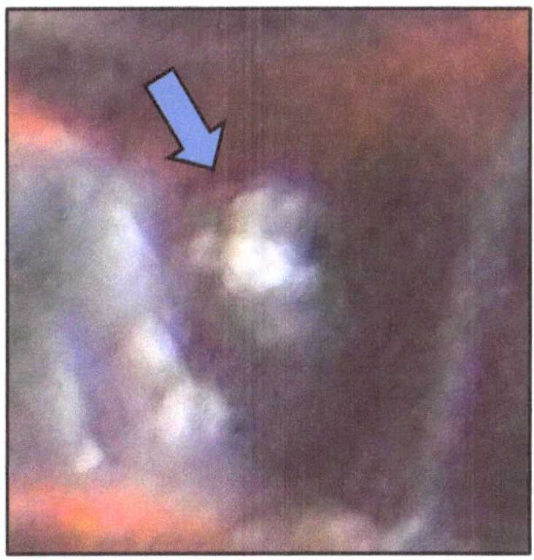

During biblical times, people rode donkeys and camels from one place to another. Horses, however, were animals of war. They would pull chariots and carry soldiers. The Horse Gate was close to the king's stables, so it was easy for the men to ride their horses out of this gate to war.

Third Picture

You may recall that I discovered the image of the four living creatures on the last day of January. The next day, of course, was the first of February. It was also Katarina and Leila's birthday. I decided to take some pictures of them since the sunlight was perfect in the kitchen that afternoon. That's when I noticed that all the pictures from the miracle button were still on the memory card. I thought I had deleted them, but there they were! The last picture, which we will call the third picture, became the photo of interest that day. I didn't even look at the other ones until about a month later.

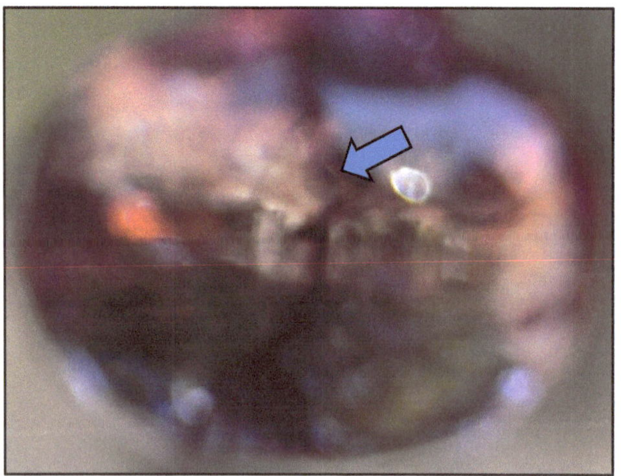

The third picture is blurry since it represents movement. In the center of the photo, towards the top, is an image of a white horse. You can see the top of its head. There is also a hoof by the side of its face. I believe this could be the Lord's horse. John tells us, "I saw heaven standing open and there before me was a white horse, whose rider is called Faithful and True" (Revelation 19:11). Then, in verse 14, it says, "The armies of heaven were following him, riding on white horses and dressed in fine linen, white and clean." Since we see a great deal of white in the clouds on the left side of the picture, it is possible that it represents the armies of Heaven. We will take a closer look at it later.

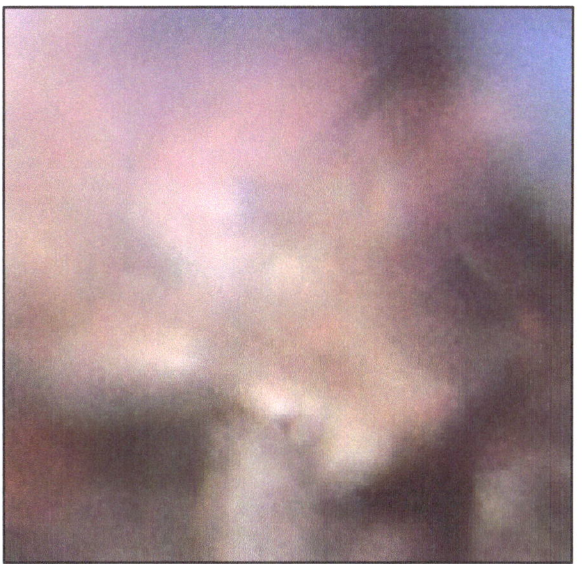

Dan

Rachel had two sons, Joseph and Benjamin. And Rachel's servant, Bilhah, was the mother of Dan and Naphtali (Genesis 35:24-25). It is interesting to note that three of the four sons may make up the east side of the New Jerusalem.

The tribe of Dan was the most efficient of the warriors. They were a large group, numbering around 62,700 men

(Numbers 1:38-39). The tribe was given a small, yet fertile piece of land by the Mediterranean Sea. They decided, however, to take some land south of modern-day Lebanon instead. Since Dan fell into idolatry, their tribe was left out of the 144,000 listed in Revelation.

When Moses blessed the Israelites, this is what he said about Dan: "Dan is a lion's cub, springing out of Bashan" (Deuteronomy 33:22). Months ago I noticed a small cub in the first picture. I didn't know what to think of it. Since it is near the Horse Gate, the gate of Dan, I believe it could represent this tribe.

Cub

I also discovered a snake in the second picture, which I think points to the tribe of Dan as well. When Jacob told his sons what would happen to them in the days to come, this is what he said about Dan: "Dan will provide justice for his people as one of the tribes of Israel. Dan will be a snake by the roadside, a viper along the path, that bites the horse's heels so that its rider tumbles backward. I look for your deliverance, Lord" (Genesis 49:16-18).

Since some of the picture's images are too small for print, I may not get to share everything I had hoped. I will, however, do my best to explain what I see.

As you may already know, the three gates in our study represent the end times. First, we have the day of the Lord and perhaps a part of the tribulation with the Horse Gate. Then we look to the Lord's return to Jerusalem with the East Gate. And the last gate is the Inspection Gate, which reminds us that the Lord will judge each one of us. Those who have died without Christ will receive judgment according to what they have done as recorded in the books (Revelation 20:12).

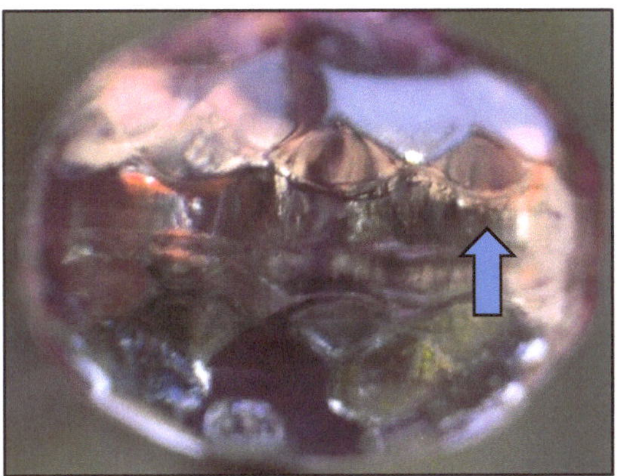

The book of life, however, belongs to Jesus the Lamb (21:27). He tells us that the one who is victorious dresses in white. He will never blot out the name of that person from the book of life, but will acknowledge that name before His Father and His angels (3:5).

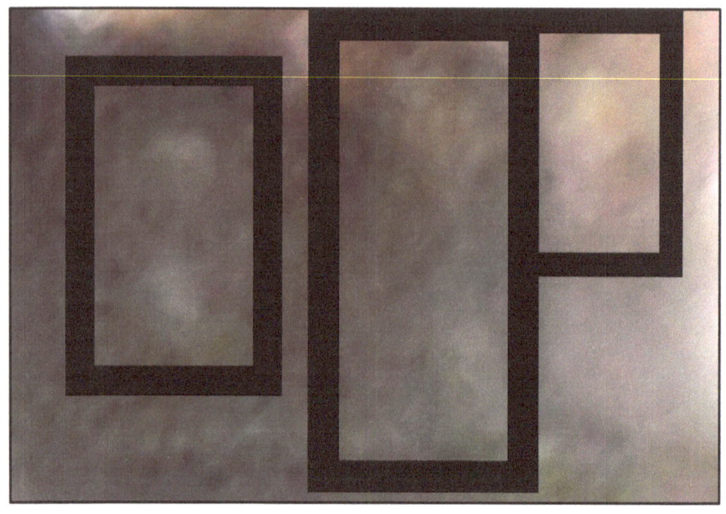

I know it is challenging to see the images in the picture above, but I will point them out anyway. The first box highlights either an older man writing in a book or a bride. The second box shows us a young woman dressed as a bride. And the third box draws our attention to an older man reading a book, which I think is the book of life.

Sheep & Goats

Only one image startled me when I first saw it. You may have already noticed the black goat by the Inspection Gate. He's not very attractive, but neither are sinful deeds.

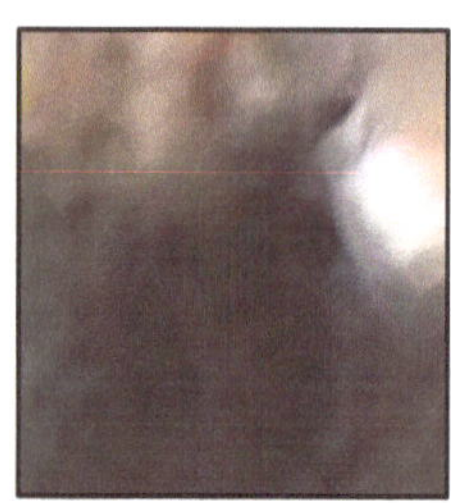

Jesus tells His disciples, "When the Son of Man comes in his glory, and all the angels with him, he will sit on his glorious throne. All the nations will be gathered before him, and he will separate the people one from another as a shepherd separates the sheep from the goats" (Matthew 25:31-32). The sheep will inherit the Kingdom of Heaven (v. 34), and the goats will go into the eternal fire prepared for the devil and his angels (v. 41).

Bulls & Goats

Hebrews 10:4 tells us that "it is impossible for the blood of bulls and goats to take away sins." Only the blood of Jesus purifies us from all sin (1 John 1:7).

In the picture below, we can see two bulls. The goat is sitting on the neck of one bull, while the other, a reddish bull, is near the center of the picture.

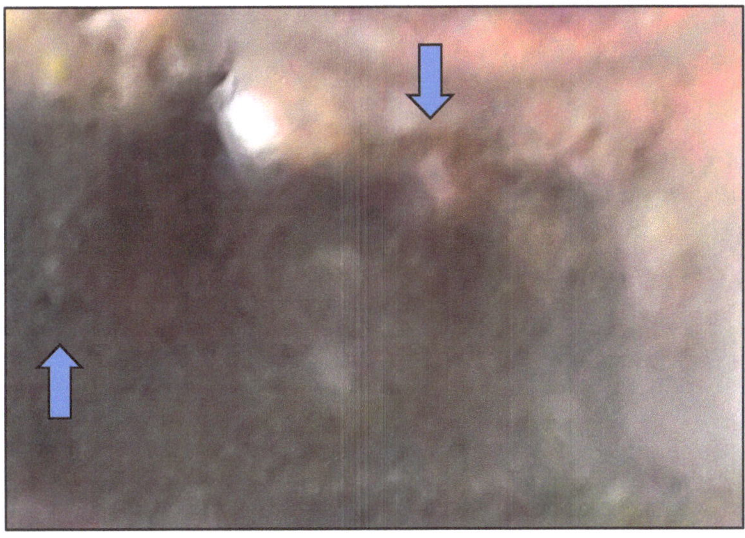

It is possible that the reddish bull in the picture could be a red heifer instead. The Lord told Moses and Aaron to have the Israelites bring them a red heifer without defect or blemish, one that had never been under a yoke (Numbers 19:1-2). The priest had the heifer taken outside the camp and slaughtered (v. 3). The blood was then sprinkled and the heifer burned (vv. 4-5). And they used the ashes for purification from sin (v. 9).

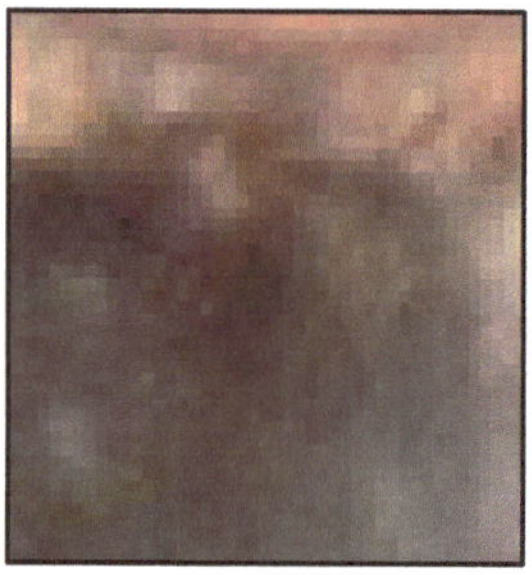

The "Miphkad altar" is the name of the altar of sacrifice used for the red heifer. "Miphkad" means "numbering," like in a census. A shepherd counting his sheep also comes to mind. The Miphkad Gate is another name for the Inspection Gate (Nehemiah 3:31, KJV). This is where David would meet with his troops to inspect them. The Miphkad altar was east of the gate, situated on the Mount of Olives. This is where several important events took place, including the beginning of the triumphal entry, Jesus' ascension into Heaven (Luke 24:51), and, of course, His glorious return which is yet to come (Zechariah 14:4; Acts 1:11). Jesus also suffered and died outside the city gate (Hebrews 13:11-12). I personally believe He died on the Mount of Olives near the Miphkad altar.

In the second photo, which was actually taken before the other two, we can see Zechariah's prophecy of the Lord's return. Zechariah tells us, "On that day his feet will stand on the Mount of Olives, east of Jerusalem, and the Mount of Olives will be split in two from east to west, forming a great valley, with half of the mountain moving north and half moving south" (Zechariah 14:4).

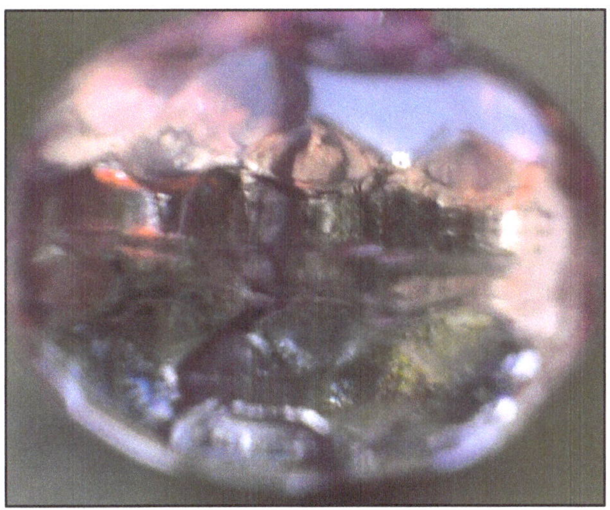

In the picture above, we are looking at a heavenly view of God's plan for earth from "outside the camp." Zechariah's prophecy will be fulfilled on earth before the New Jerusalem comes down out of Heaven.

Joseph

Look at how many miles we have traveled! According to Scripture, it has been about 1400. We will linger at the last gate a little longer and consider Jacob's son, Joseph, the prince among his brothers. Since Joseph was dearly loved by his father, he receives the longest blessing (Genesis 49:22-26). Verse 26 explains that "your father's blessings are greater than the blessings of the ancient mountains, than the bounty of the age-old hills." This reminds me of the Mount of Olives, of the blessings we receive through the offering of Jesus for our sins. In Deuteronomy 33:17, Moses blesses Joseph by saying, "In majesty he is like a firstborn bull." As already mentioned, it is impossible for the blood of bulls and goats to take away sins. So, as we look at each animal at the Miphkad Gate, may we remember our Father's love. "For God so loved the world that he gave his one and only Son, that whoever believes in him shall not perish but have eternal life" (John 3:16).

Angels

As we come to a close on our study of gates, we learn that the gates in the New Jerusalem will never be shut (Revelation 21:25). There won't be any night and nothing dangerous will try to enter. Plus, an angel will be positioned at each one of the gates (v. 12).

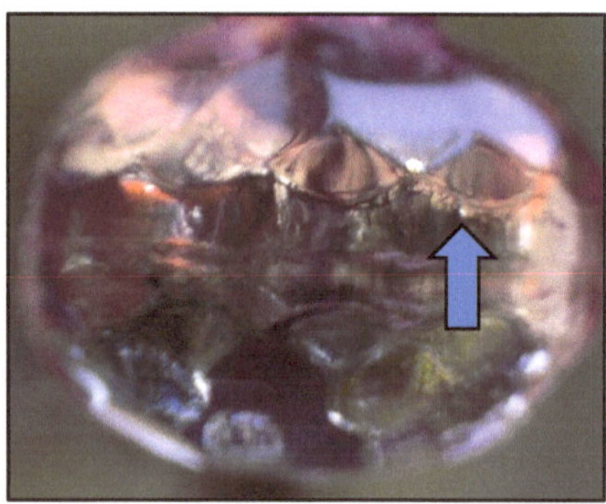

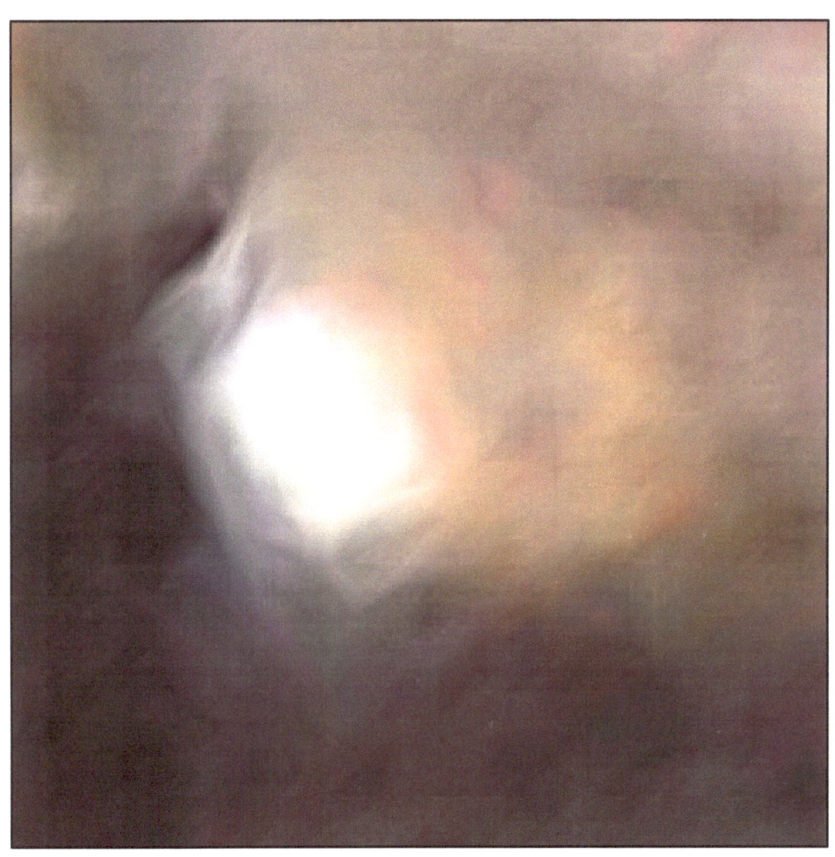

"In my thirtieth year, in the fourth month on the fifth day,
while I was among the exiles by the Kebar River,
the heavens were opened and I saw visions of God."

Ezekiel 1:1

5

EZEKIEL

The first chapter of Ezekiel has helped clarify a number of things for me. What I thought was a branch (in the picture) suddenly became a storm and a river. The prophet describes what he saw that day. He says, "I looked, and I saw a windstorm coming out of the north—an immense cloud with flashing lightning and surrounded by brilliant light. The center of the fire looked like glowing metal…" (Ezekiel 1:4). The King James Version calls the storm a "whirlwind" and describes the color as "amber."

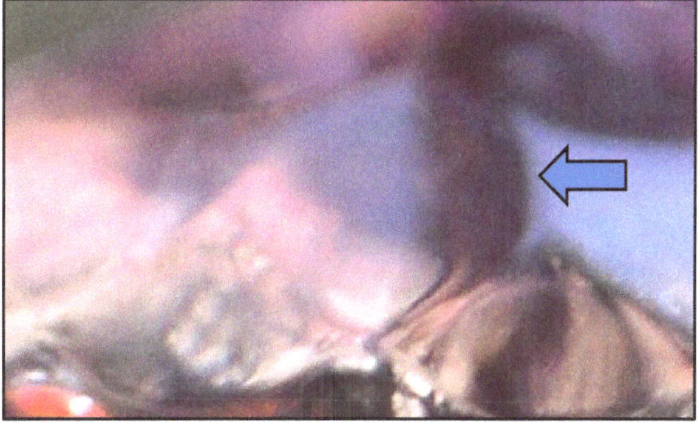

Verse 5 then explains that "out of the midst thereof came the likeness of four living creatures" (KJV).

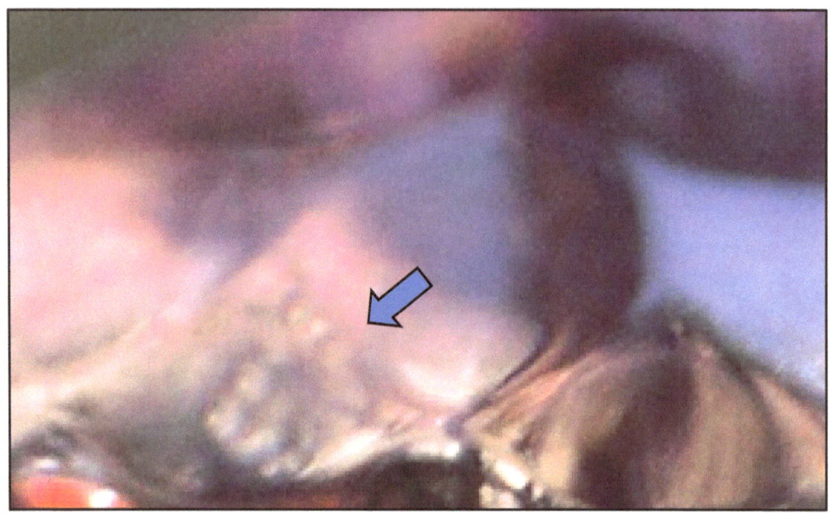

We are unable to see the burnished bronze feet, but verse 13 tells us that the creatures' appearance was like burning coals of fire. The New King James Version says it was like torches going back and forth among the living creatures. If you look closely at the human face and the ox, you can see specks of gold.

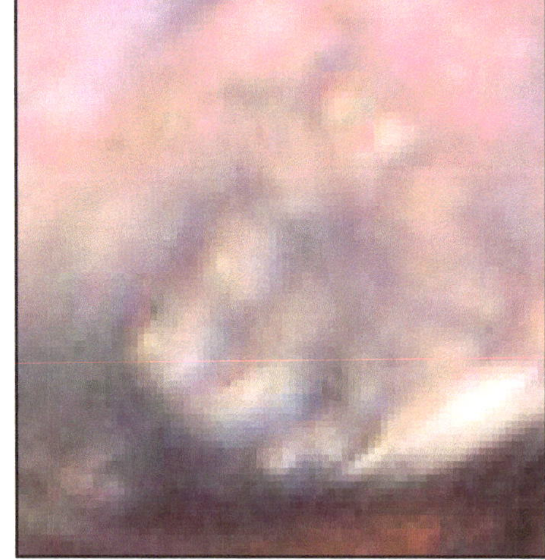

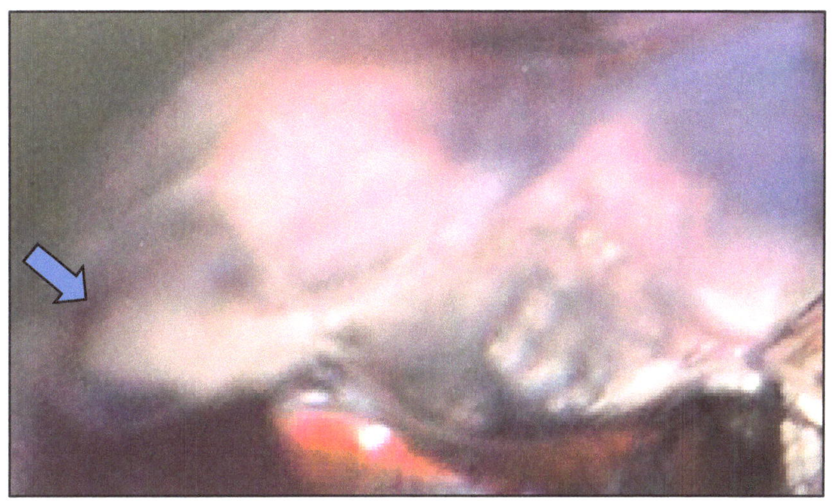

Each living creature has four wings. It is difficult to see where they begin and where they end. Ezekiel 1:11 tells us that "each had two wings spreading out upward, each wing touching that of the creature on either side; and each had two other wings covering its body." In the picture below please note the human hands, which, according to Scripture, are located underneath the wings (v. 8).

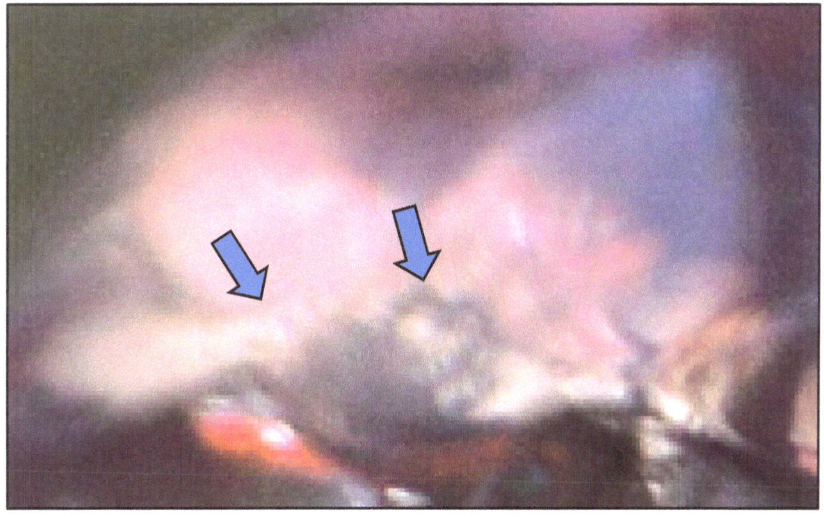

Revelation 7:1 speaks of four angels standing at the four corners of the earth. Their purpose is to hold back the four winds, so they won't blow on the land, sea, or any tree. "Four winds" implies all directions. In the context of Revelation 7, the winds are holding back the judgments listed in chapter 6. God's people have been given time to receive a seal that will protect them from harm (v. 3).

Proverbs 30:4 also provides an interesting description of the wind. It says, "Who has gathered the wind in His fists?" (NKJV). In the picture below, the creatures appear to have a grip on the wind.

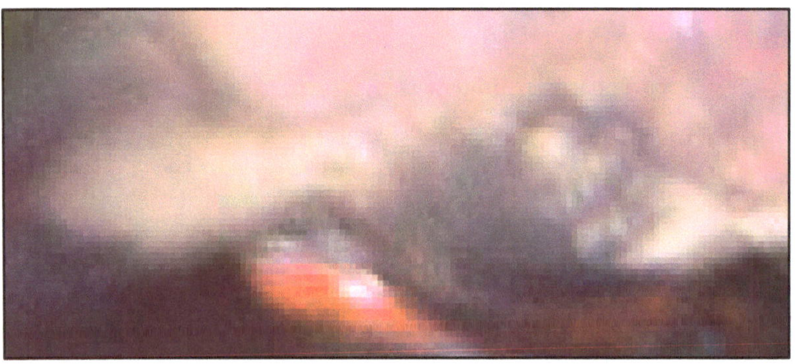

If you could take a ride in any car, which one would you choose? God certainly doesn't need a vehicle to go from one place to another, but He has chosen the cherubim. They are similar to, if not the same as, the four living creatures. Second Samuel 22:11 says, "He mounted the cherubim and flew; he soared on the wings of the wind." The first chapter of Ezekiel paints a picture of the creatures' constant motion around the throne of God. The clouds are the Lord's chariot pulled by His heavenly creatures as they ride through the air (Psalm 104:3).

As already mentioned, it was difficult to cover up the spot in between the two golden buildings. The colorful light around the rim was especially bright. As I began to read through the first chapter of Ezekiel, I immediately thought the spot could possibly be a wheel. It just happens to appear in all the pictures, although the details vary from photo to photo.

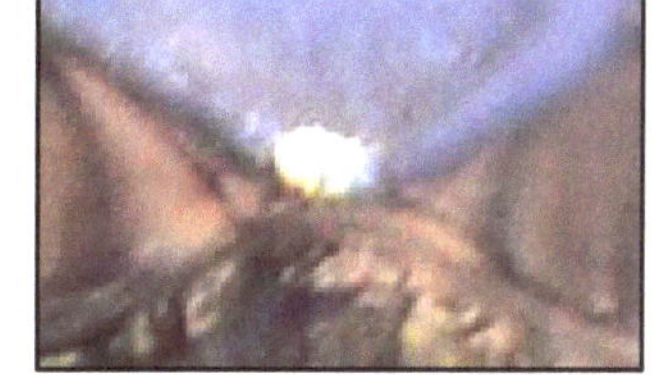

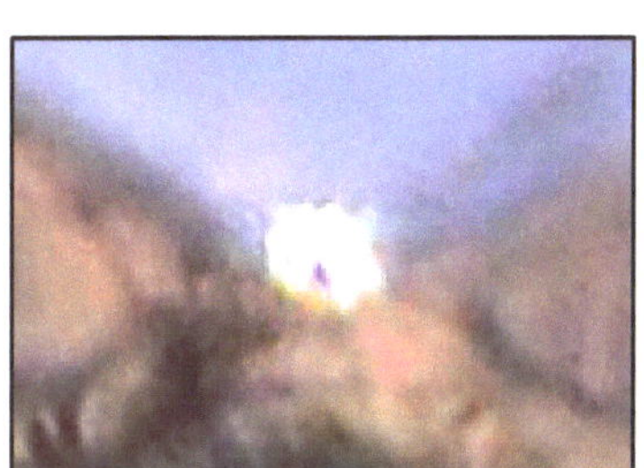

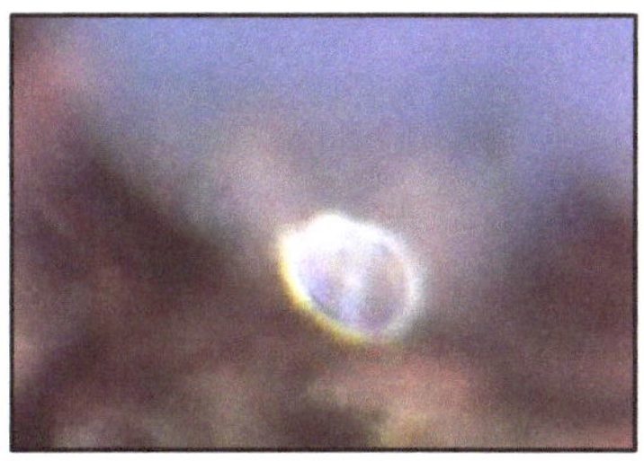

Ezekiel says that the wheels sparkled like topaz (NIV) or beryl (KJV), which is a gold-colored stone (1:16). They also "appeared to be made like a wheel intersecting a wheel." Wherever the living creatures moved, the wheels would move beside them (v. 19). The rims were also full of eyes all around (v. 18). The omniscient, all-knowing God could see everything, including sin and apostasy, so He was moving to judge.

"Spread out above the heads of the living creatures was what looked something like a vault, sparkling like crystal, and awesome" (Ezekiel 1:22). Verse 26 then tells us that above the vault was what looked like a throne of lapis lazuli (NIV) or sapphire stone (KJV). Remember our study on foundations? We learned that the color may resemble violet-blue. I have pointed out what could be the throne of God.

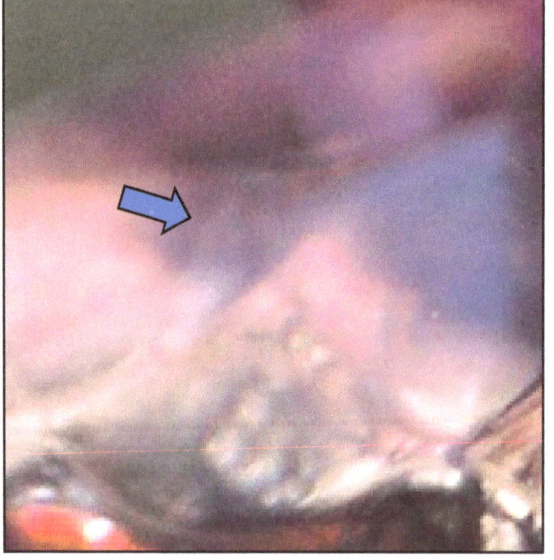

I always imagined God's throne as immovable, fixed somewhere in Heaven. It didn't occur to me that His throne could move until I started researching Ezekiel. Daniel 7:9 provides a vivid description of the throne. It says, "His throne was flaming with fire, and its wheels were all ablaze." We have already seen that "he makes the clouds his chariot" (Psalm 104:3). Chariots, of course, have wheels.

Although each image is interesting in its own way, the one below is especially vibrant. To me, it goes along beautifully with Ezekiel's description of the glory of the Lord (Ezekiel 1:28). You can see the bright purple throne on our left. It likely corresponds with the verse that tells us "His throne was flaming with fire." Please note the bright yellow on the throne. Ezekiel then says that there was a figure like that of a man (v. 26). In the photo, I think He is standing on the right side instead of sitting on the throne. From his waist up it looks like glowing metal, like He is full of fire (v. 27). And from the waist down it looks like fire.

Ezekiel describes the light as brilliant. He says it is "like the appearance of a rainbow in the clouds on a rainy day" (v. 28).

It is important to note the position of the throne and the figure of the man in this photo. They are in the same place as the "wheel" in the other pictures.

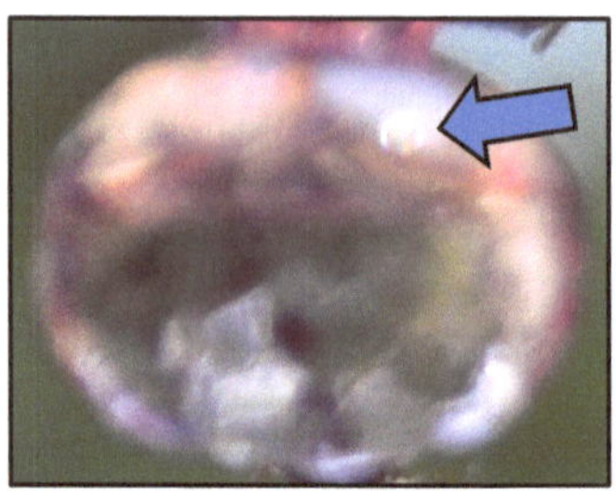

I came across a lovely description from the Dead Sea Scrolls. I think it sheds some light on this scene as well. The English translation says, "The cherubim bless the image of the Throne-Chariot above the firmament, and they praise the majesty of the fiery firmament beneath the seat of his glory. And between the turning wheels, angels of holiness come and go, as it were a fiery vision of most holy spirits; and about them flow seeming rivulets of fire, like gleaming bronze, a radiance of many gorgeous colors, of marvelous pigments magnificently mingled."

The first time we see the cherubim in Scripture is right after the fall. The Lord banished man from the Garden of Eden (Genesis 3:23). After He drove him out, God placed cherubim and a flaming sword on the east side of the garden (v. 24). The sword turned every way to guard the way to the tree of life. The flashing back and forth of the flaming sword is similar to the motion of the wheels in Ezekiel.

Next, we see the cherubim in the tabernacle and temple. Their image was woven into the curtains made from finely twisted linen as well as blue, purple, and scarlet yarn (Exodus 26:1; 2 Chronicles 3:14). When Solomon built the temple, craftsmen carved cherubim on the walls (2 Chronicles 3:7). Two olive-wood doors leading to the inner sanctuary also had cherubim, palm trees, and flowers (1 Kings 6:31-32). It is interesting to note that the millennial temple will have intricate carvings of cherubim and palm trees as well (Ezekiel 41:25).

The ark of the covenant is perhaps the most well-known piece from the tabernacle and temple. The atonement cover had a gold cherub on each end (Exodus 25:19). Their wings spread upward, overshadowing the cover (v. 20). This is symbolic of the cherubim in Heaven. Ezekiel 1:11 tells us that their wings spread out upward and that they touched that of the creature on either side. On the ark of the covenant, the cherubim faced each other, looking toward the cover. In Exodus 25:22, the Lord says to Moses, "There, above the cover between the two cherubim that are over the ark of the covenant law, I will meet with you and give you all my commands for the Israelites." The ark of the covenant was a model of God's throne (Hebrews 8:5). In Heaven, He sits enthroned between the cherubim (Psalm 80:1; 99:1; Isaiah 37:16). It is there that He gives commands, judges the nations, and, of course, shows mercy.

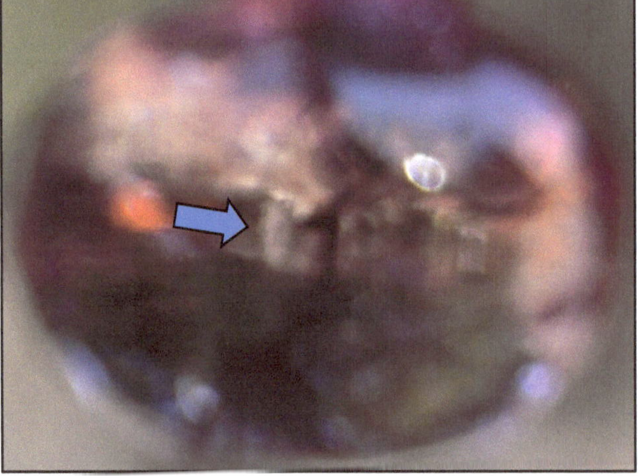

When I first saw the third picture, I immediately thought that the object underneath the horse's head and hoof resembled the ark of the covenant. It looks like a rectangular box with an open lid. I also think it resembles a tomb. Interestingly enough, the Hebrew word for "ark" is *arown*, which means "ark," "chest," and "coffin."

When Mary Magdalene visited the Lord's tomb, she bent over to look inside and saw two angels in white (John 20:11-12). They had taken a seat where Jesus' body had been. The last part of this verse is significant. It tells us that there was one angel at the head and one angel at the foot. The scene was just like the cherubim over the mercy seat! It was like the heavenly cherubim beside the throne of God!

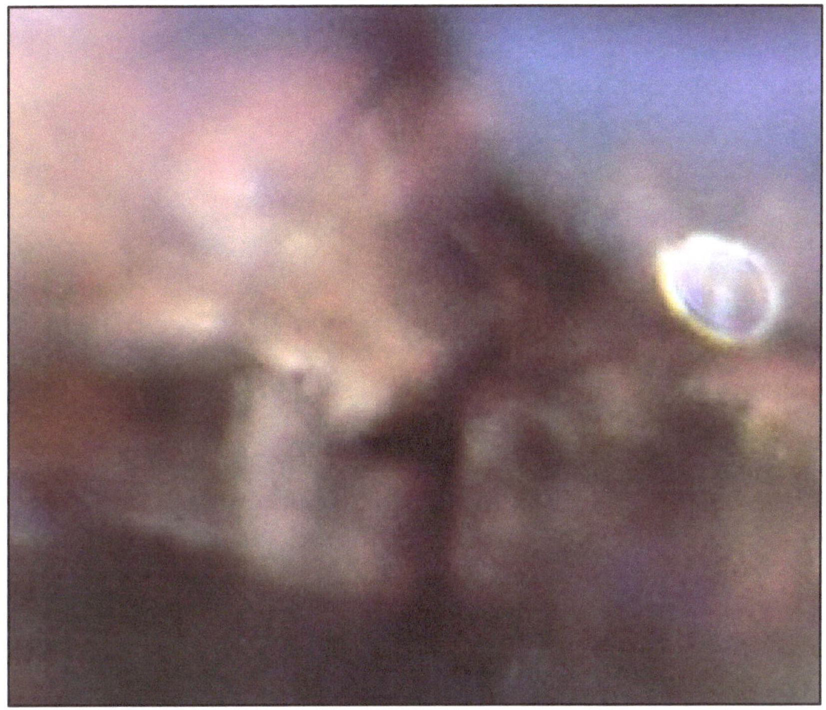

When the seventh angel blows his trumpet, God's kingdom will be announced (Revelation 11:15). The time will arrive for judging the dead as well as rewarding the Lord's servants (v. 18). The beloved disciple describes the scene for us. He explains, "Then God's temple in heaven was opened, and within his temple was seen the ark of his covenant. And there came flashes of lightning, rumblings, peals of thunder, an earthquake and a severe hailstorm" (v. 19).

Someday when the Lord returns to bless Jerusalem, He will also judge those who lived contrary to His ways. Oftentimes the Lord will manifest in a storm. Isaiah tells us, "See, the Lord is coming with fire, and his chariots are like a whirlwind" (Isaiah 66:15).

When Elijah and Elisha "were walking along and talking together, suddenly a chariot of fire and horses of fire appeared and separated the two of them…" (2 Kings 2:11). Elijah went up to Heaven in a whirlwind, and Elisha saw it and cried out, "My father! My father! The chariots and horsemen of Israel!" (v. 12). I'm not sure which man's experience was more intense. I can't imagine being taken up in the Lord's chariot, but witnessing it would be overwhelming as well.

Ezekiel's visions of God began with a windstorm coming out of the north (Ezekiel 1:1, 4). He describes it as "an immense cloud with flashing lightning and surrounded by brilliant light." The Lord will sometimes manifest in a cloud, which is often called the "shekinah glory." It was first introduced to the Israelites in a pillar of cloud by day and a pillar of fire by night (Exodus 13:21). The cloud represents the glory of God.

In the Gospel of Mark, Jesus describes His return. He says, "At that time people will see the Son of Man coming in the clouds with great power and glory" (13:26).

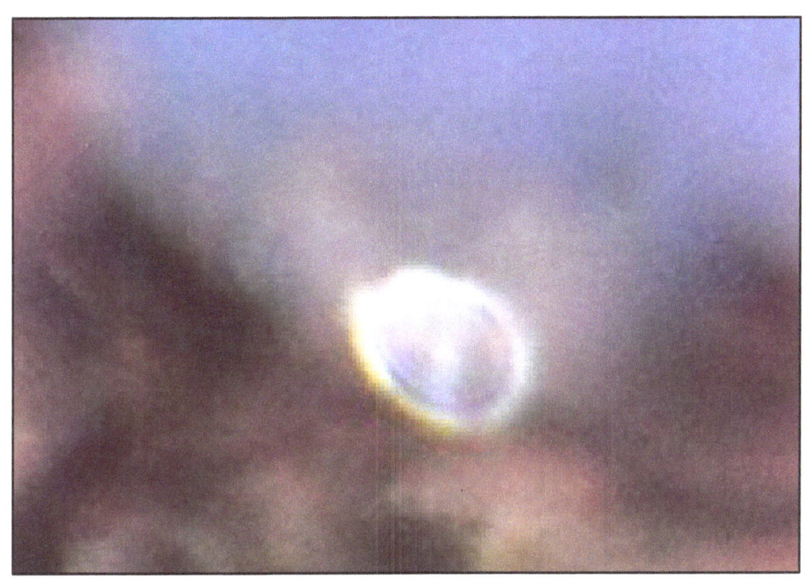

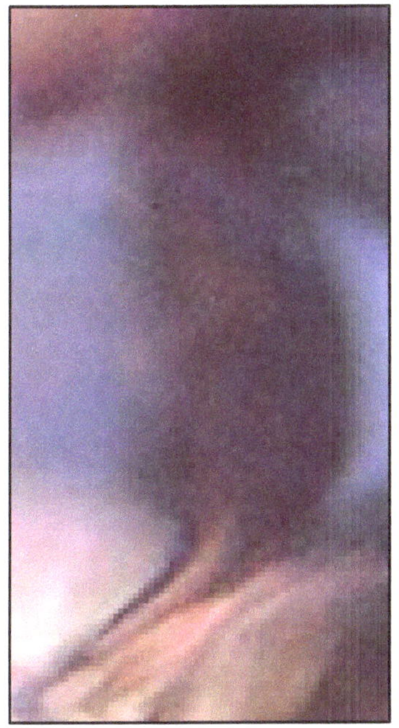

Glory cloud
& storm

There are many similarities between chapters 1 and 10 in the Book of Ezekiel. Therefore, I will attempt to focus on a few topics not yet covered in this study. For example, Ezekiel 10:12 tells us that the cherubim's entire bodies, including their backs, hands, and wings, were completely full of eyes. This represents God's ability to see everything and, of course, know everything. So, are you ready to look at a couple of eyes? I think I found several in the second picture, although the two boxes highlight the most obvious ones.

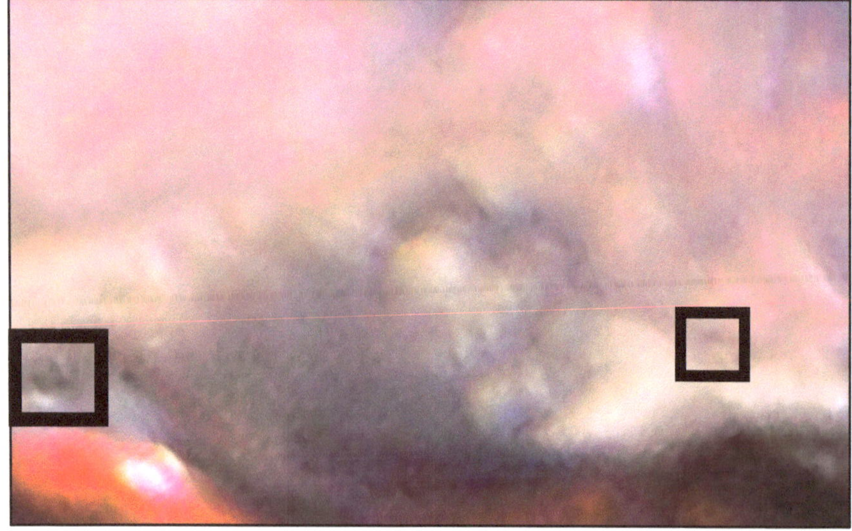

Judgment

God judged Jerusalem because of their idolatry. He spared the righteous, but coals of fire were scattered over the city (Ezekiel 10:2). The Lord commanded the man in linen to "take fire from among the wheels, from among the cherubim" (v. 6). One of the cherubim reached out his hand to the fire, took some of it, and then placed it in the hands of the man in linen (v. 7). It is interesting to note that God uses angels in judgment. When we arrive at the Book of Revelation, we will definitely take a moment to look at this particular assignment more carefully.

Due to the sin and idolatry, the glory of God departed from Solomon's temple. When this happened, the cherubim were standing on the south side (v. 3). "The cloud filled the temple, and the court was full of the radiance of the glory of the Lord" (v. 4). This scene reminds me of the return of God's glory described in chapter 43.

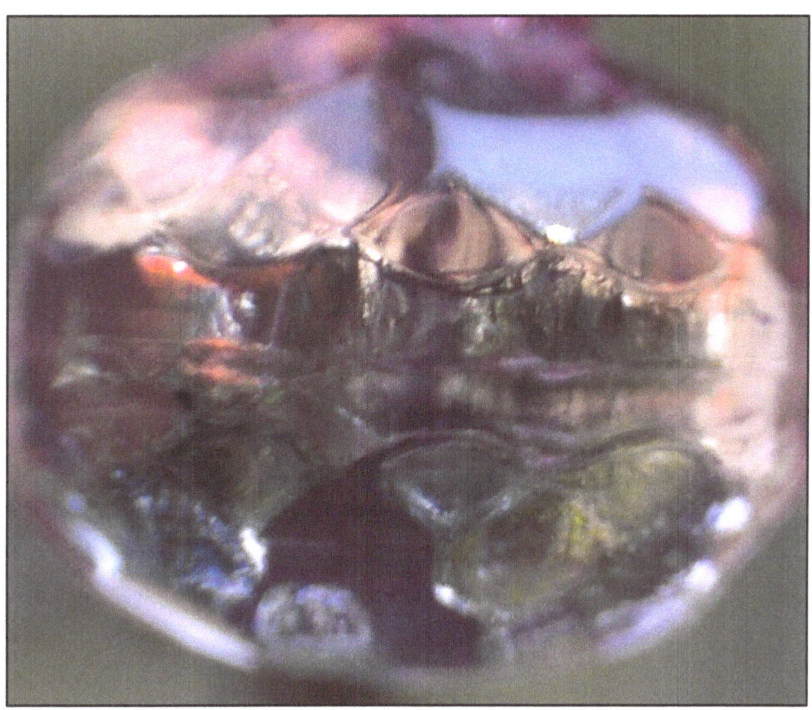

The cherubim that Ezekiel saw in chapter 10 have the same appearance as those by the Kebar River (v. 22). Even though one face was like a cherub (v. 14), we will focus on the face of the ox in chapter 1.

The ox is the king of all domestic beasts. Since this particular animal is helpful in farming, it has been highly prized by people in both past and present cultures. It is possible that the tribe of Ephraim had an ox on their banner (or standard). Ephraim was on the west side of the tabernacle along with Manasseh and Benjamin (Numbers 2:18-24). All of the men assigned to the camp of Ephraim totaled 108,100. Although there are different interpretations, the Gospel of Mark could be associated with the ox since we see Jesus as a servant.

The next banner in our study is on the north side. Just as we have to look up to see a bird in flight, we find the eagle in the direction that points up. The tribe of Dan was the leader of Asher and Naphtali (vv. 25-31). All of the men assigned to the camp of Dan numbered 157,600. It is likely that the Gospel of John corresponds with the eagle since we read about our Heavenly Lord, the Son of God.

It is not surprising that the tribe of Judah was the leader of the east side of the camp (vv. 3-9). And the lion was the image on their banner. The camp of Judah included both Issachar and Zebulun. They had a grand total of 186,400 men, making it the most populated side of the tabernacle.

The Gospel of Matthew presents Jesus as the King of the Jews. The lion, of course, is also a king since he is the strongest of all the wild animals.

Finally, we arrive at the south side, the camp of Reuben (vv. 10-16). Their banner had the face of a man, symbolizing Jesus as the Son of Man. Simeon and Gad were a part of this camp, and they had a total of 151,450 men. It is possible that the Gospel of Luke, written by a Gentile physician, points to Jesus' humanity.

It is difficult to see the details, but I noticed a lion's face on the right side of the pearl gate. The face could be a part of a banner or shield. At first I thought it represented the tribe of Judah, but it may serve as an emblem for Jerusalem. It is possible, therefore, that the New Jerusalem will embrace this symbol as well.

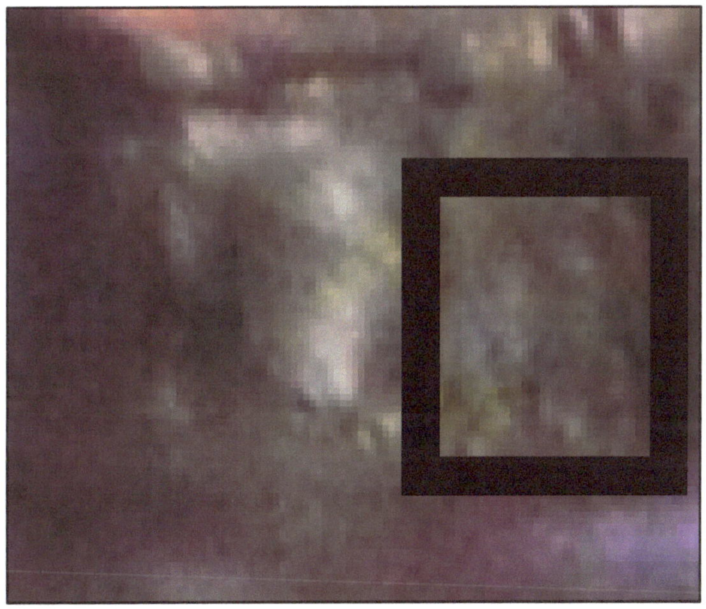

"Hear us, Shepherd of Israel, you who lead Joseph like a flock. You who sit enthroned between the cherubim, shine forth before Ephraim, Benjamin and Manasseh."

Psalm 80:1

6

SHEPHERD-KING

Psalm 80:1 may refer to our Shepherd-King's throne in Heaven or its earthly representation in the tabernacle or temple. According to the Strong's Concordance, the Hebrew word for "shepherd" is *ra'ah*. It means "to tend a flock," "to rule," and "to associate with as a friend."

The kings of Israel were known as shepherds, although many of them didn't do what they should have. Instead of caring for the flock, they focused on themselves (Ezekiel 34:2). The Sovereign Lord explains, "You have not strengthened the weak or healed the sick or bound up the injured. You have not brought back the strays or searched for the lost. You have ruled them harshly and brutally. So they were scattered because there was no shepherd…" (vv. 4-5).

The Lord, however, promises to care for His sheep in the millennial kingdom. He says, "I myself will tend my sheep and have them lie down…" (v. 15). Psalm 23:1-3 suddenly comes to mind. Perhaps you can recite it from memory. "The Lord is my shepherd; I shall not want. He makes me to lie down in green pastures; He leads me beside the still waters. He restores my soul" (NKJV). When a sheep can finally lie down to rest, this means that all its needs have been met. No parasites will bother the sheep, there is plenty of food and water, and it is safe from its enemies.

The Good Shepherd

Jesus is not just one of a handful of good shepherds. He is the one and only Good Shepherd! He tells us that "the good shepherd lays down his life for the sheep" (John 10:11). A hired hand doesn't care about the sheep (v. 13). Rather, he abandons them and runs away when he sees a wolf coming (v. 12).

According to the Strong's Concordance, the Hebrew word for "good" is *kalos.* It means "beautiful," "valuable," "virtuous," "better," and "worthy." When I discovered the image of a shepherd in the first picture, I thought it was beautiful. You can see the purple robe and its long train flowing down the steps.

As a Gentile believer, I find comfort in Jesus' words. The Good Shepherd explains, "I have other sheep that are not of this sheep pen. I must bring them also. They too will listen to my voice, and there shall be one flock and one shepherd" (v. 16).

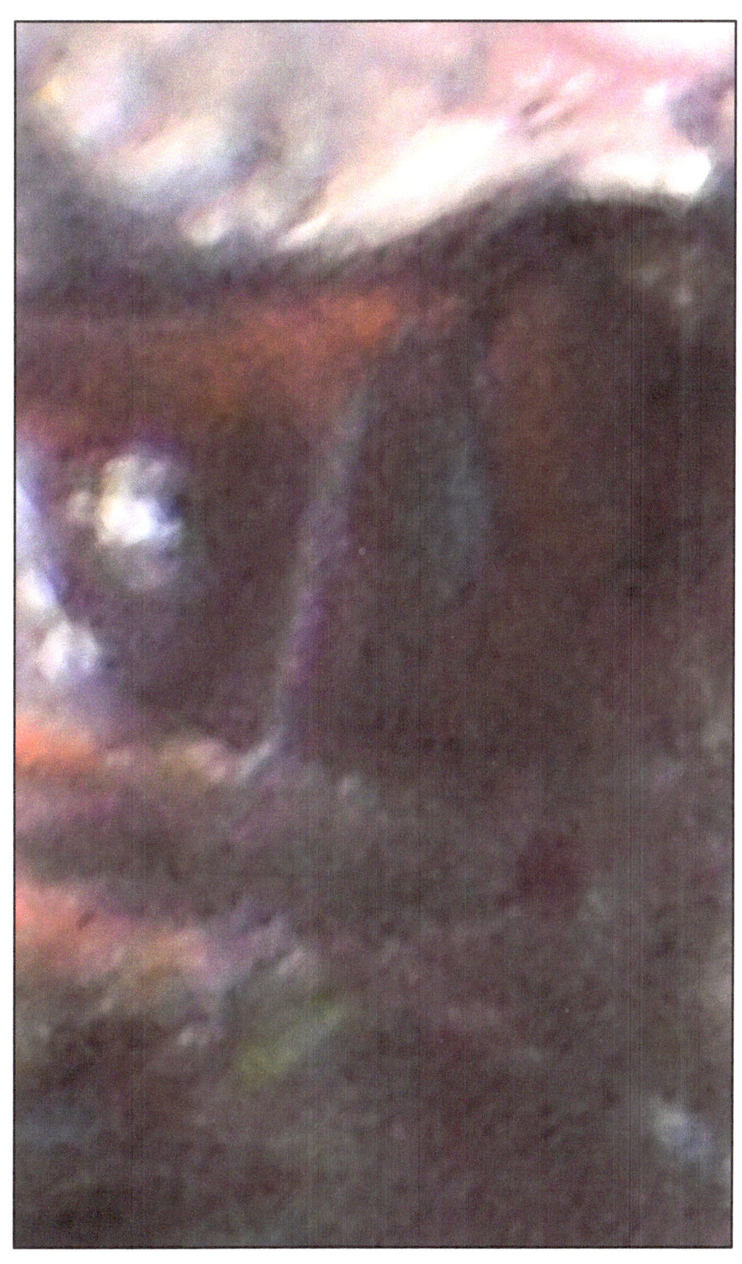

When Jesus comes as the heavenly warrior, He will ride on a white horse (Revelation 19:11). The armies of Heaven will follow the Lord on white horses as well (v. 14). Please note what looks like a white horse's head in the distance.

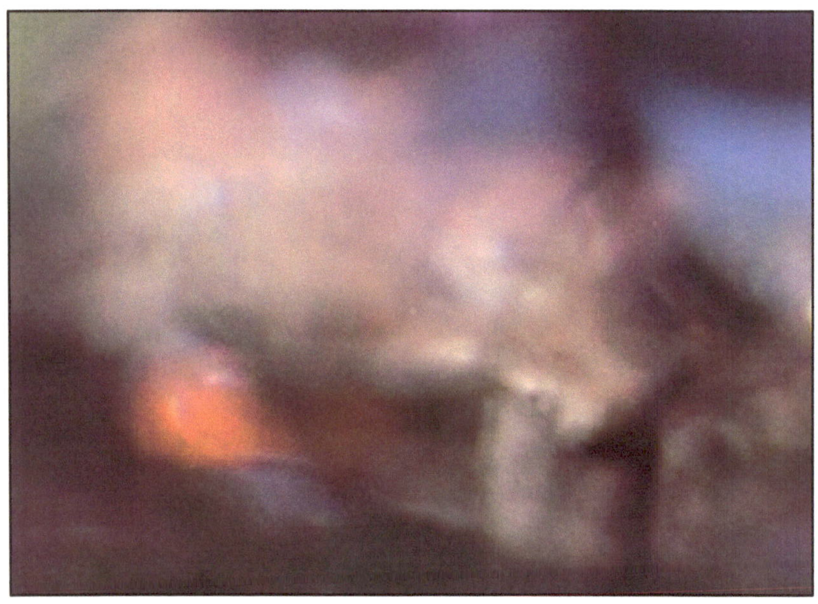

Jesus will wear many crowns and have a robe dipped in blood (vv. 12-13). His robe and thigh will say "KING OF KINGS AND LORD OF LORDS" (v. 16). This name points to His reign as King and Lord of all the earth. No one will be able to conquer Him. We will forever lift Him up as the Lord of all creation.

In the second photo, the Shepherd-King has lowered His head. It looks like He is wearing a crown. Psalm 132:18 tells us that "his head will be adorned with a radiant crown."

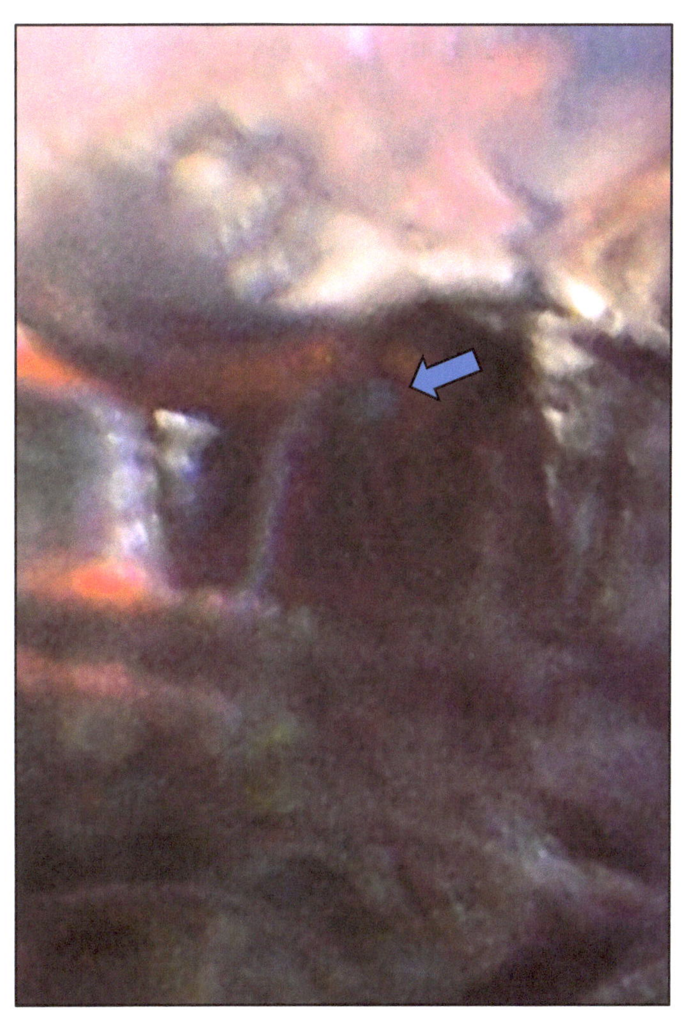

KING OF KINGS

&

LORD OF LORDS

The thought of Jesus being flogged and mocked is horrible to me. Whenever Kirk and I watch *Jesus of Nazareth*, my hands quickly cover my eyes during the crucifixion. I remember sobbing as a child as I watched this life-changing scene on T.V. And to think that Jesus went through all of this for me…and for you. It is a sobering thought.

The King of kings deserves many crowns of honor as well as a royal robe. That is why the twenty-four elders lay their crowns before His throne (Revelation 4:10). In three of the four gospels, however, we read about a crown of thorns and a robe (Matthew 27:27-31; Mark 15:16-20; John 19:1-3). When Jesus is sentenced to be crucified, the soldiers make fun of Him. They twist together a crown of thorns for His head and clothe Him in a purple robe (Mark 15:17; John 19:2). Matthew describes it as a scarlet robe (Matthew 27:28). So, which color was the robe—purple or scarlet? It is likely that it was a purplish-red or a reddish-purple. Since the hues are similar to one another, each disciple did his best to describe it as he saw it.

The head covering in the first picture appears scarlet, while the robe is both purple and blue. Did you happen to notice the hint of blue? It reminds me of the heavenly veil that separated the holy place from the most holy place in the tabernacle. The Lord said to Moses, "Make a curtain of blue, purple and scarlet yarn and finely twisted linen, with cherubim woven into it by a skilled worker" (Exodus

26:31). The ark of the covenant was then placed beyond the veil (v. 34). When Jesus was on the cross, He cried out with a loud voice and then gave up His spirit (Matthew 27:50). The next two verses say, "At that moment the curtain of the temple was torn in two from top to bottom. The earth shook, the rocks split and the tombs broke open" (vv. 51-52).

Seraphim

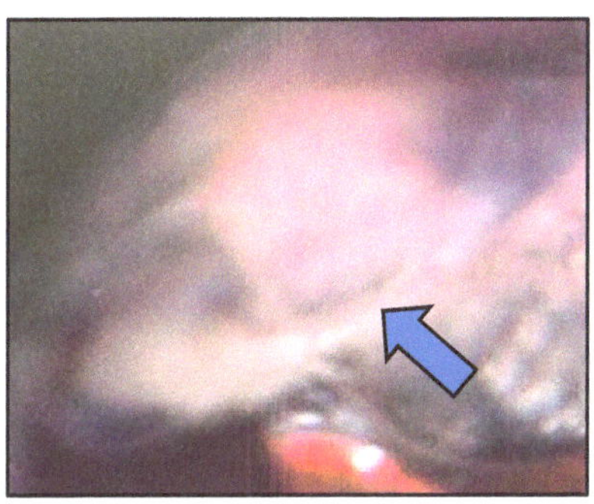

I hadn't planned on writing about seraphim, but I think they are definitely worth mentioning. We learn about these heavenly creatures in the Book of Isaiah. When the prophet sees the Lord seated on the throne, he notices seraphim above (Isaiah 6:1-2). Since each seraph covers his face with two of the six wings, I began to think that the creature next to the throne could be one. Please note the eyes peeking over the wings in the picture above.

"The train of his robe filled the temple."

Isaiah 6:1

It was surprising to find several skulls in the first picture. I quickly realized, however, that Ezekiel prophesied to the dry bones (Ezekiel 37:1-14). Since Israel was in captivity at the time, they had little, if any, hope of being restored as a nation.

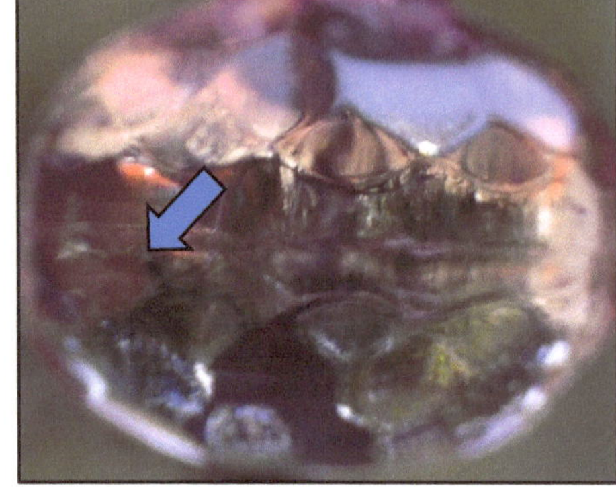

The Sovereign Lord told Ezekiel to say, "Dry bones, hear the word of the Lord!" (v. 4). Even though Ezekiel did the prophesying, it was actually the Lord's words. There was a rattling sound, and the bones came together (v. 7). Tendons, flesh, and skin covered the bones (v. 8). Breath from the four winds then entered the slain, and they came to life (vv. 9-10). The Lord told Ezekiel that "these bones are the people of Israel" (v. 11). In verse 10, Ezekiel describes them as a vast army.

Breath of life

Skulls

The breath of life that went into the people is similar to the creation of man. Genesis 2:7 tells us that "the Lord God formed a man from the dust of the ground and breathed into his nostrils the breath of life, and the man became a living being."

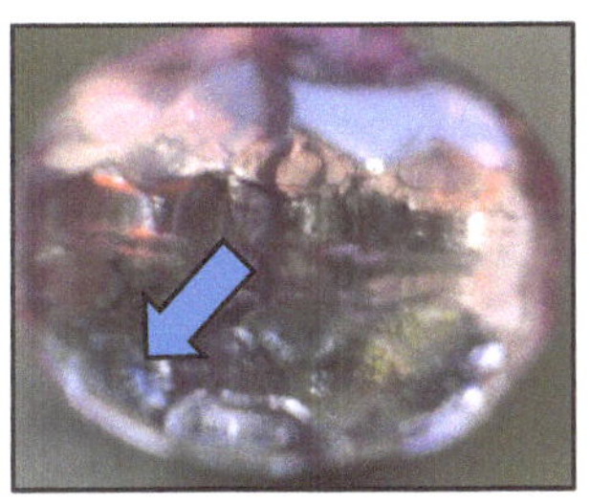

A girl & some friends in the river

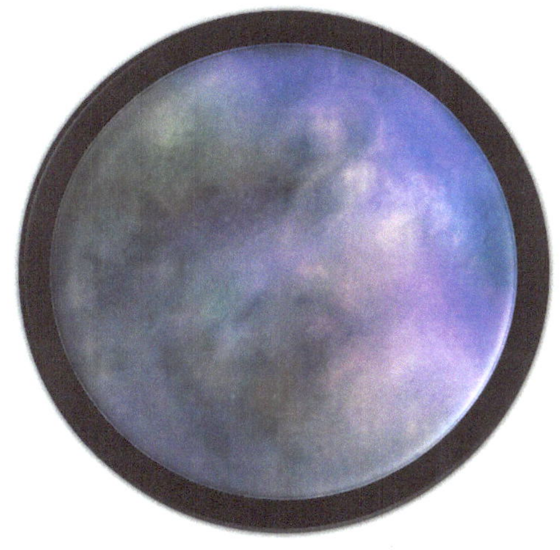

Interpreting each photo certainly takes time. Sometimes months may pass before I see something clearly. In fact, I had planned on pointing out the "breath of life" in the shepherd's picture. I thought I saw a white puff of air near His hood. Just now, however, I zoomed in to analyze the details. It was the first time I ever looked at it closely in this format, and I discovered something very interesting. To me, it seems as if we are looking at the profile of the Lord!

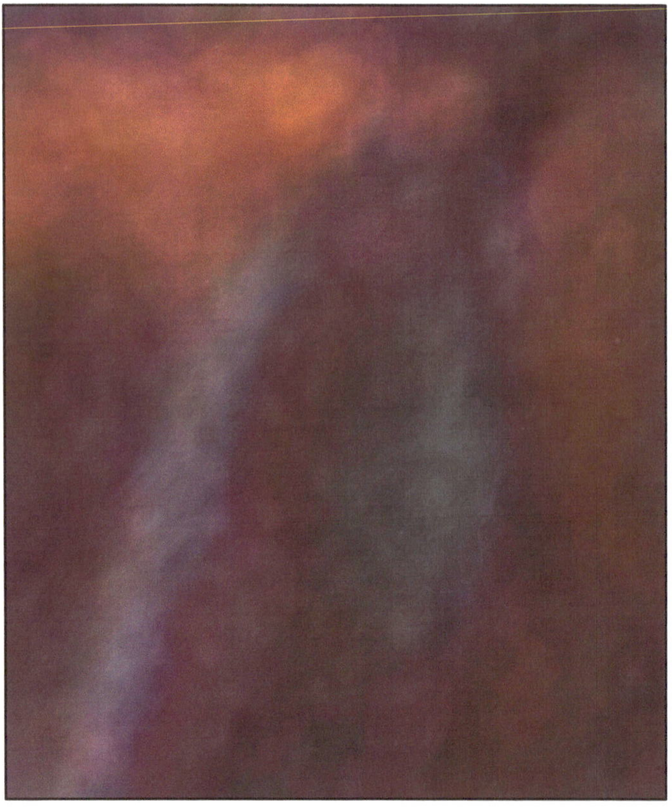

When we visited Jerusalem, I experienced a miracle at the Western Wall. It was one of the most significant moments of my life. It was a time of intercessory prayer that focused on end times. It also strengthened me in spirit, soul, and body. Since that visit (to the remains of the temple where Jesus walked and taught and worshiped) I have never been the same. A verse from a well-known psalm suddenly comes to mind. It says, "One thing I ask from the Lord, this only do I seek: that I may dwell in the house of the Lord all the days of my life, to gaze on the beauty of the Lord and to seek him in his temple" (Psalm 27:4).

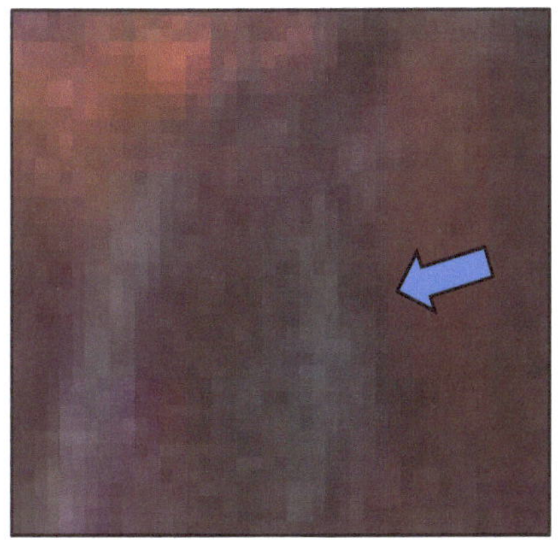

When looking at a digital photo up close, it is very easy to make something out of nothing. For example, at times I think I see animals or people when, in reality, it probably isn't anything at all. Other times, when the image is more obvious, I tend to consider it carefully. Well, there is another face that I think is worth considering in this picture. It reminds me of the Ancient of Days. He even looks like He is wearing a crown or wreath.

Ancient of Days

It is possible that the title "Ancient of Days" refers to the Father or the Son, depending on the interpretation. This name, as well as the white hair, points to God's eternality.

In Daniel's vision, he sees someone like a son of man coming with the clouds of Heaven. Daniel explains that the son of man "approached the Ancient of Days and was led into his presence. He was given authority, glory and sovereign power; all nations and peoples of every language worshiped him. His dominion is an everlasting dominion that will not pass away, and his kingdom is one that will never be destroyed" (Daniel 7:13-14).

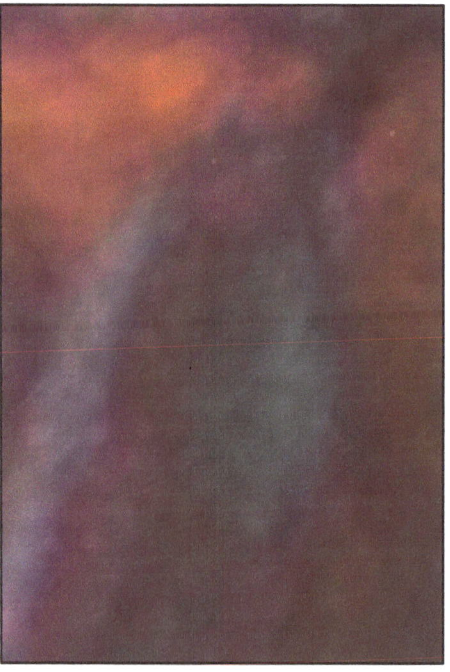

Son of Man

&

Ancient of Days

It would be wonderful to stay right here and study the face of the Lord all day. He is beautiful, and His voice is powerful. In fact, Ezekiel provides an interesting description of God's voice. He says, "When the creatures moved, I heard the sound of their wings, like the roar of rushing waters, like the voice of the Almighty, like the tumult of an army" (Ezekiel 1:24). Even though I have never been to Niagara Falls, I imagine the sound of the waterfall is similar to the sound of their wings. In Ezekiel 10:5, the prophet tells us that "the sound of the wings of the cherubim could be heard as far away as the outer court, like the voice of God Almighty when he speaks."

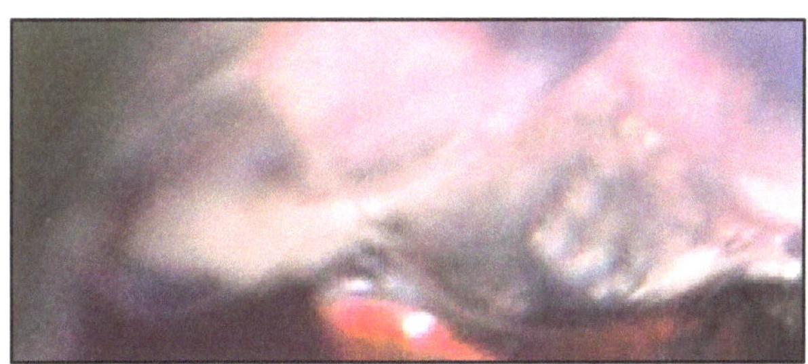

In Psalm 29, David compares the Lord's voice to a number of things. He tells us that "the God of glory thunders" (v. 3). He says His voice is powerful, majestic, breaks the cedars of Lebanon, strikes with flashes of lightning, shakes the Desert of Kadesh, twists the oaks, and strips the forests bare (vv. 4-9). All of these things seem possible in light of creation. You may recall how "God said, 'Let there be light,' and there was light" (Genesis 1:3). His voice is obviously powerful!

"The man brought me back to the entrance to the temple, and I saw water coming out from under the threshold of the temple toward the east (for the temple faced east)."

Ezekiel 47:1

7

RIVER

There are many similarities between Ezekiel 47 and Revelation 22, and yet they refer to different periods of time. Ezekiel 47 describes the millennium, whereas Revelation 22 refers to the eternal state. A great deal of our study has been on the millennium. However, we can look forward to the last two chapters of Revelation which focus on eternity. For now, let's continue with the thousand-year reign.

Ezekiel describes the river in detail. He says that the man led him through water that was ankle-deep, to his waist, and then deep enough to swim in (Ezekiel 47:3-5). He tells us that no one could cross the river. The water flowed east where it entered the Dead Sea (v. 8). When the water emptied into the sea, the salt water became fresh and swarms of living creatures lived (v. 9).

I figured there was more to the picture of the river than what I could initially see, so one day I decided to look at it more carefully. The first creature I noticed was a little seal or sea lion.

Then I saw what looks like a whale. Even though its mouth appears open, I think it is likely closed. The nose is just a little darker in color.

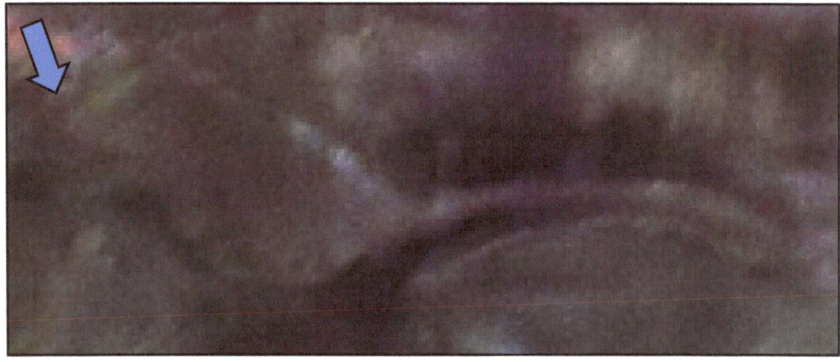

When I first noticed the whale, I got a little teary-eyed. It was the only time I felt a little overwhelmed by the images. I began to see so many creatures. It was like I was stepping into the story of creation. "And God said, 'Let the water teem with living creatures…'" (Genesis 1:20). The word "teem" means "to bring forth abundantly" (KJV). Verse 21 tells us that "God created the great creatures of the sea and every living thing with which the water teems and that moves about in it, according to their kinds…."

God likes to follow patterns, so it is possible that a similar process will take place when He restores Israel. On that day, when the Lord resettles towns and rebuilds ruins, the people will say, "This land that was laid waste has become like the garden of Eden" (Ezekiel 36:33-35).

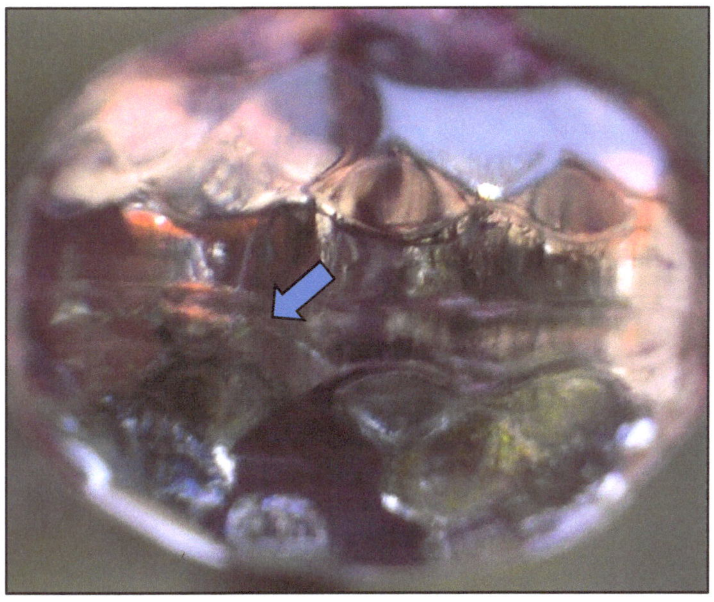

There will be a large number of fish because of the fresh water (Ezekiel 47:9). In fact, fishermen will stand along the shore to spread their nets.

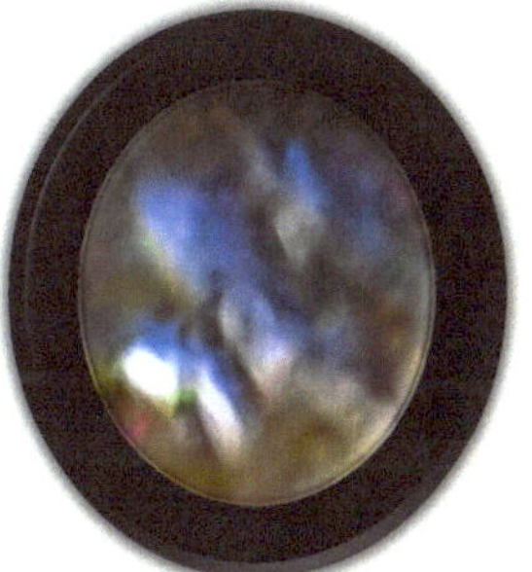

And there will be many kinds of fish, like the fish of the Mediterranean Sea (v. 10).

I have placed a box around the largest fish I could find.

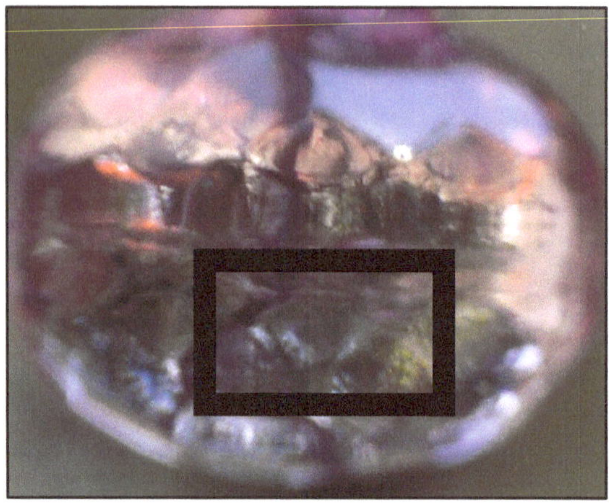

There are even some smaller fish nearby.

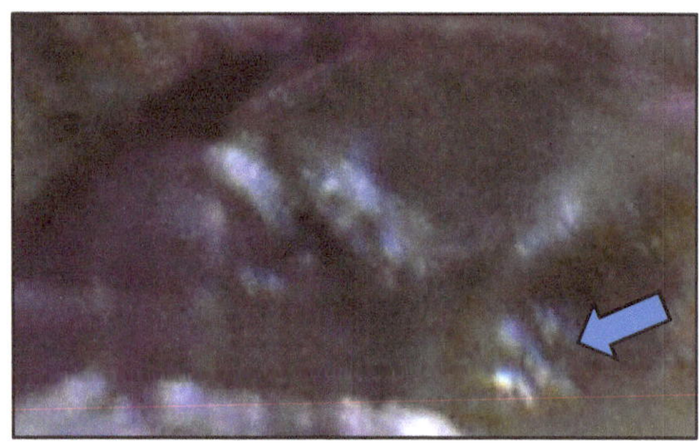

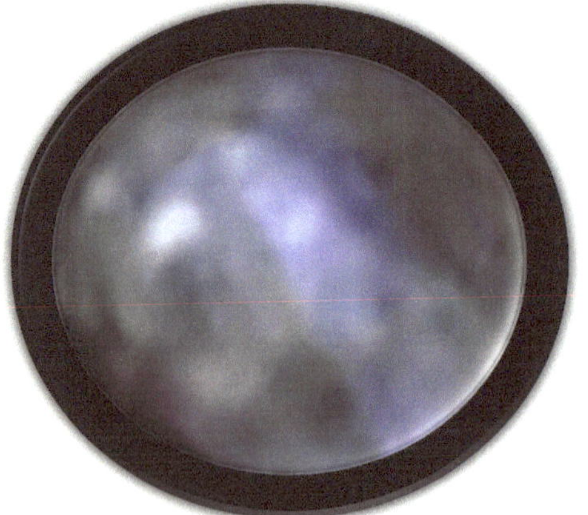

A frog above the eye of the large fish

Ezekiel saw many trees on the banks of the river (Ezekiel 47:7). He also mentions how the swamps and marshes will remain salty (v. 11). Given the scale of the *painting*, it is certainly possible that the green on either side of the river represents trees, swamps, and marshes.

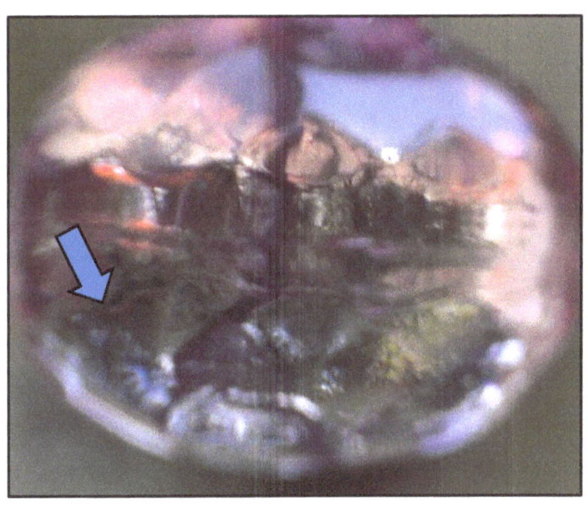

Here we have a turtle in the marsh. The arrow points to its face.

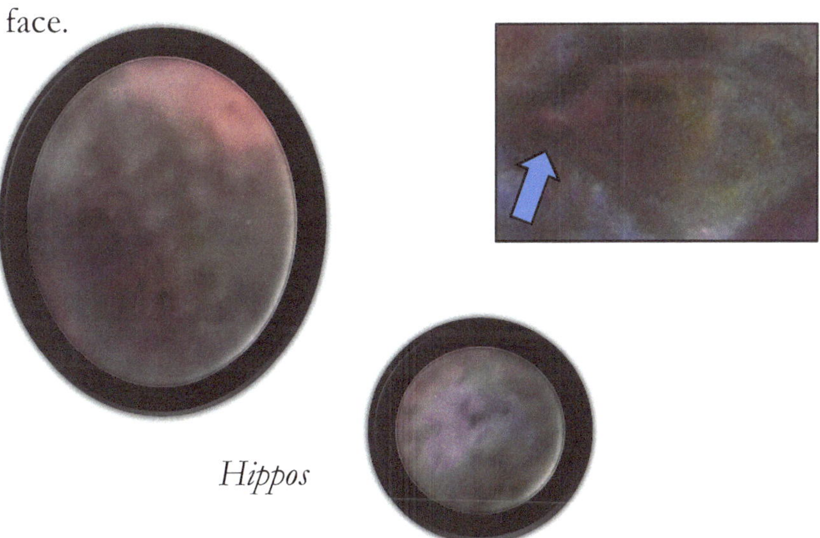

Hippos

Psalm 68:30 speaks of a "beast among the reeds." Some people believe the "beast" is a crocodile. You may have already noticed what looks like a crocodile in the first and second pictures.

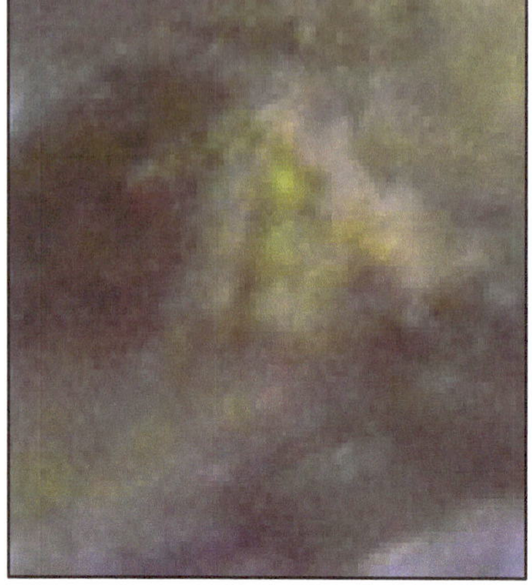

The crocodile may refer to Egypt since verse 31 says, "Envoys will come from Egypt."

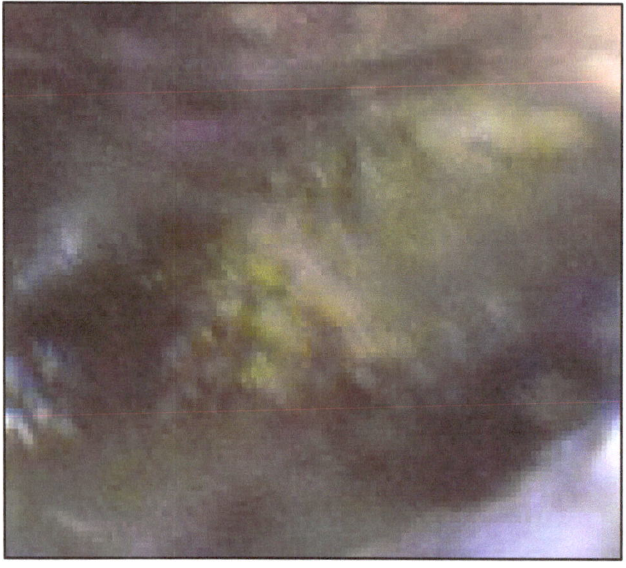

Right next to the East Gate is a large stone cat, which could also represent Egypt.

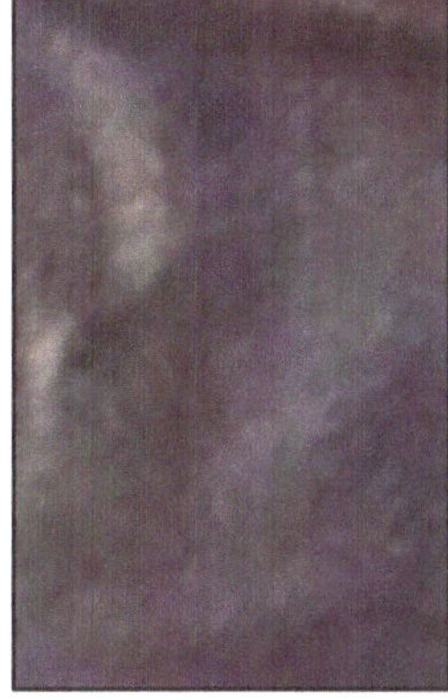

People will travel to Jerusalem from all over the world to worship the Lord. Isaiah 60:3 says, "Nations will come to your light, and kings to the brightness of your dawn." Verse 6 explains that "herds of camels will cover your land, young camels of Midian and Ephah." Below is an image of the backside of a camel. I lightened the area around its face to see it better.

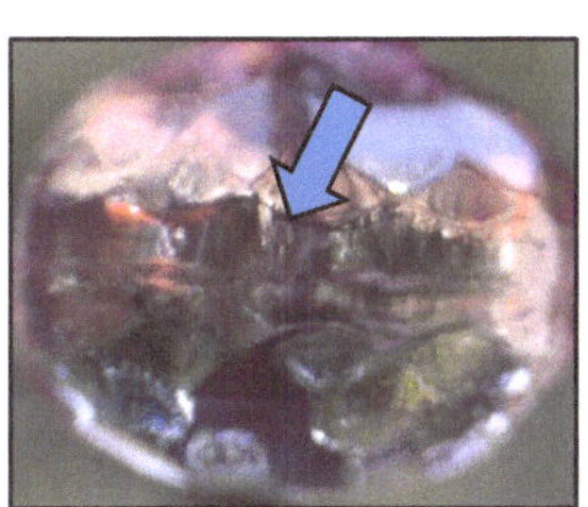

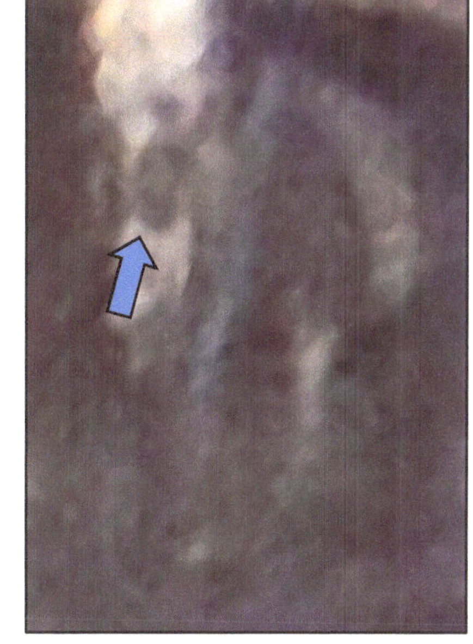

When I first noticed the two critters below, I wasn't sure what they were. Their ears seemed too long for wolves, but then I realized that they are jackals.

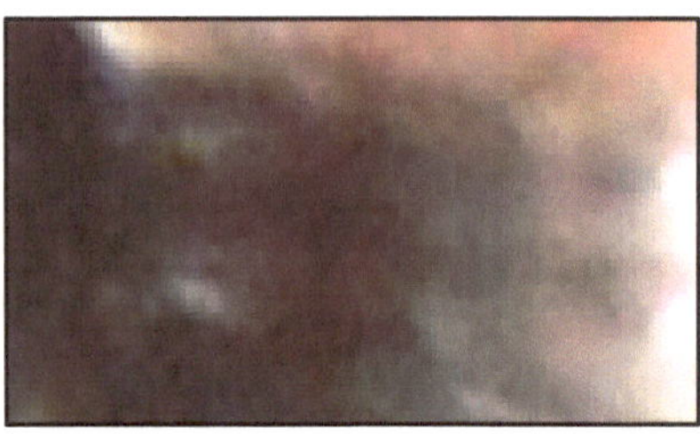

Although the following verse has a serious message, I had to chuckle when I first read it. It says, "Son of man, prophesy against the prophets of Israel who are now prophesying" (Ezekiel 13:2). There certainly is a lot of prophesying going on in this verse! Since the prophets were living in a poor spiritual and natural state, they were like "jackals among ruins" (v. 4). God had never called them, and as a result they ended up leading the nation astray. Thankfully, the Sovereign Lord made a promise to cleanse Israel from all their sins (36:33).

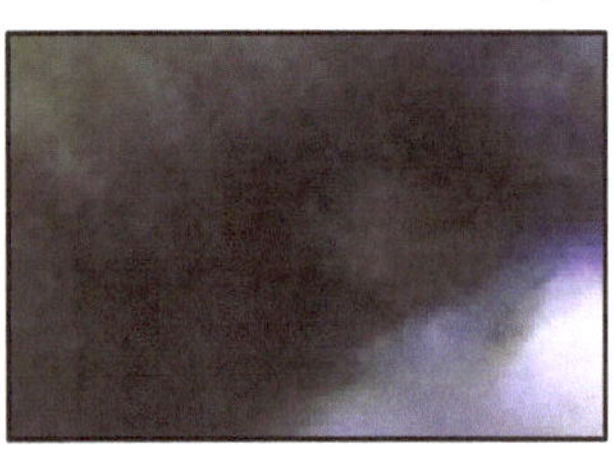

On a much lighter note, here are two more animals you may enjoy. The first one is a hedgehog. Perhaps you spotted her by the crocodile. I think she has one of the most precious faces. And then we have a purple duck. Yes, a purple duck! He is likely a mallard.

Along the river and near the East Gate, I am beginning to find layers of images. Most of them are of baby animals. God will certainly make all things new, won't He? It's a baby jungle out there!

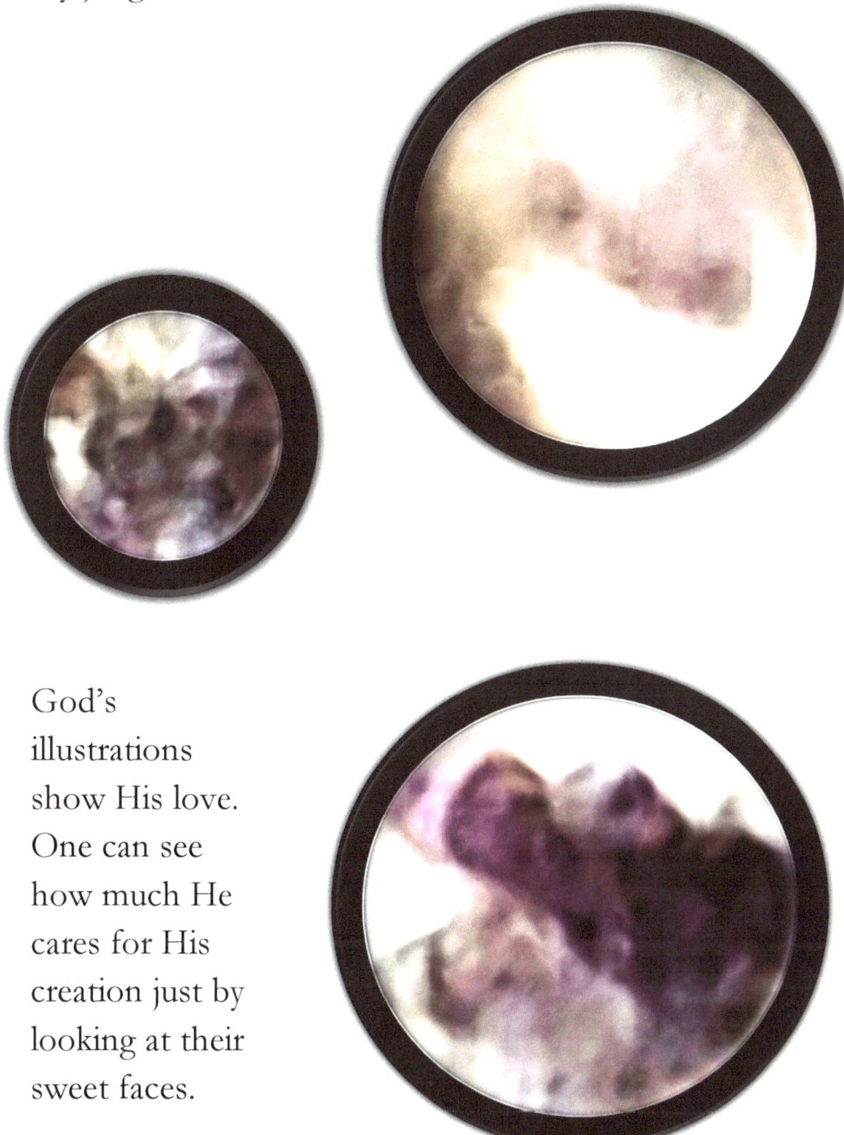

God's illustrations show His love. One can see how much He cares for His creation just by looking at their sweet faces.

Elephants and monkeys and bears, oh my! Wouldn't it be amazing to interact with wild animals without any fear of harm? I have always wanted to hold a koala.

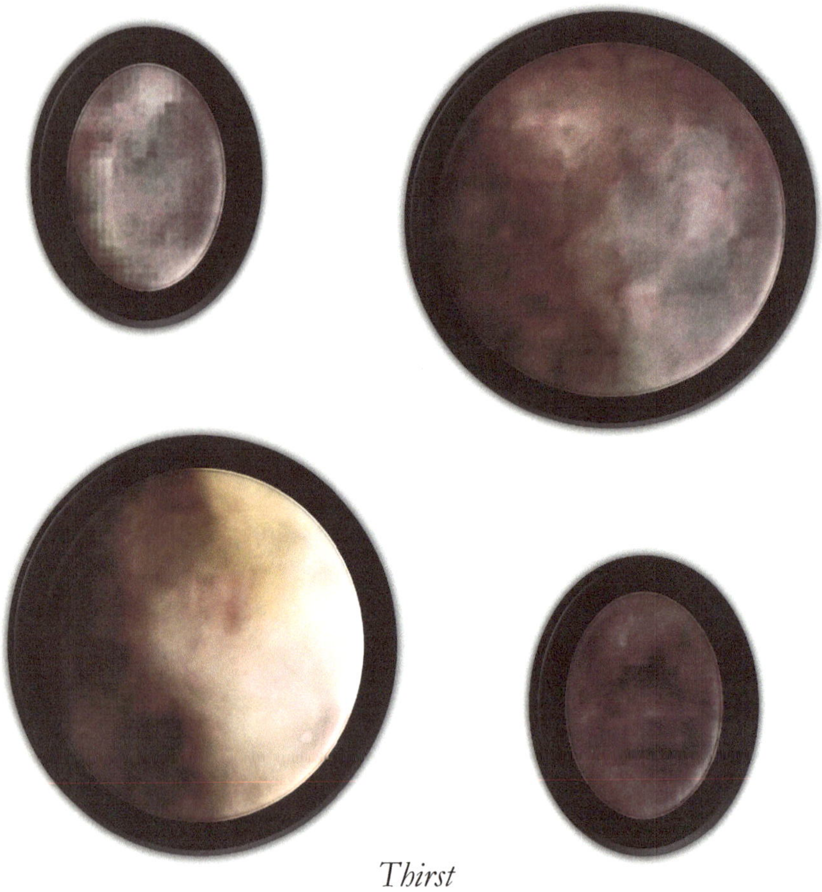

Thirst

In John 4:1-26, Jesus meets the Samaritan woman at the well where He asks her for some water (v. 7). When she brings up the fact that Jews do not associate with Samaritans, He explains, "If you knew the gift of God and who it is that asks you for a drink, you would have asked him and he would have given you living water" (vv. 9-10). He tells her that everyone who drinks from the well will be thirsty again, but whoever drinks the water He gives them will never thirst (v. 13). In fact, the water will become a spring welling up to eternal life (v. 14).

The river of the water of life flows from the throne of God in His eternal kingdom (Revelation 22:1). This illustrates how eternal life flows from God to all His people. During the millennial reign, creatures will live wherever the river flows. God's water will bring life. It brings life to the natural realm as well as the spiritual. I love Psalm 42 since it paints a vivid picture of both the natural and the spiritual. It says, "As the deer pants for streams of water, so my soul pants for you, my God" (v. 1). When I found the image of the donkey in the second photo, I noticed another animal's head above it. At first I thought it looked like a deer, but then I figured it was the donkey's mother. When I researched donkeys and deer, however, I reached the conclusion that it looks more like a deer. Therefore, the image can remind us of the living water that comes from the throne. God will meet the needs of all His creation. Yes, even the sweet donkeys and deer!

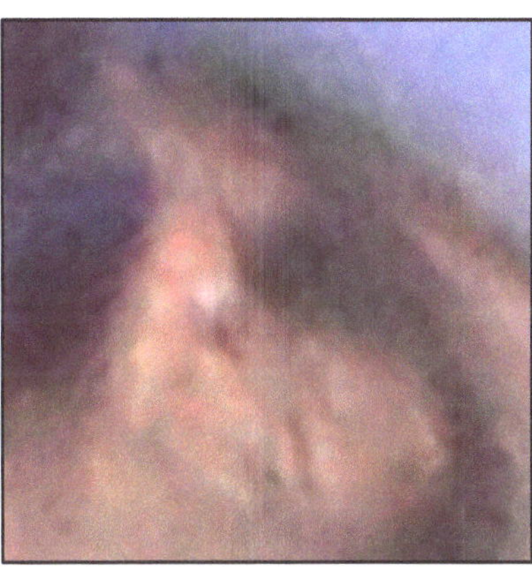

"Blessed is the one who reads aloud the words of this prophecy, and blessed are those who hear it and take to heart what is written in it, because the time is near."

Revelation 1:3

8

REVELATION

The beloved disciple is one of my favorite people in the Bible. He was a part of Jesus' inner circle, which included Peter, James, and John. It is believed that John wrote the Book of Revelation. After being exiled to the island of Patmos, he received a heavenly vision as well as insight into end times. He explains, "I, John, your brother and companion in the suffering and kingdom and patient endurance that are ours in Jesus, was on the island of Patmos because of the word of God and the testimony of Jesus" (Revelation 1:9). John then hears a loud voice like a trumpet. The Lord tells him to write what he sees and then send it out to the seven churches (vv. 10-11).

When I first noticed a man kneeling on the red stone, I immediately saw that he had sad eyes. John tells us that he "wept and wept because no one was found who was worthy to open the scroll or look inside" (5:4).

Some of the photos, of course, are clearer on a computer. In the picture below, it is difficult to see John's weepy eyes. It looks like he is writing, though.

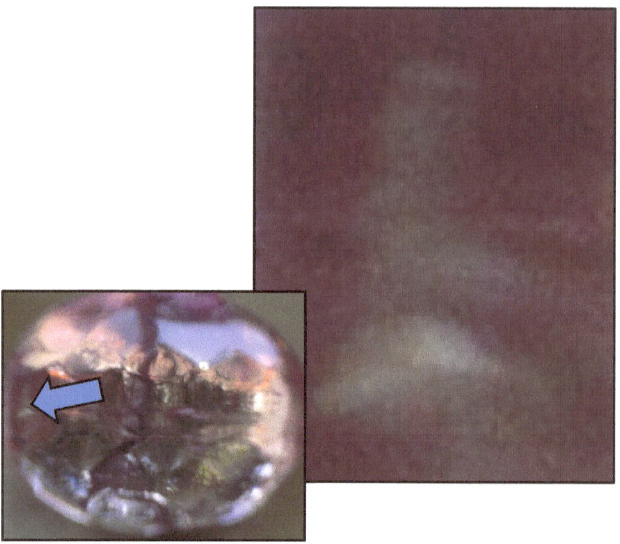

I noticed a scroll in the third photo, which I think is John's completed letter to the seven churches.

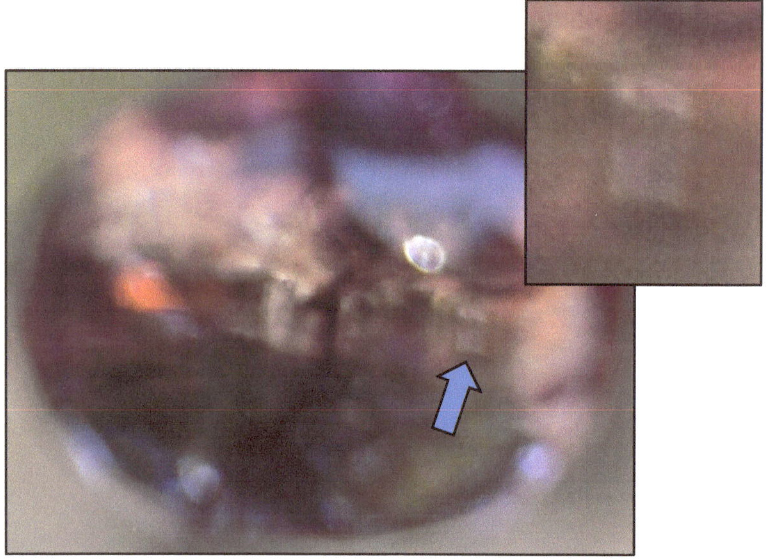

If you look closely at the first picture, you can see a floral image on John's headpiece. According to Exodus 28:36-38, the high priest wore a plate of pure gold on his turban. The words "HOLINESS TO THE LORD" were engraved in the gold. John, of course, was not a high priest, but God chose Israel for a special purpose. He says, "Although the whole earth is mine, you will be for me a kingdom of priests and a holy nation" (19:6).

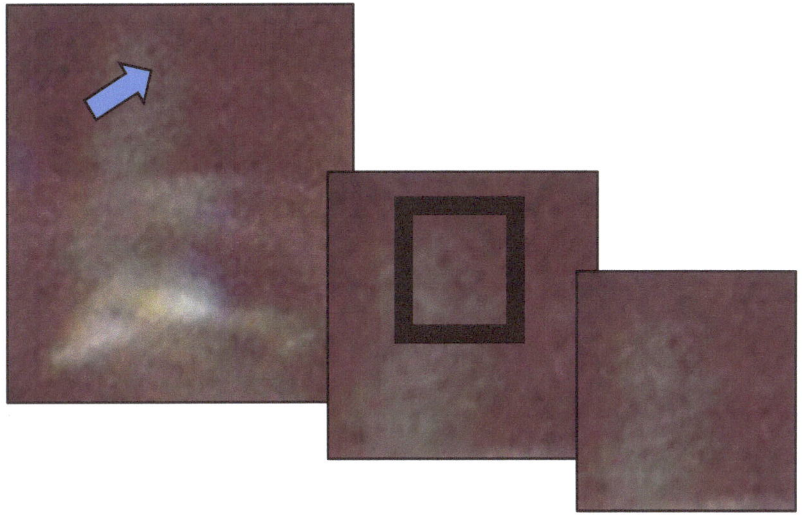

John explains that we will see the Lord's face on the New Earth, and His name will be on our foreheads (Revelation 22:4).

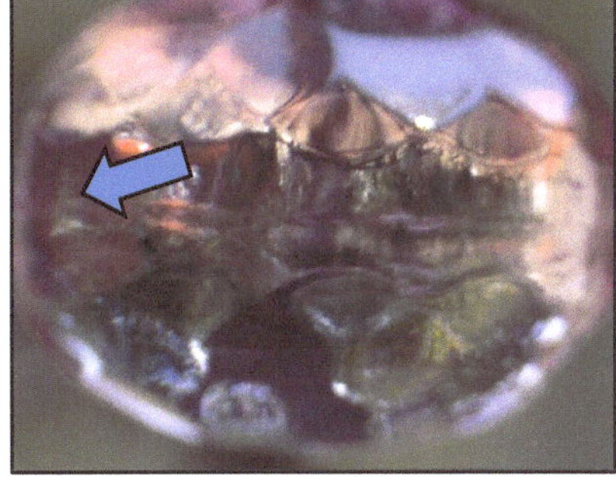

When John turned around to see who was speaking to him, he saw seven golden lampstands (1:12). The lampstand symbolizes the church, how it shines in a dark world. "And among the lampstands was someone like a son of man, dressed in a robe reaching down to his feet and with a golden sash around his chest" (v. 13). His hair was "white like wool, as white as snow" (v. 14). I considered the possibility that the figure on the right could be the Son of Man, Jesus. When John saw Him, he fell at His feet (v. 17). In Revelation 15:6, however, there are seven angels with golden sashes around their chests as well. I tend to think that the figure fits the context of the angels better. We will definitely take a look at this again later.

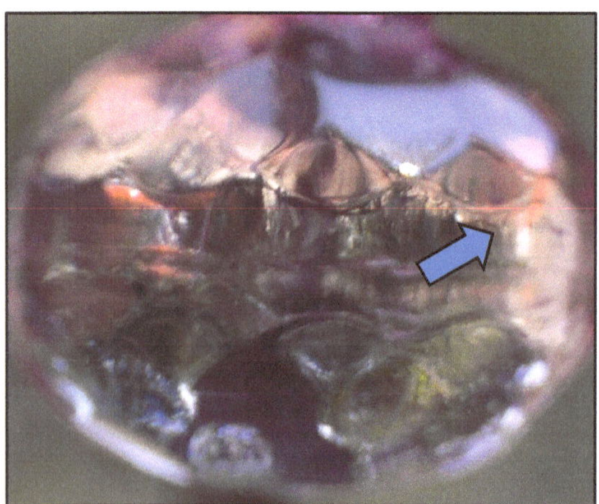

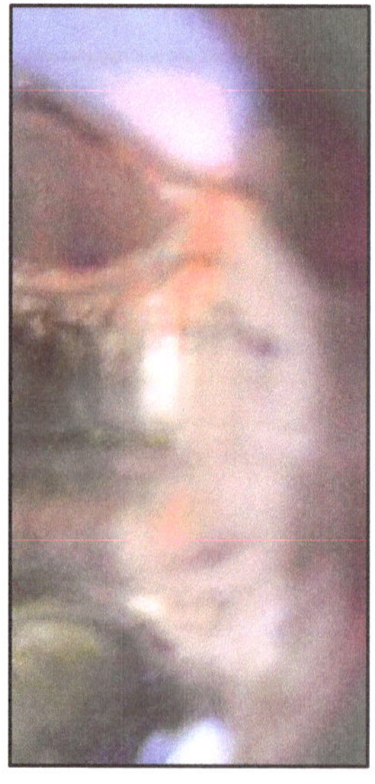

So, perhaps you are wondering, how it is possible to see God. In 1 Timothy 6:15-16, it says, "God, the blessed and only Ruler, the King of kings and Lord of lords, who alone is immortal and who lives in unapproachable light, whom no one has seen or can see. To him be honor and might forever." Some people in the Bible got blessed with a glimpse of God, although it was not the fullness of God. That would be too overwhelming. As we continue to analyze the photos, please keep in mind that we are looking at impressions of Heaven. The photos are not actually Heaven. For example, the profile of the Lord is an impression, not necessarily an exact representation. And it certainly is not the Lord Himself. It is only a photograph.

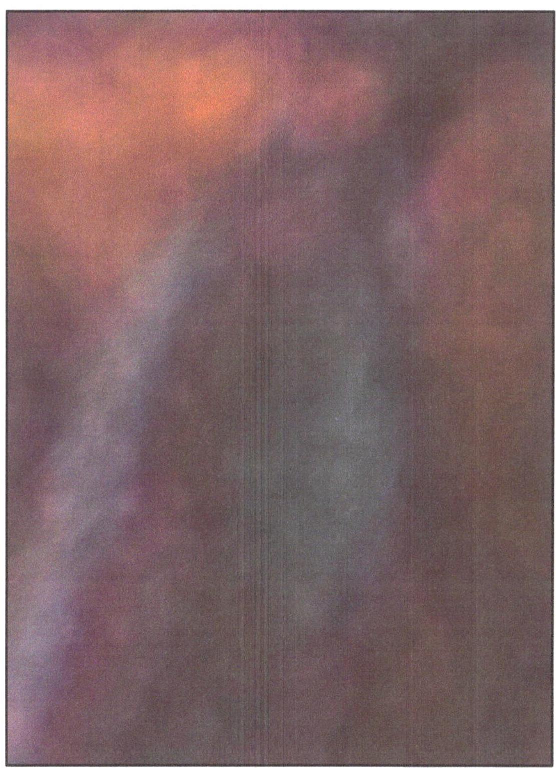

John saw a door standing open in Heaven (Revelation 4:1). Someone who had an appearance of jasper and ruby was sitting on a throne, and a rainbow that shone like an emerald encircled it (vv. 2-3). Twenty-four elders dressed in white and wearing gold crowns were also seated on thrones (v. 4). The next verse reminds me of the third photo. It tells us that "from the throne came flashes of lightning, rumblings and peals of thunder" (v. 5).

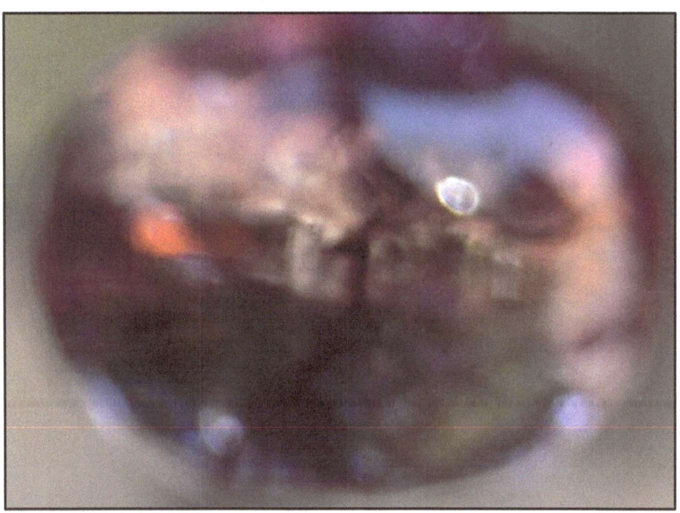

"Also in front of the throne there was what looked like a sea of glass, clear as crystal" (v. 6).

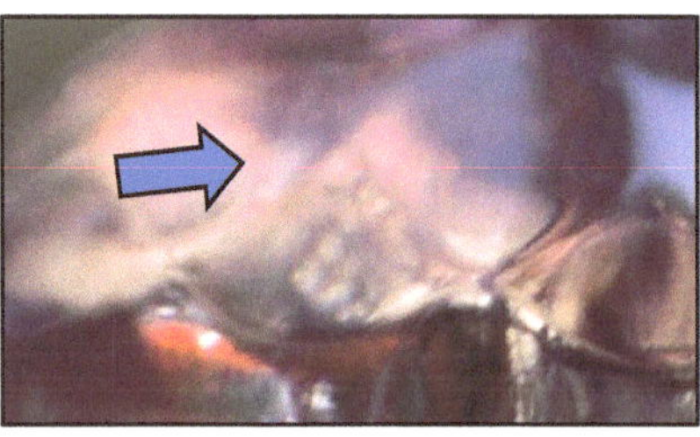

“In the center, around the throne, were four living creatures, and they were covered with eyes, in front and in back” (v. 6).

The first living creature was like a lion.

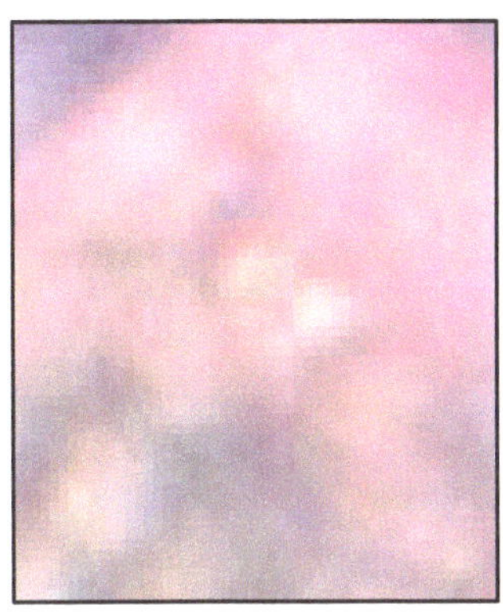

The second was like an ox.

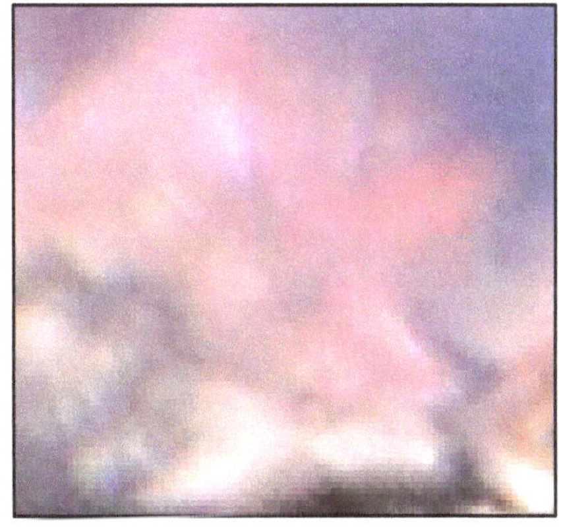

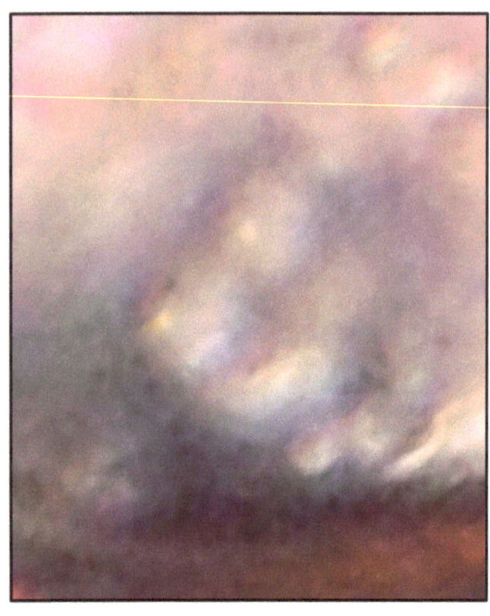

The third had a face like a man.

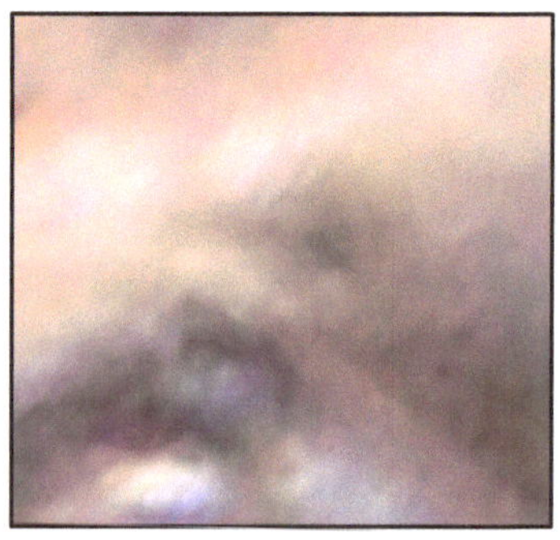

The fourth was like a flying eagle.

The four living creatures, also known as cherubim, constantly glorify God. "Day and night they never stop saying: 'Holy, holy, holy is the Lord God Almighty,' who was, and is, and is to come" (v. 8). One thing I love about the man and the eagle is that they look like they are singing. Just imagine the creatures beside the throne of God, worshiping Him with a beautiful song! Whenever the living creatures give glory, honor and thanks to him, the twenty-four elders fall down and worship (vv. 9-10). "They lay their crowns before the throne and say: 'You are worthy, our Lord and God, to receive glory and honor and power, for you created all things, and by your will they were created and have their being'" (vv. 10-11).

Scroll & Lamb

The one who sat on the throne held a scroll in His right hand with seven seals (5:1). It also had writing on both sides. John wept since no one was found worthy to open the scroll or look inside of it (v. 4). Of course, it is possible that we see the image of a scroll in the third photo. However, as already noted, it could also represent the letter to the seven churches.

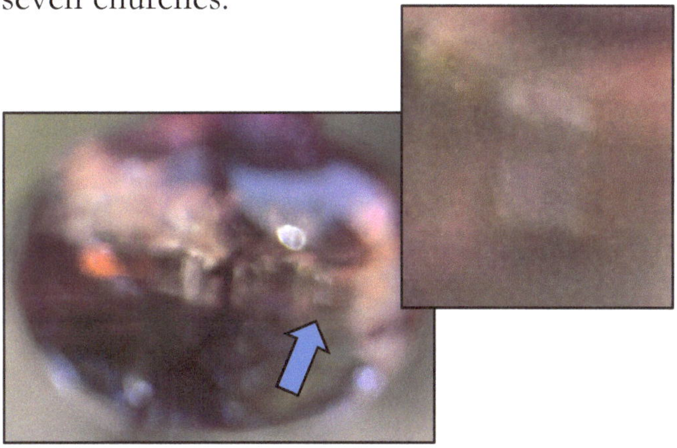

John saw a mighty angel proclaiming in a loud voice, "Who is worthy to break the seals and open the scroll?" (v. 2). Then one of the elders said to John, "Do not weep! See, the Lion of the tribe of Judah, the Root of David, has triumphed. He is able to open the scroll and its seven seals" (v. 5).

John then saw a Lamb, looking as if it had been slain (v. 6). He was standing at the center of the throne, encircled by the four living creatures and the elders. The Lamb took the scroll from the right hand of the one who sat on the throne (v. 7). Then the four living creatures and the twenty-four elders fell down before Him (v. 8). Each one held a harp and golden bowls full of incense. In the second photo, we actually get to see a heavenly harp. Now if we could just hear it…although we will be a part of Heaven's music one day.

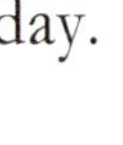

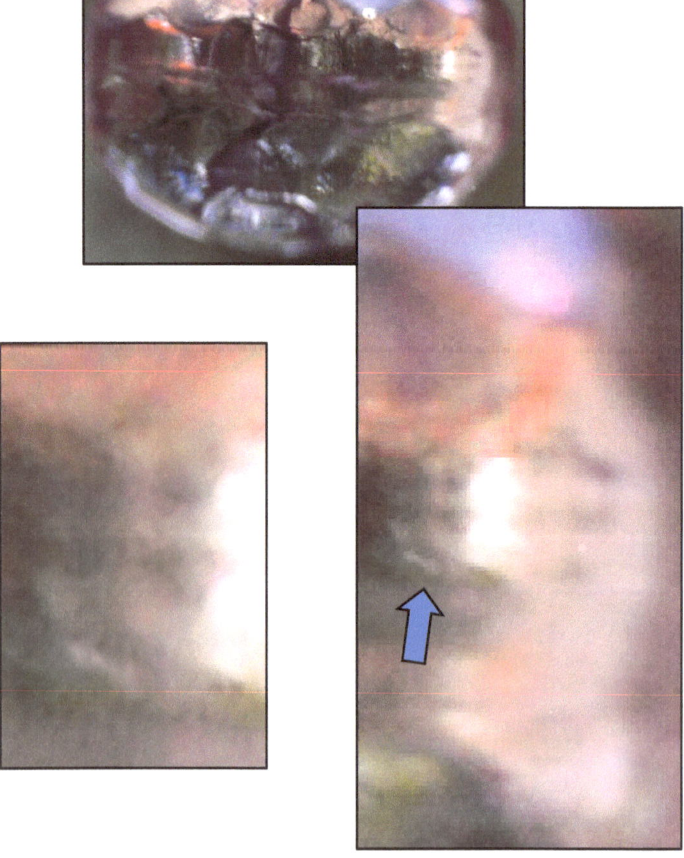

The bowls are more obvious in the first photo, although they are visible in the second photo as well.

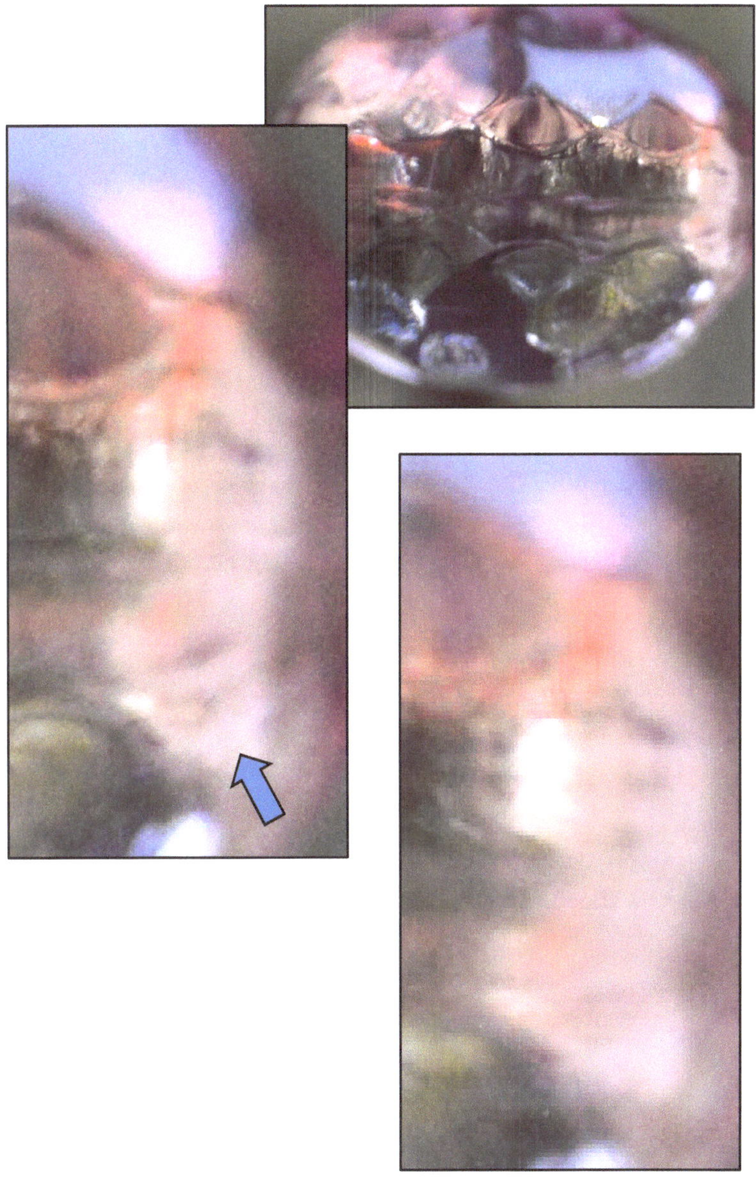

The golden bowls full of incense are the prayers of God's people (v. 8).

When the Lamb opened the seventh seal, Heaven was silent for about half an hour (8:1). Then seven trumpets were given to the seven angels who stand before God (v. 2). And another angel held a golden censer. "He was given much incense to offer, with the prayers of all God's people, on the golden altar in front of the throne" (v. 3).

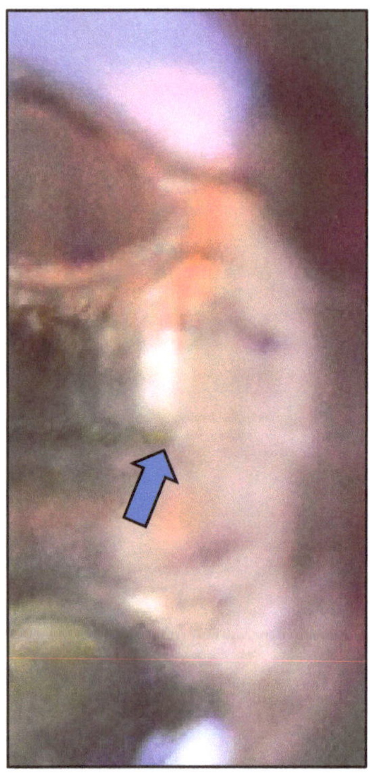

Golden Censer

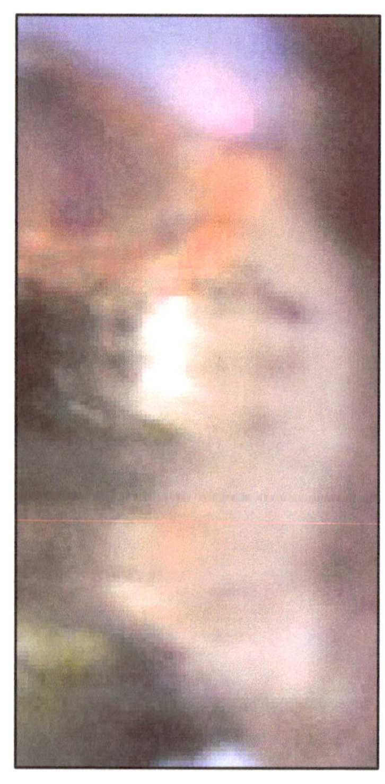

The smoke of the incense along with people's prayers went up before God (v. 4). Then the angel filled the censer with fire from the altar and hurled it to the earth. "There came peals of thunder, rumblings, flashes of lightning and an earthquake" (v. 5).

Eight months after I took the miracle pictures, we spent a weekend preparing our taxes. Kirk does most of the work, but I help when I can. Anyway, I had a little extra time, so I decided to take a closer look at the other photos. Just for fun I decided to crop each button to see if there was anything interesting. I didn't think I would find much. Usually when I take a series of photos, there will be several duds that lead up to one really nice shot. Well, I was pleasantly surprised to find some of the most beautiful images I have ever seen! I will introduce them gradually throughout the rest of our study.

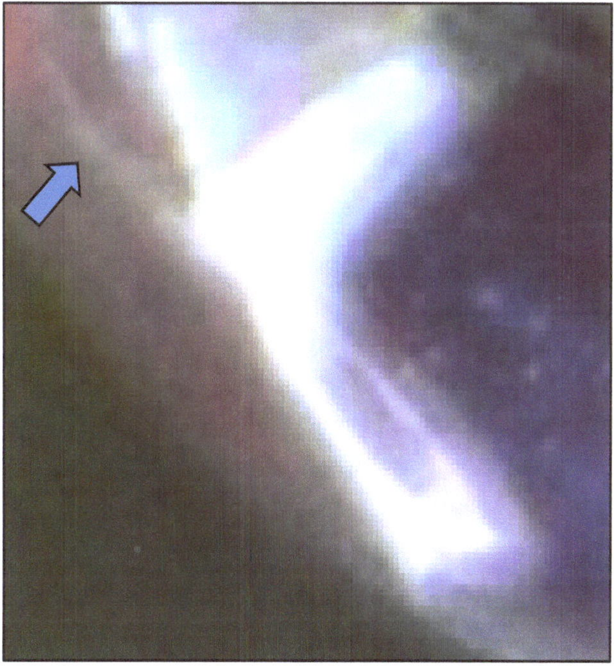

The angel above looks like he is holding something, possibly a trumpet or a sickle.

The seven angels holding the seven trumpets were prepared to sound them one by one (Revelation 8:6). Hail, fire, and blood got hurled to the earth (v. 7). As John watched, he heard an eagle calling out in a loud voice: "Woe! Woe! Woe to the inhabitants of the earth, because of the trumpet blasts about to be sounded by the other three angels!" (v. 13).

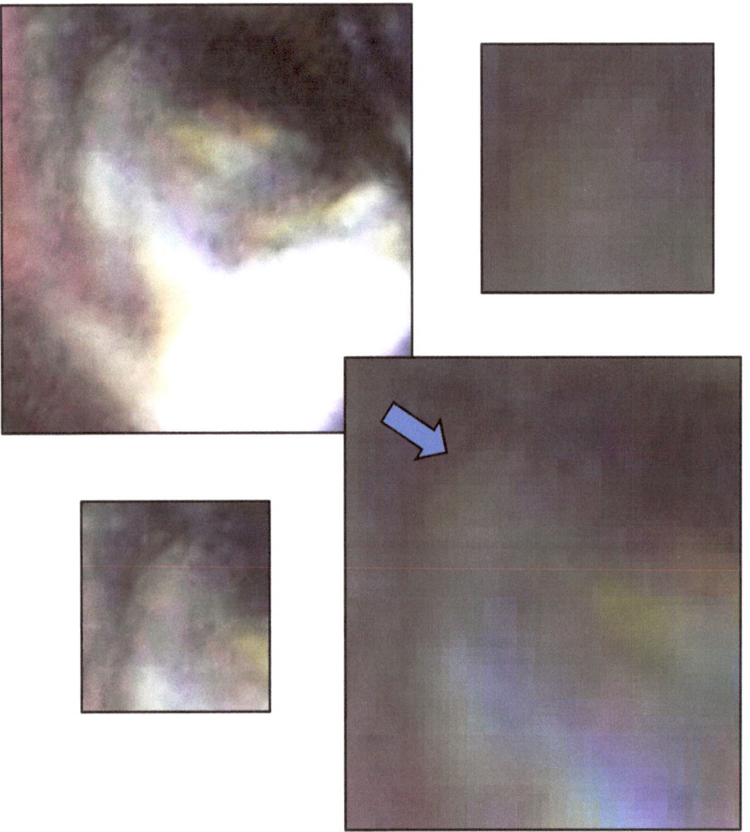

To me, the photo above looks like an eagle with its mouth open. The heavenly messenger provides a warning of the last three trumpet judgments. The first four focus on nature, while the last three will be upon humanity.

John saw another mighty angel coming down from Heaven. "He was robed in a cloud, with a rainbow above his head; his face was like the sun, and his legs were like fiery pillars" (10:1).

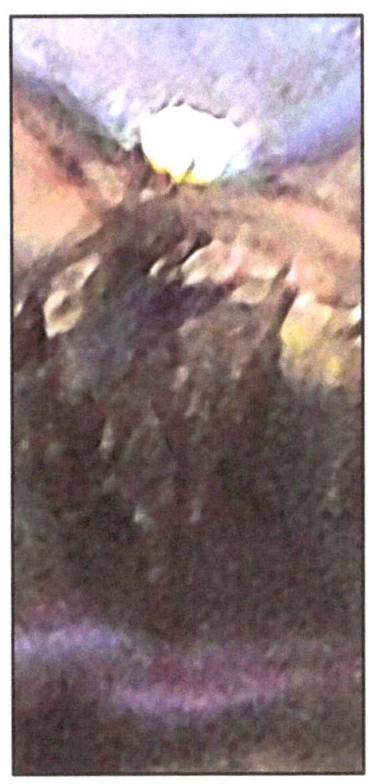

Mighty Angel

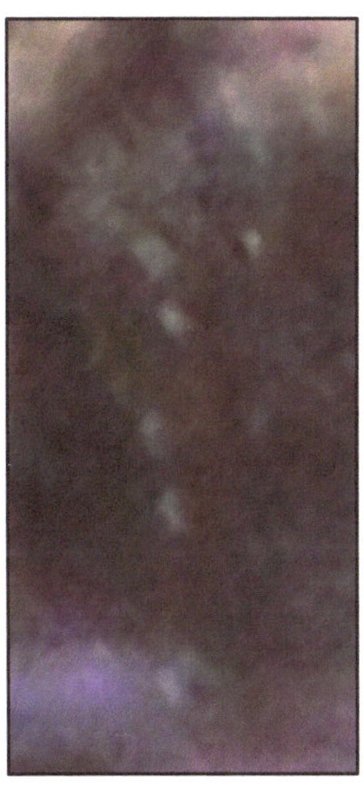

Even though the colorful details of the angel are not visible in the photos, there are some interesting things to note. First of all, as we have already seen, the white spot above his head possesses a rainbow in a few of the other pictures. Also, in the second photo, it looks like a cloud surrounds him. Unfortunately, the image doesn't translate well into this format.

Some people believe the mighty angel is Jesus. However, I tend to think that the angel is a messenger, perhaps Michael. At first I thought he had a large wing on his left side (our right). But as I studied the image on my computer, I decided it could be another angel.

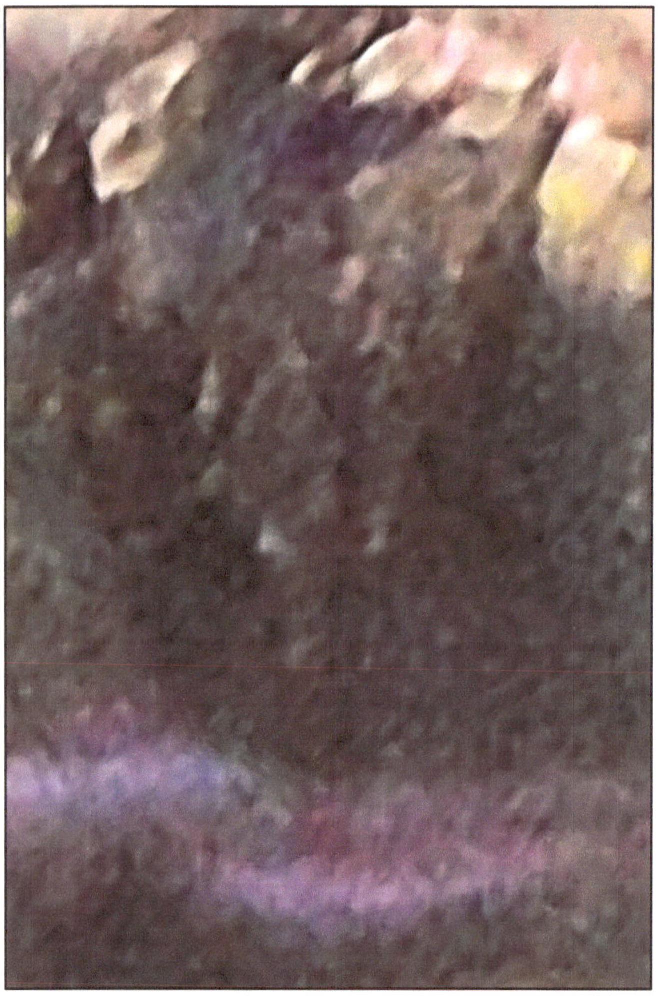

John tells us that the angel was holding a little scroll (10:2). In the photo it looks like he is reading it. Please note the position of his head, particularly his face.

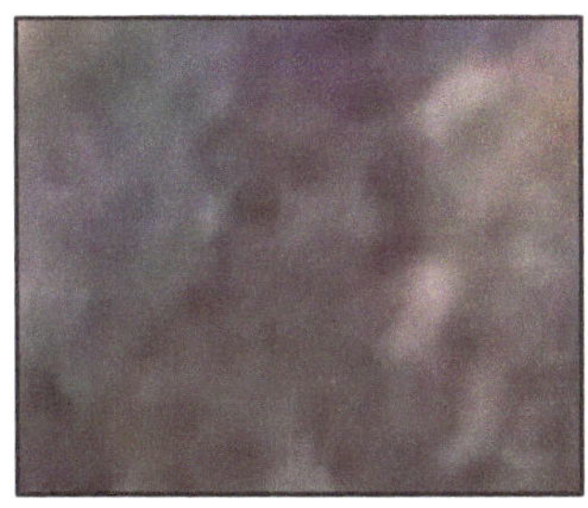

Reading the little scroll

When the four living creatures stand still, they lower their wings (Ezekiel 1:24). Therefore, I assume angels function in a similar way. At first glance, the mighty angel looks like a soldier. In fact, I thought he was wearing a military vest. Then one day I realized his wings were down. The wings, I think, look like a vest. If you look carefully, you can see how they come down under his arms from behind.

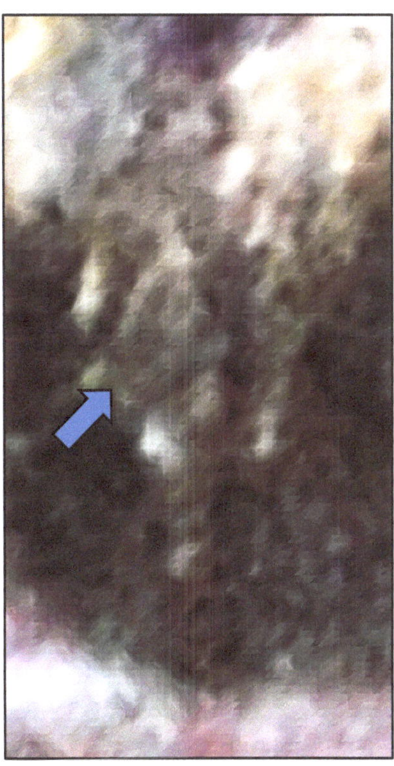

"Then I looked, and there before me was the Lamb, standing on Mount Zion, and with him 144,000 who had his name and his Father's name written on their foreheads."

Revelation 14:1

9

HARVEST

The Lamb is symbolic for Jesus the Messiah. In Revelation 14:1, He is standing on Mount Zion with God's people. The conflict is over, so the mountain has become a place of victory and rest.

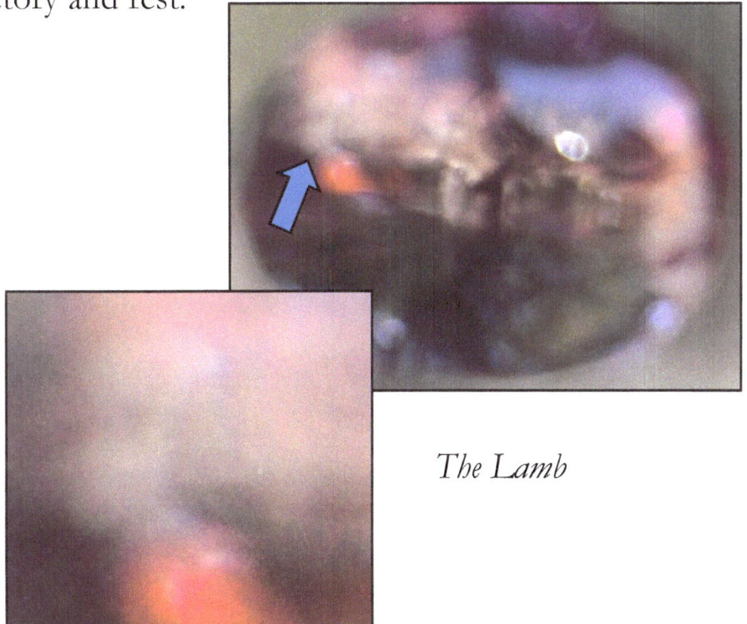

The Lamb

At this moment, John hears a sound from Heaven like the roar of rushing waters and like a loud peal of thunder (14:2). He says it was like harpists playing their harps. Then the people sang a new song before the throne (v. 3).

Parable of the Weeds

In the gospels, Jesus often tells a simple story to illustrate a spiritual lesson. For example, He uses the parable of the weeds to teach about the end of the age (Matthew 13:36-43). Here is an overview of the parable:

Sower: Son of Man

Field: world

Good Seed: people of the kingdom

Weeds: people of the evil one

Enemy: the devil

Harvest: end of the age

Harvesters: angels

The Son of Man will send out His angels to weed out all evil from His kingdom (v. 41). The weeds will get pulled up and burned in the fire (v. 40). Of course, the Lord does not want anyone to perish (2 Peter 3:9). "But the day of the Lord will come like a thief. The heavens will disappear with a roar; the elements will be destroyed by fire and the earth and everything done in it will be laid bare" (v. 10).

Harvesting the Earth

The pictures of the angels are some of the most beautiful images I have ever seen. To think that we get a glimpse of Heaven is truly a gift. I do not take sharing the photos with you lightly.

John says, "I looked, and there before me was a white cloud, and seated on the cloud was one like a son of man with a crown of gold on his head and a sharp sickle in his hand" (Revelation 14:14). As you can see, the angel in the photo is sitting down. There is a wing by his side, and a second angel is to his left.

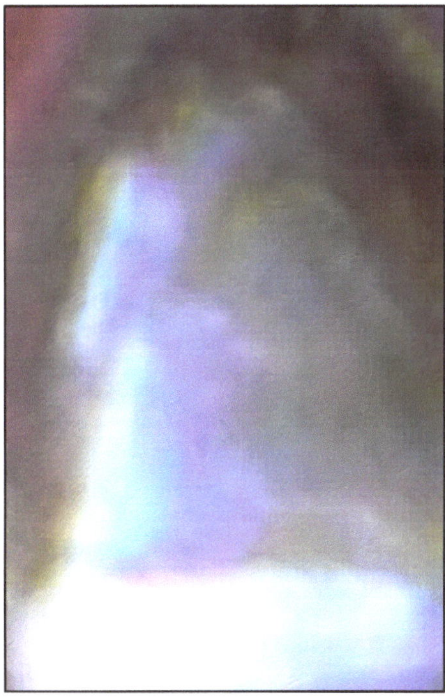

Then another angel (probably the angel on the left) came out of the temple and called to the one sitting on a cloud, "Take your sickle and reap, because the time to reap has come, for the harvest of the earth is ripe" (14:15). So he swung his sickle over the earth to harvest it (v. 16).

Next to the angels, we find a planet that looks like Earth.

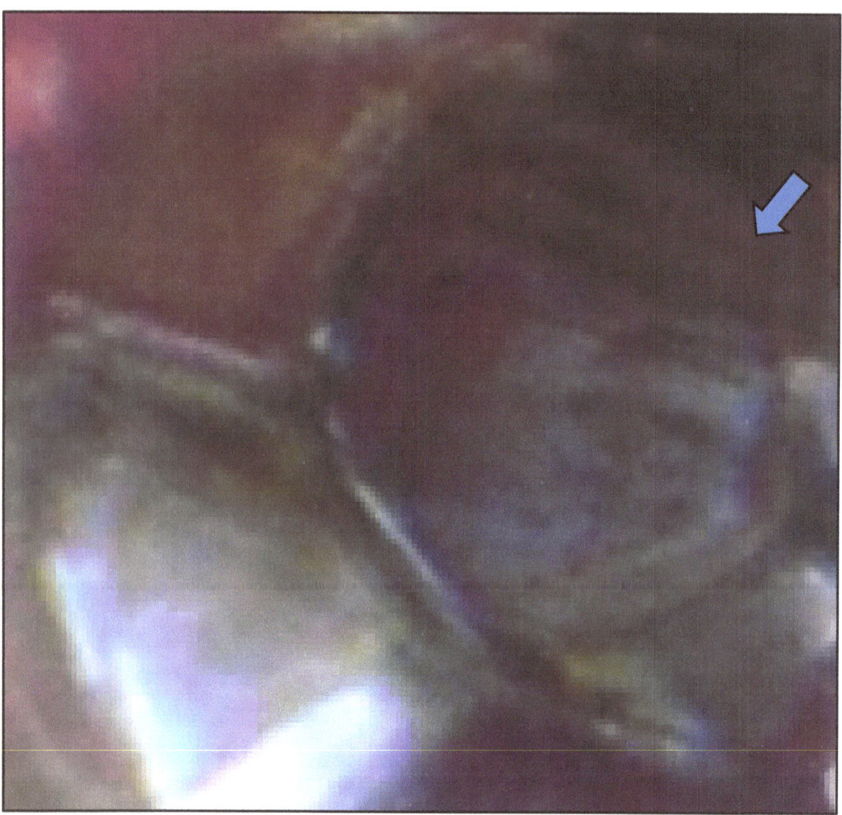

Then another angel with a sharp sickle came out of the temple in Heaven (v. 17). In the last chapter, we took a look at this particular angel, although it is not clear whether he is holding a sickle or a trumpet. What do you think? I tend to think it is a sickle even though it has less of a curve.

Did you happen to notice the smaller planet in the distance? This could be the New Earth. Some people believe God will recreate the earth we live on now. Others believe there will be an entirely new earth. The photos don't solve the mystery for us. Rather, they give us several snapshots of God's plan for Earth, whether recreated or made new.

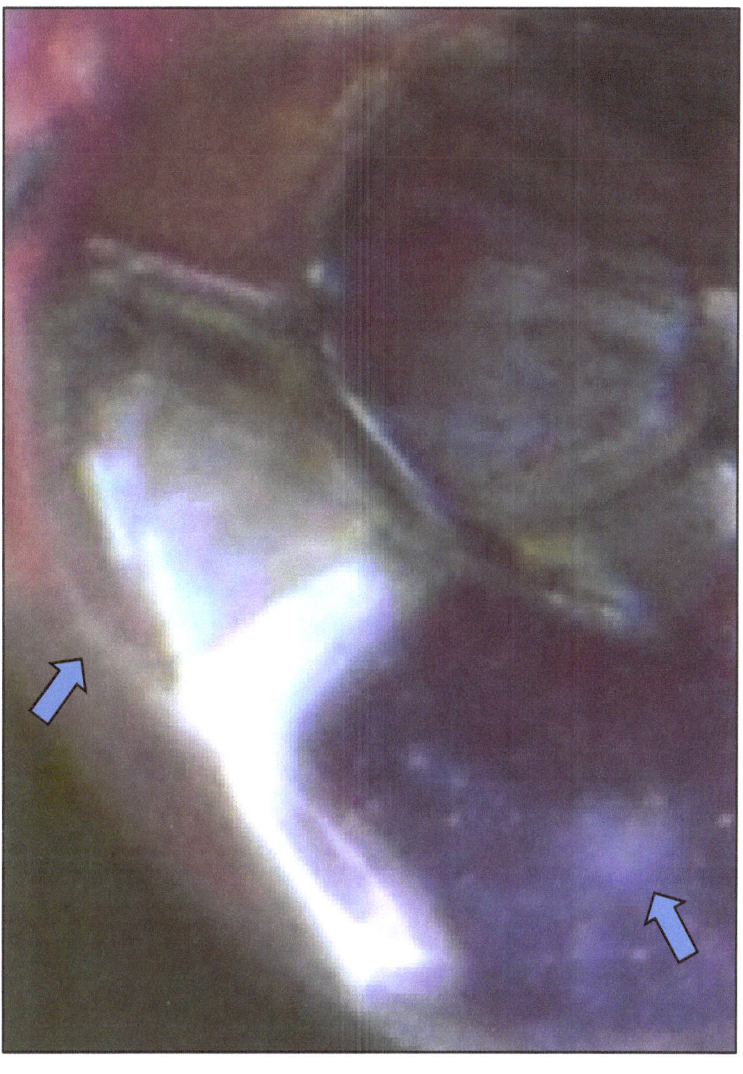

I couldn't leave you hanging without showing you the next photo. You may recognize the eagle and rainbow in the upper left-hand corner. Also, the New Earth has moved into full view.

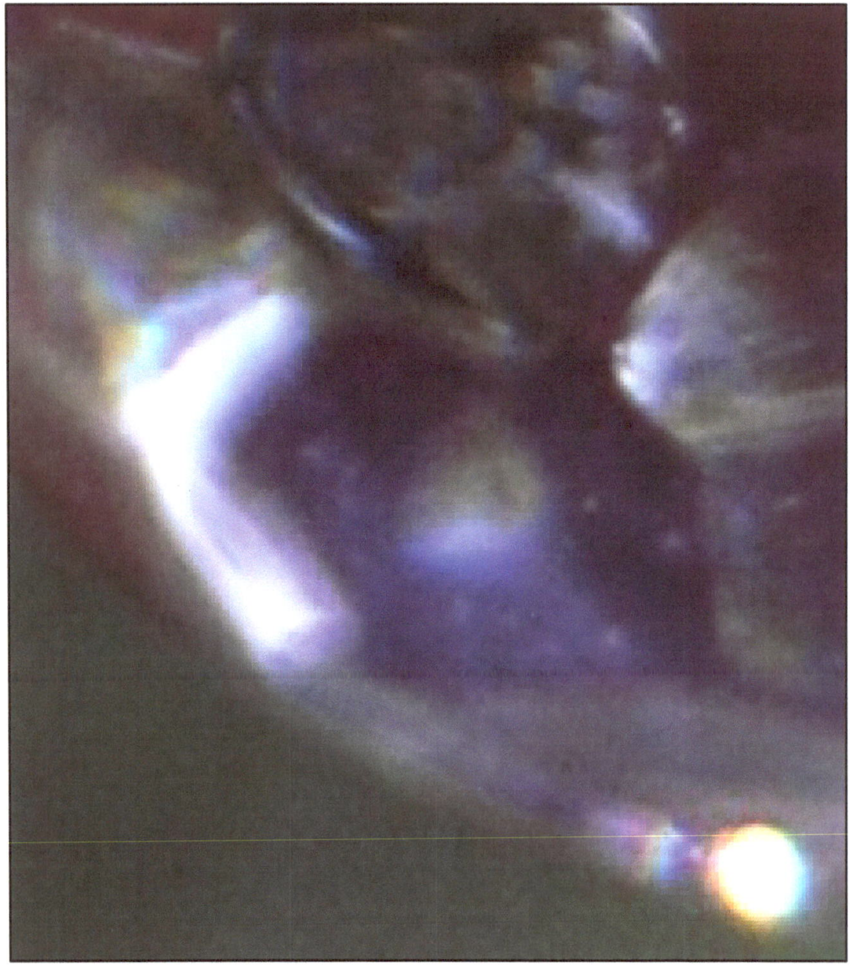

Angels travel at the speed of light, perhaps even faster. It reminds me of a rocket blasting off into space. The way John describes the angel in Revelation 10:1 is also fitting. He tells us that "a rainbow was above his head" and "his face was like the sun." I've never seen anything quite like it.

We also get a glimpse of the angel's speed in the first picture.

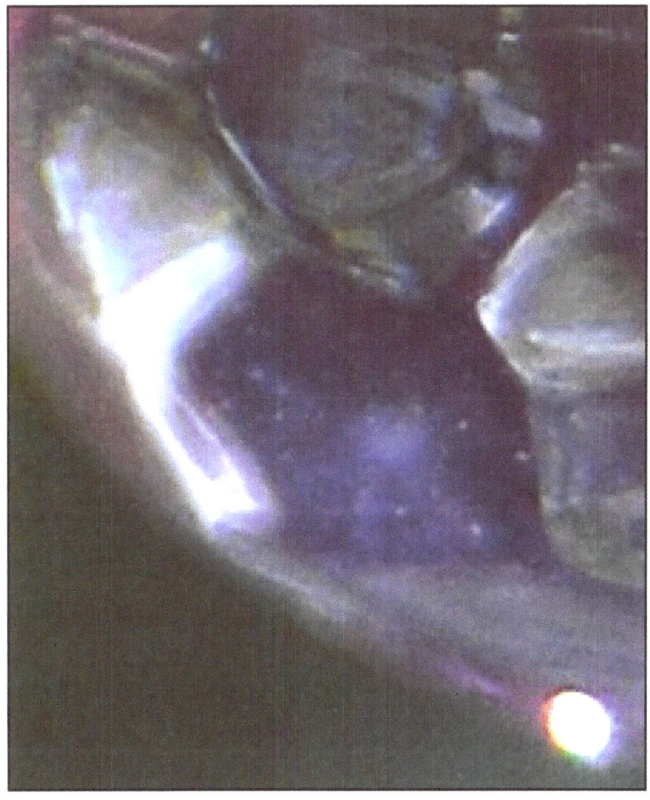

When I asked Kirk about it, he said that the concave part of the angel's body would make him fly faster. Of course, angels are spirit beings, but they are also made of matter. According to Scripture, they can take on the form of a man (Genesis 18:1-19; Mark 16:5).

I often pray that God will send His angels to protect those I love. After seeing the images of the angels, the heavenly realm has become more real to me. "Are not all angels ministering spirits sent to serve those who will inherit salvation?" (Hebrews 1:14).

I'm not a big fan of fire. In fact, I probably would have preferred Noah's ark over the trumpets and bowls. God, however, has prepared us "for such a time as this" (Esther 4:14). He will be with us. He is with us, *Immanuel.* Thank You, Lord!

At the sound of the first trumpet, hail and fire mixed with blood will come to the earth (Revelation 8:7). Then a blazing mountain will get thrown into the sea (v. 8). That will take place after the second trumpet. Then, after the third, a great star will fall from the sky (v. 10). In chapter 16, John outlines the seven bowls. He tells us that the fourth angel will pour out his bowl on the sun (v. 8). Intense heat will scorch people with fire.

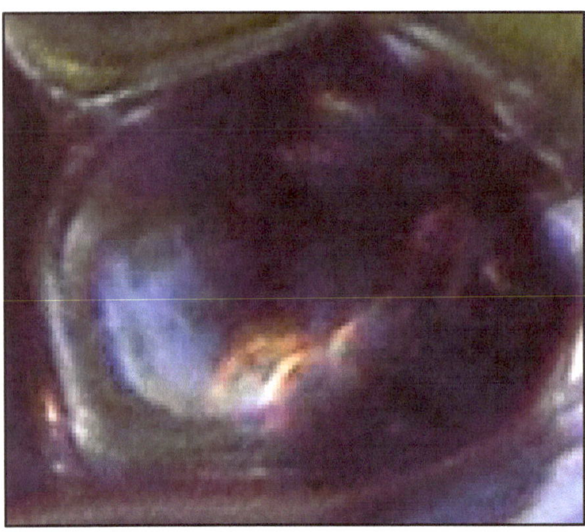

The frog may symbolize deception in the last days (Revelation 16:12-14).

In the picture above, we have another interesting image of the earth. It looks as though fire is falling from Heaven.

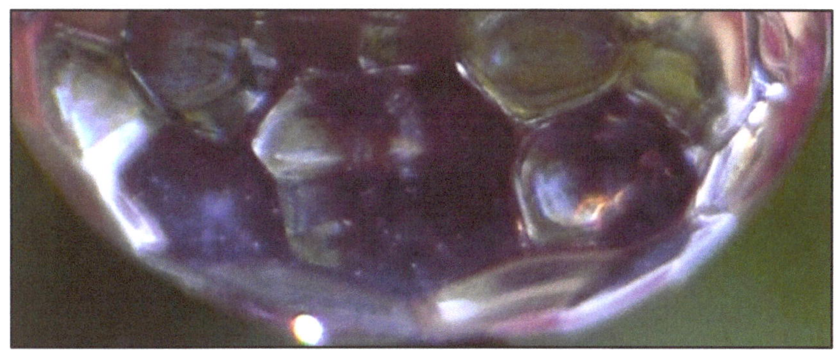

Now let's take a look at the entire scene. On the left we have an angel sitting down. He is harvesting the earth. The angel below him is flying with a trumpet or sickle in his hand. The New Earth is in the distance. On the right side we see fire falling to the earth. There is also another angel, and he is extremely beautiful!

I also spotted something very unusual in the center of the photo. You may have noticed it too. It looks like the Horsehead Nebula. Apparently, it is found in the constellation Orion, and it consists of dust and gas. As I zoomed in on the image, I noticed the creature has the face of a lion. Therefore, perhaps a Lionhead Nebula exists as well! It's just a fun thought.

Like a caring apostle, Peter asks an important question about the last days. His words are worth considering, don't you agree? He explains, "Since everything will be destroyed in this way, what kind of people ought you to be?" (2 Peter 3:11). He then provides the answer. Peter tells us that we ought to live holy and godly lives as we look forward to the day of God and speed its coming. "That day will bring about the destruction of the heavens by fire, and the elements will melt in the heat. But in keeping with his promise we are looking forward to a new heaven and a new earth, where righteousness dwells. So then, dear friends, since you are looking forward to this, make every effort to be found spotless, blameless and at peace with him" (vv. 11-14).

Man in Linen

We have finally arrived at one of the most spectacular images in the collection. As we read through a couple of verses in Daniel, we find answers about this heavenly being. Daniel receives a visit from a man who resembles the lovely one in this picture. He describes the following things: his linen clothes, a belt of fine gold around his waist, a body like topaz, a face like lightning, eyes like flaming torches, and arms and legs like the gleam of burnished bronze (Daniel 10:4-6). Even though wings are not mentioned in this passage, it looks like there could be one in the photo. Notice the gorgeous golden color along his side. It also could be a burnished bronze arm. The King James Version describes his arms and feet as polished brass.

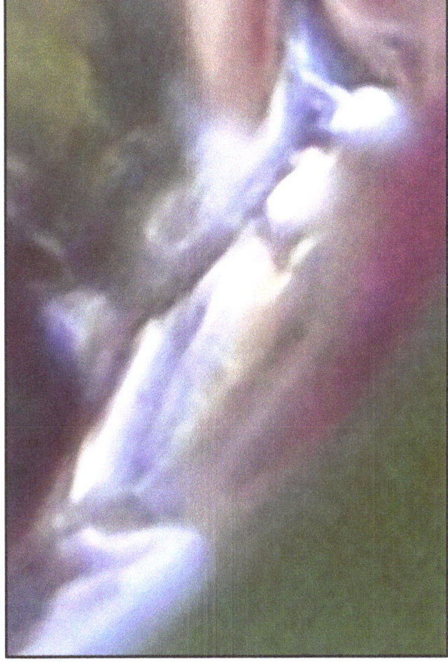

It is possible that the image represents a theophany. According to Edward J. Young, a theophany is "a preincarnate appearance of the eternal Son" (225). In Revelation 1:13-16, John sees someone like a son of man dressed in a robe with a golden sash around his chest. His eyes were like blazing fire, his feet like bronze, and "his face was like the sun shining in all its brilliance."

In Song of Solomon (also known as Song of Songs), we read about the beloved, the lovely one. The King James Version tells us that "his hands are as gold rings set with beryl: his belly is as bright ivory overlaid with sapphires. His legs are as pillars of marble, set upon sockets of fine gold…" (5:14-15). To me, this section of Scripture describes this picture beautifully.

As our study on the harvest comes to a close, let's take a moment to return to the angel holding the bowls. John describes seven angels with seven plagues. "They were dressed in clean, shining linen and wore golden sashes around their chests" (Revelation 15:6). One of the four living creatures gave them seven golden bowls filled with wrath (v. 7). Then the temple filled with smoke from the glory and power of God, and no one could enter it until the end of the seven plagues (v. 8). So, what do you think? Is it possible that the photos represent Revelation 1, 5, 8, or 15?

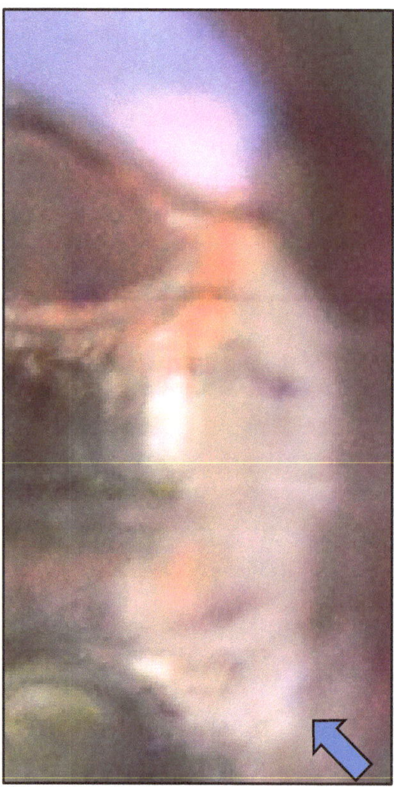

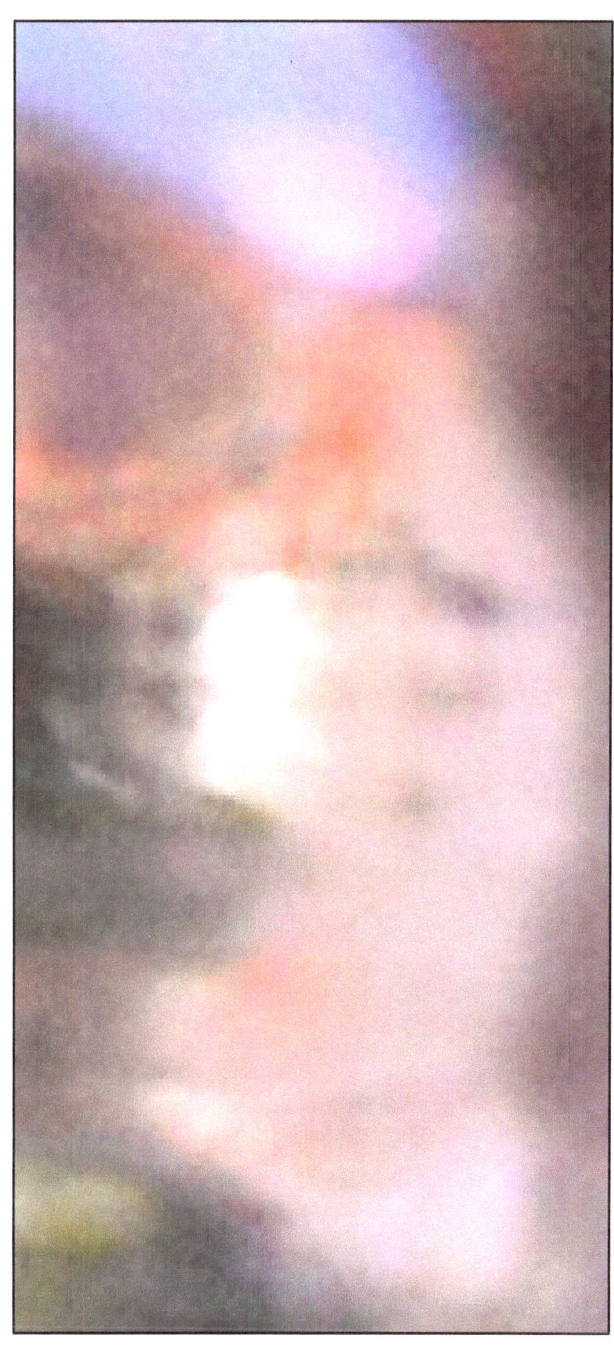

"Then I saw 'a new heaven and a new earth,'
for the first heaven and the first earth had passed away,
and there was no longer any sea."

Revelation 21:1

10

NEW HEAVEN & EARTH

I was a ballet dancer and teacher for many years. Our director was from Holland, so she used to walk along the shore of the North Sea. Since her company was in Minnesota where there is only fresh water, she taught us to soak our feet in a bowl of salt water to heal the sores on our toes.

On the New Earth, much like in Minnesota, no salty bodies of water will exist. The river of life, however, will flow from the throne of God down the middle of the street and into ponds and lakes, perhaps even Great Lakes like Superior. Sea creatures will likely be created to live in fresh water. Therefore, water will remain an important part of our lives. It will not have a negative side to it. For example, continents will no longer be separated, and no one will have to worry about shark attacks.

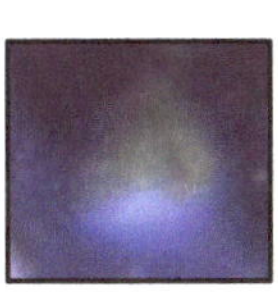

John tells us that he "saw the Holy City, the new Jerusalem, coming down out of heaven from God, prepared as a bride beautifully dressed for her husband" (Revelation 21:2).

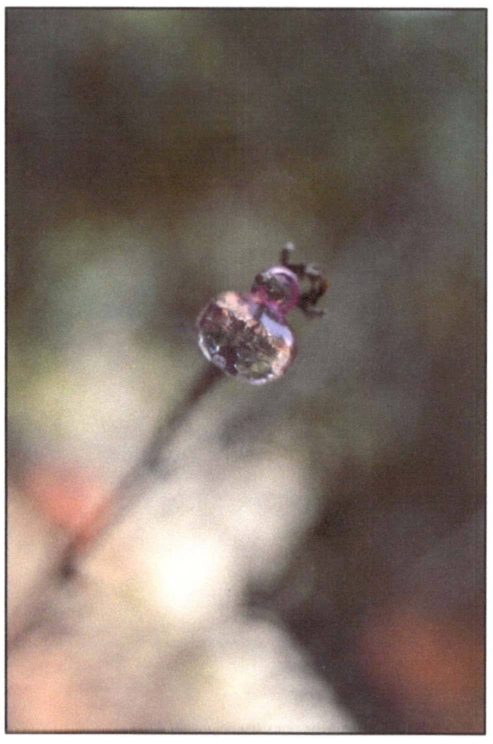

John then hears a voice from the throne saying, "Look! God's dwelling place is now among the people, and he will dwell with them. They will be his people, and God himself will be with them and be their God" (v. 3). Just as Heaven is special because God is there, so the New Jerusalem will be special because of Him as well. *Jehovah-Shammah*, the Lord is there (Ezekiel 48:35). We will finally get to experience Heaven on Earth! No more death, mourning, crying, or pain, for our God will wipe away every tear from our eyes (Revelation 21:4).

Let's take one last look at the first picture of the universe (or heavenly realm). As already noted, it represents the harvest and fire.

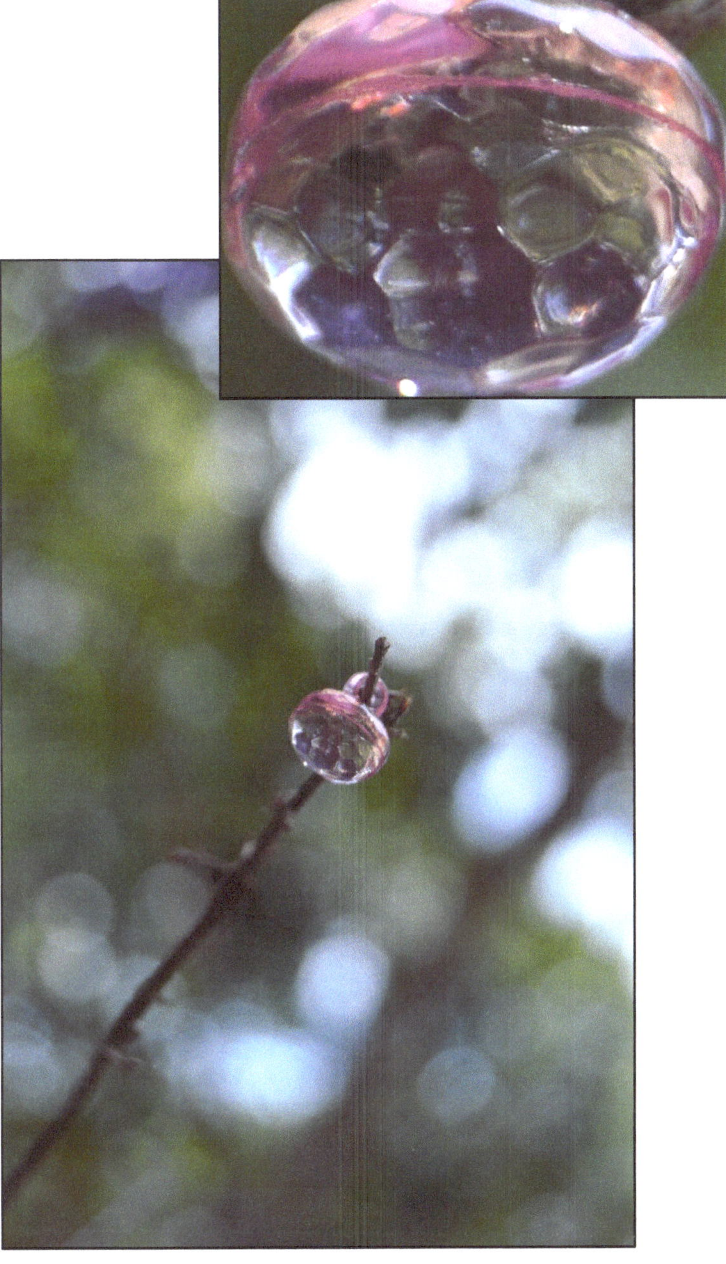

The second photo of the universe, I think, represents the new creation. John explains that the one seated on the throne said, "I am making everything new!" (Revelation 21:5).

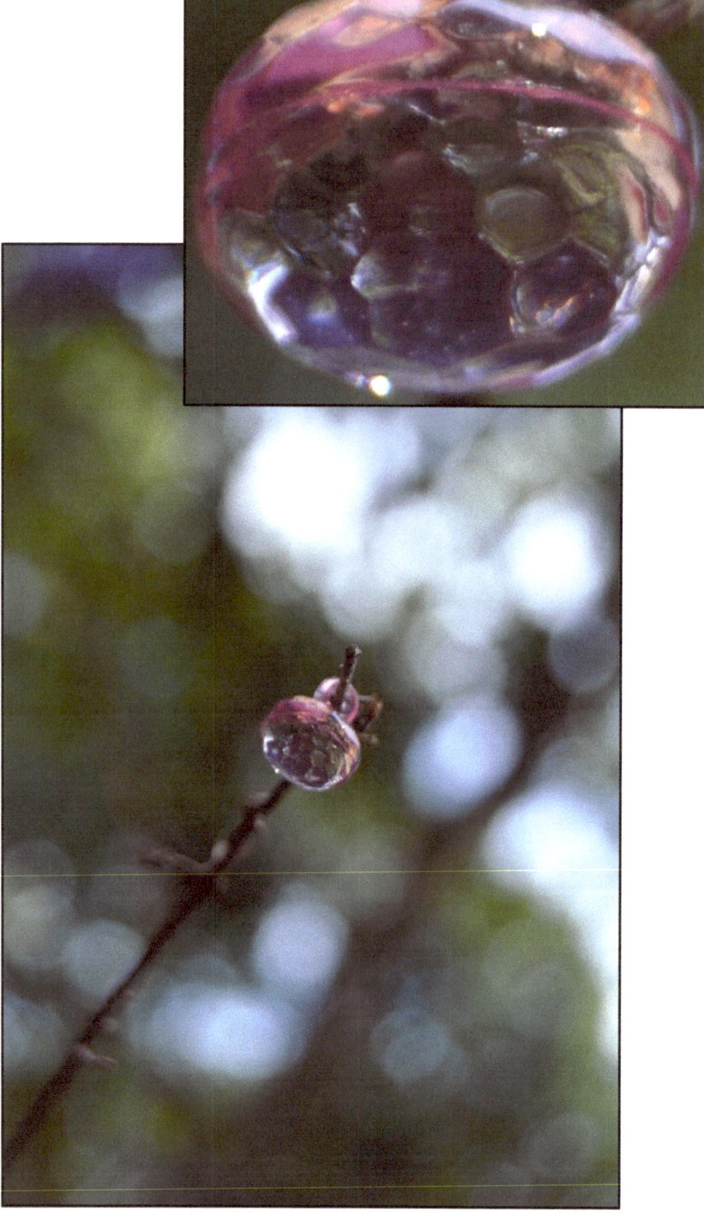

So, let's go all the way back to creation where we read about water and light. It tells us that "in the beginning God created the heavens and the earth. Now the earth was formless and empty, darkness was over the surface of the deep, and the Spirit of God was hovering over the waters" (Genesis 1:1-2). I find it fascinating that aquatic animals are beginning to emerge. The large fish near the center of the picture is probably the most obvious one.

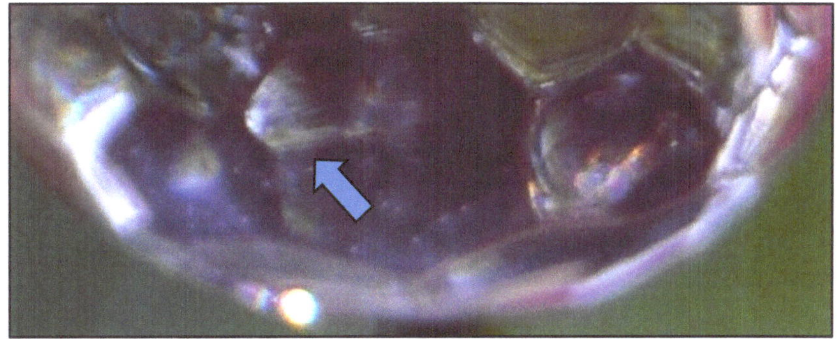

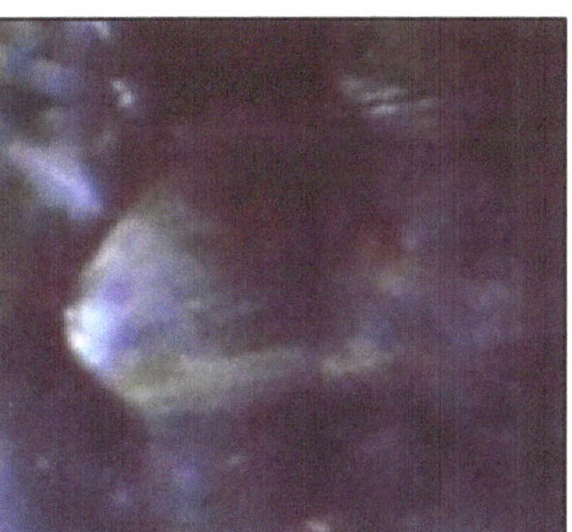

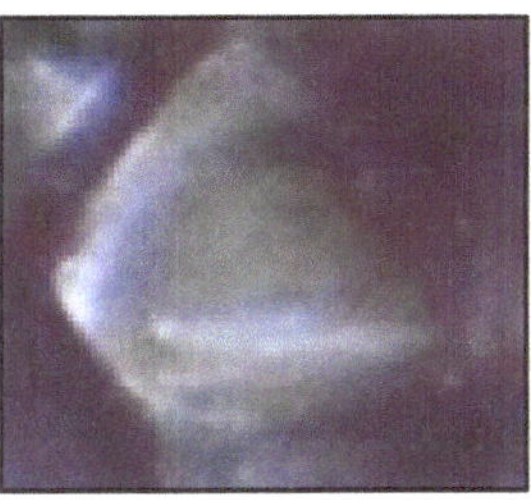

Fish in the first picture

That's not to say that fish exist in space. Rather, the photos show us the New Heaven and the New Earth being created simultaneously.

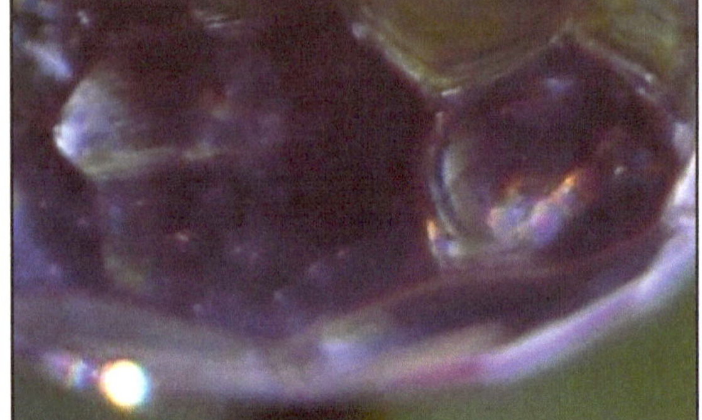

"And God said, 'Let there be light,' and there was light" (v. 3). In the photo above, bolts of light appear in the colors of a rainbow. There are even a couple of bolts near the fish as well as a possible DNA strand. The DNA is violet-blue.

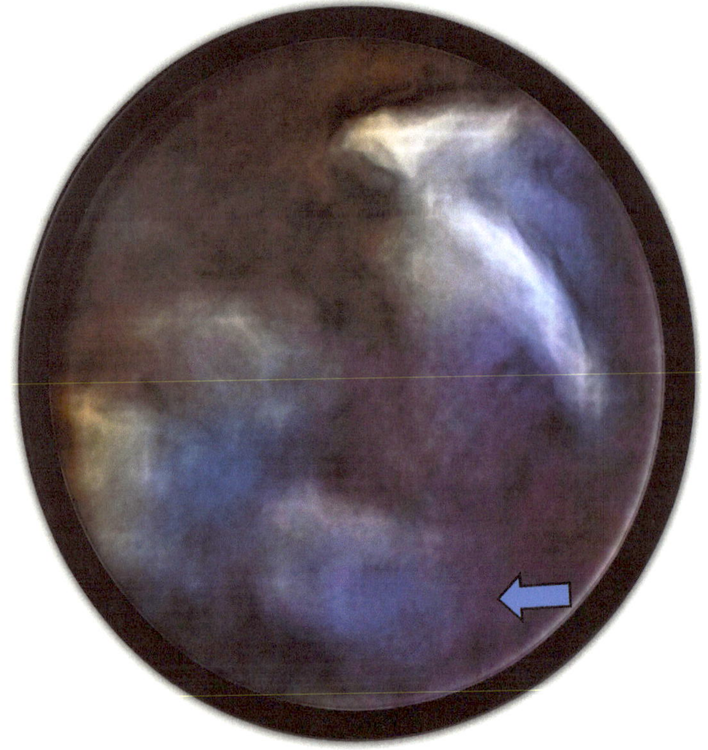

Just recently I discovered that certain bolts of light could be angels in motion.

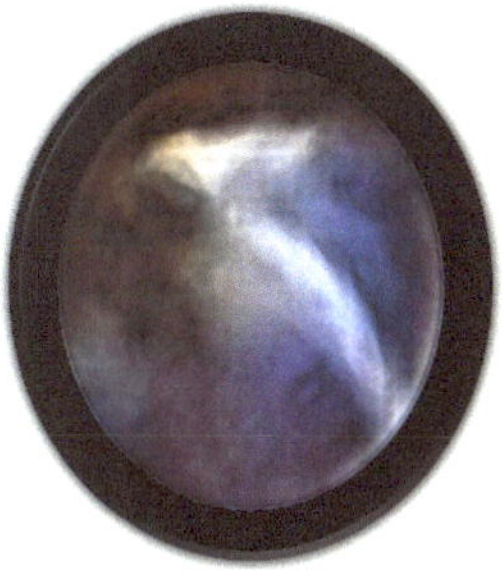

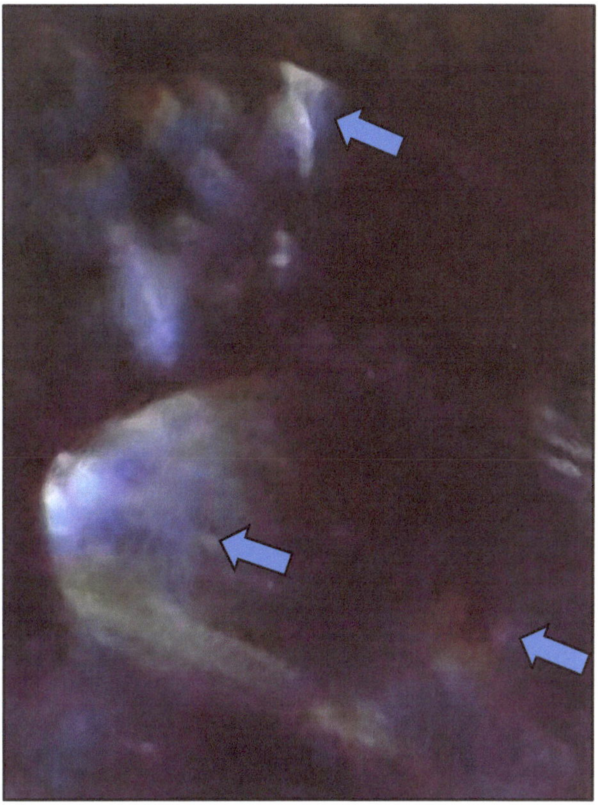

There is also a woman dressed as a bride and a child sitting cross-legged looking down. They are tiny specks on the fish. We will take a closer look at them in the last chapter.

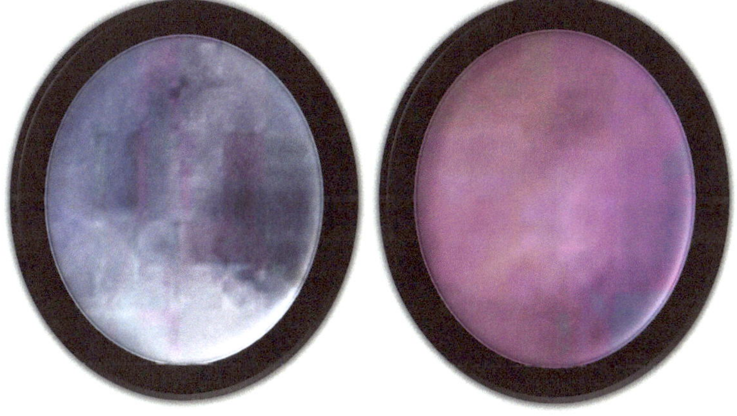

I am sure you will agree that one of the most interesting images in this book is the one below.

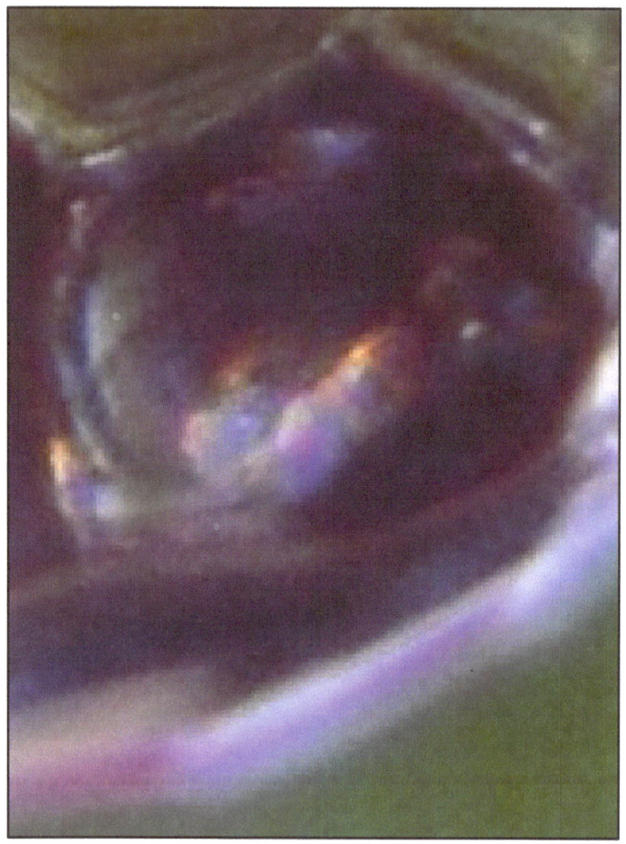

It looks like the earth is spinning, although the motion could come from the light. Perhaps it is a combination of both.

Face of a sea lion or seal

Although it is difficult to see, I am going to place a box around the face of a lion.

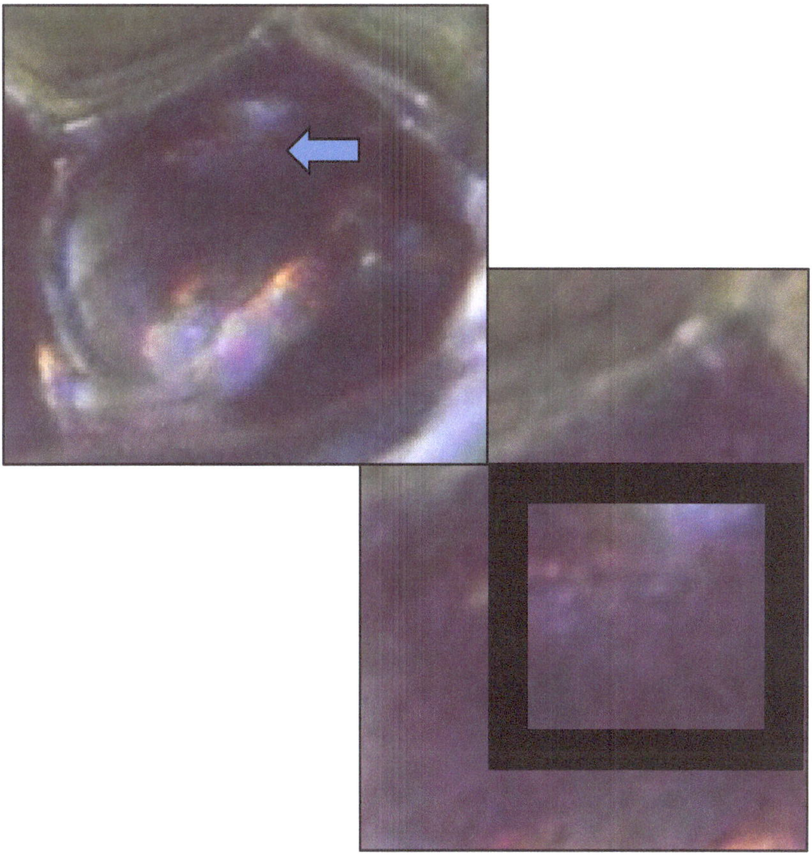

Since the face of an eagle is next to it, I think they are a part of the four living creatures.

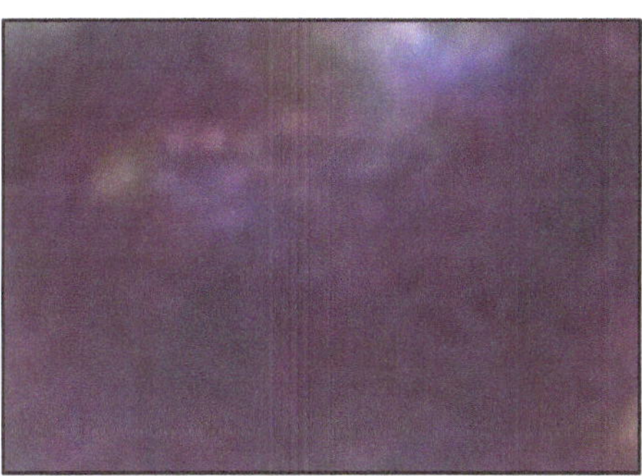

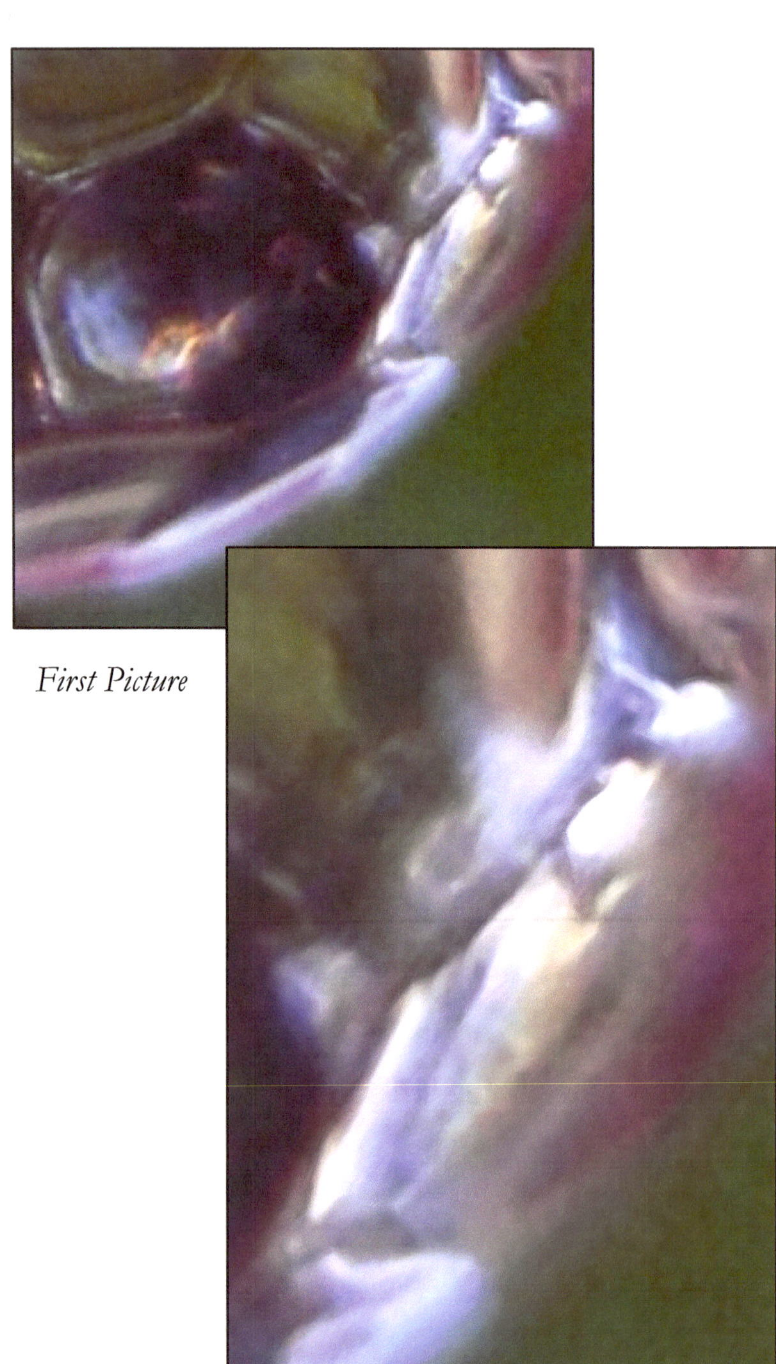

First Picture

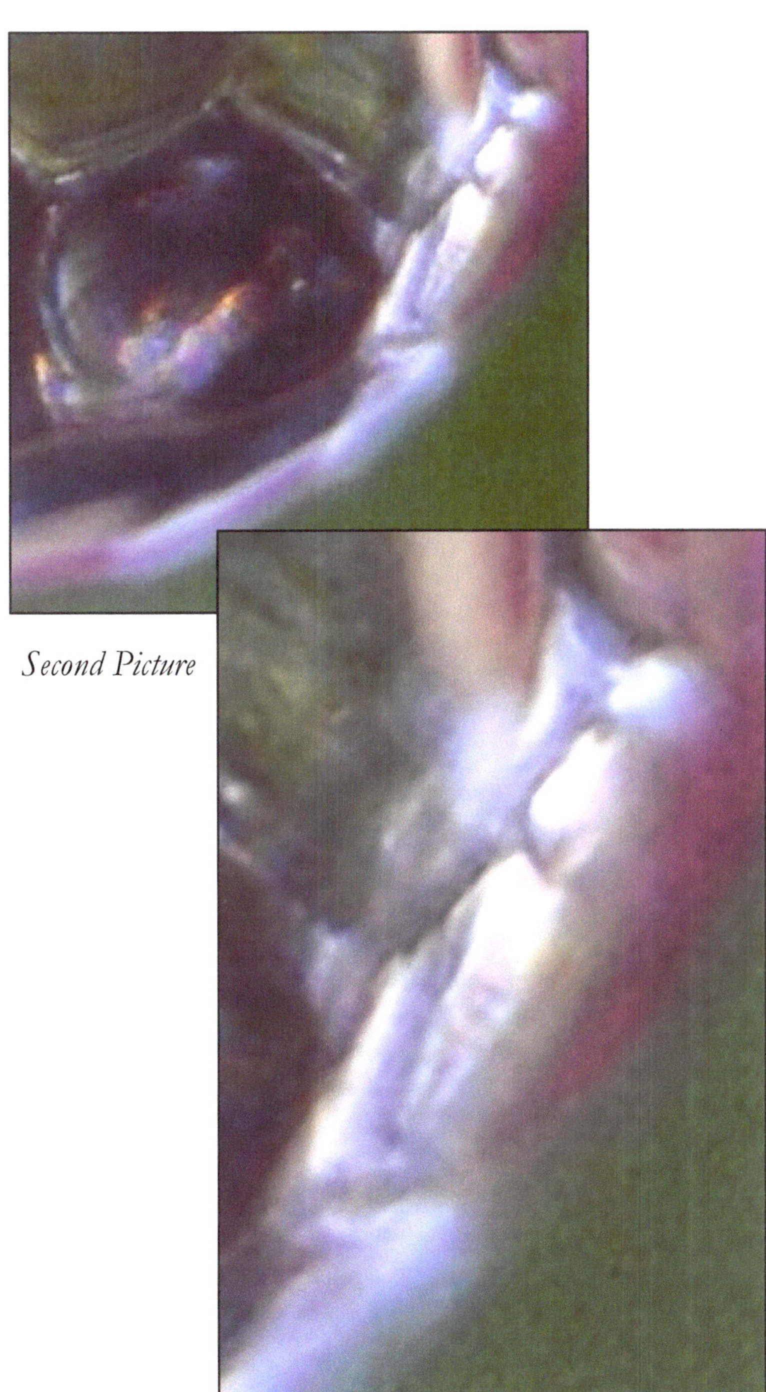

Second Picture

One of the seven angels who had the seven bowls showed John the Holy City (Revelation 21:9-10). The angel was holding a measuring rod of gold (v. 15).

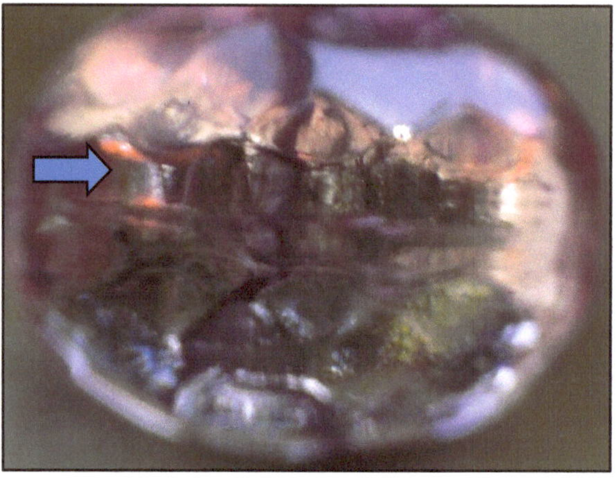

Although the image is faint, you can see a side view of the angel as he faces the waterfall by the Horse Gate. His arm is stretched out in front of him with a long rod in his hand. Perhaps he is measuring the wall or the gate.

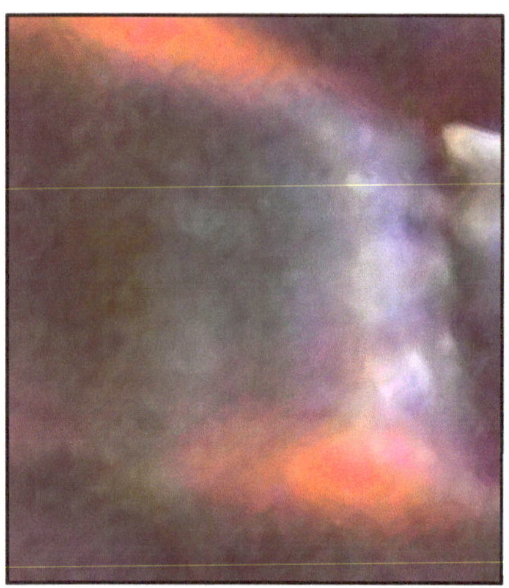

Water flows from God's throne.

Then the angel showed John the river of the water of life flowing from the throne of God (22:1). John describes it as "clear as crystal." When I took the photos, I immediately noticed the clear bubbles in the river. Of course, I wanted to cover them up, but now I realize that the bubbles are significant. They show us the purity and clarity of the water of life.

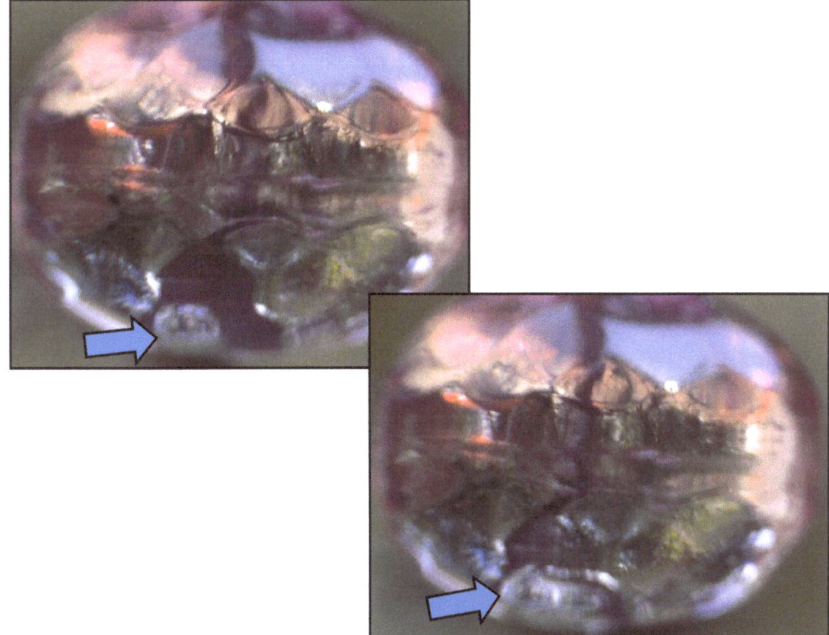

God explains, "To the thirsty I will give water without cost from the spring of the water of life" (21:6). Our natural and spiritual needs will be met on the New Earth and in the New Jerusalem. No contamination, no pollution, and, of course, no evil will exist. It will be safe for us to drink directly from the river.

"On each side of the river stood the tree of life, bearing twelve crops of fruit, yielding its fruit every month. And the leaves of the tree are for the healing of the nations" (22:2).

When Adam and Eve sinned, they had to leave the Garden of Eden (Genesis 3:24). They were separated from the tree of life. On the New Earth, however, people will be able to reach the tree of life once again.

One of the most important images in the button collection is of a cross. The King James Version tells us that "Christ hath redeemed us from the curse of the law, being made a curse for us: for it is written, Cursed is every one that hangeth on a tree" (Galatians 3:13). The tree in this verse is the cross of Christ. This is where Jesus died for our sins. He is the only one who kept the Law perfectly. He never sinned in thought, word, or deed. Since God has designed the Ten Commandments to go inside of the ark of the covenant (Exodus 25:16; Hebrews 8:5; Revelation 11:19; 15:5), it makes sense that He will judge from this place. Only Jesus kept the commandments perfectly, so it is only through His death—the sacrifice of the Perfect Lamb—that we find forgiveness. Therefore, through the death and resurrection of Jesus, we have access to the tree of life.

Let's take a moment to go back to the throne in Heaven. After the Lamb took the scroll, the four living creatures and the twenty-four elders fell down before Him and sang a new song: "You are worthy to take the scroll and to open its seals, because you were slain, and with your blood you purchased for God persons from every tribe and language and people and nation. You have made them to be a kingdom and priests to serve our God, and they will reign on the earth" (Revelation 5:8-10).

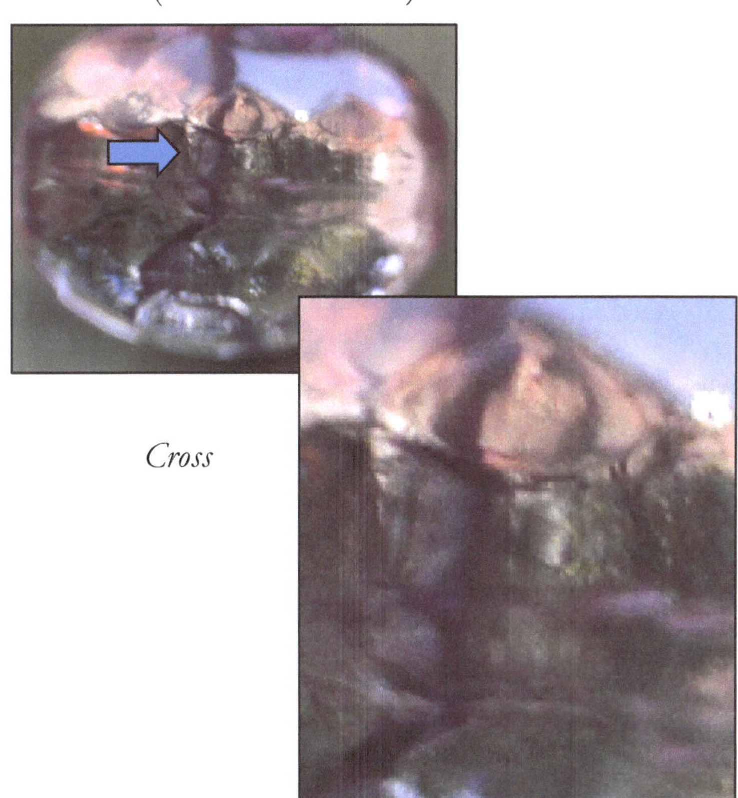

Cross

If you have never accepted the gift of salvation and you would like to, the following verse is very helpful. It says, "If you declare with your mouth, 'Jesus is Lord,' and believe in your heart that God raised him from the dead, you will be saved" (Romans 10:9). I believe the best prayer is the one from your heart, so please take a few minutes to talk with the Lord. You may even want to kneel before Him. Life doesn't get any better than on your knees.

As our study of Revelation comes to a close, we see John falling at the feet of the angel. But the angel tells him, "Don't do that! I am a fellow servant with you and with your fellow prophets and with all who keep the words of this scroll. Worship God!" (22:9). Since angels are fellow servants of God, we should never worship them. Idolatry is a dangerous path. Therefore, we need to stay faithful to the one who is Faithful and True.

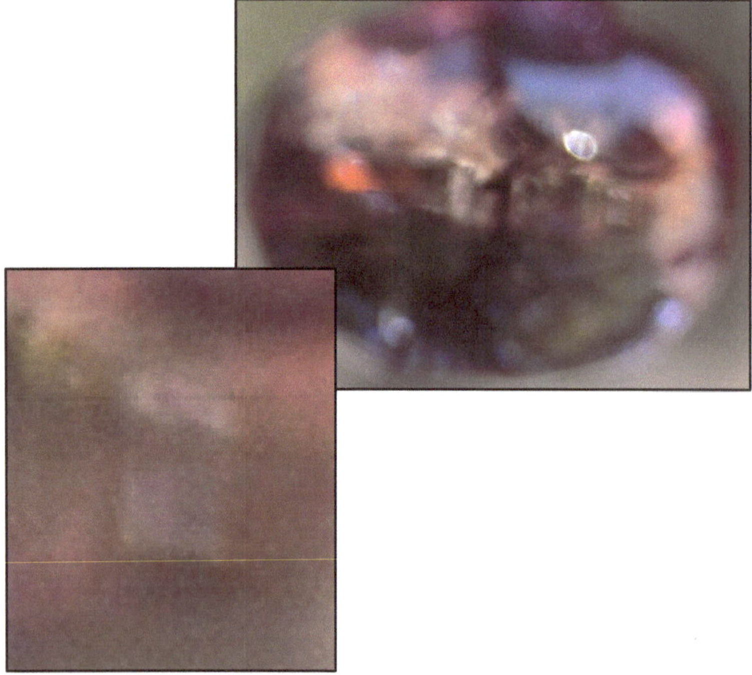

Then the angel tells John not to seal up the words of the scroll (v. 10). The message was for the seven churches, and it is for us today. We are warned not to add anything to the prophecy (v. 18), and we should never take anything from it either (v. 19). There will be consequences if we do.

The light of a perfect day is approaching, for the "sun of righteousness will rise with healing in its rays" (Malachi 4:2). Jesus, of course, is the light of the world (John 8:12). His brightness resembles the sun, while His beauty is like a shining star.

In the New Jerusalem, there will be no more night. John tells us that we will not need a lamp or the sun, for the Lord God will give us light (Revelation 22:5). Neither will the sun nor the moon have to shine on the city because of His glory (21:23).

Just last night I figured out an important detail in the last photograph. Revelation 22:16 says, "I, Jesus, have sent my angel to give you this testimony for the churches. I am the Root of the Offspring of David, and the bright Morning Star." I suddenly realized that the image below has the likeness of a star!

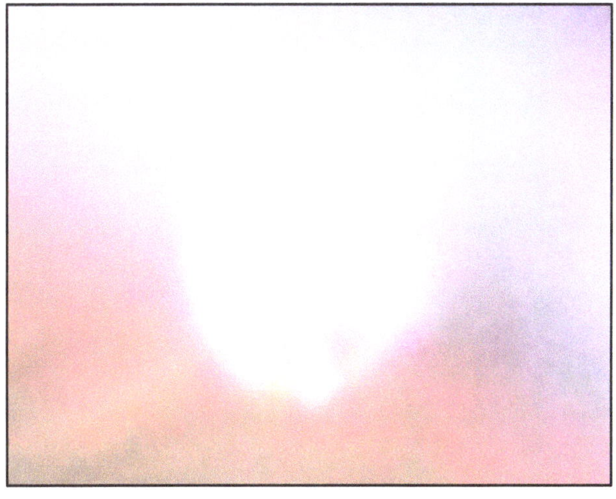

"The Spirit and the bride say, 'Come!'" (v. 17). Come to the Lord, to His salvation, to His goodness and love. What bride wouldn't enjoy a beautiful wedding photo with her beloved? Capturing the perfect picture is very popular these days. Please note a silhouette of the bride and groom inside of the star. When John saw the Holy City coming down out of Heaven, he said it was like a bride beautifully dressed for her husband. So, as we near the end our study, I leave you with a glimpse of the greatest love story ever told.

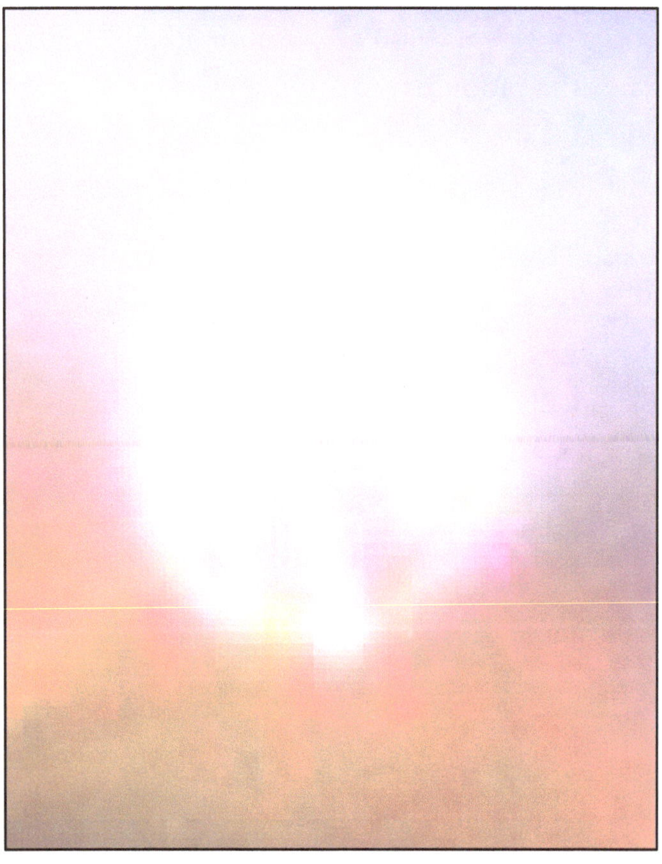

Our Lord says, "Yes, I am coming soon" (v. 20).

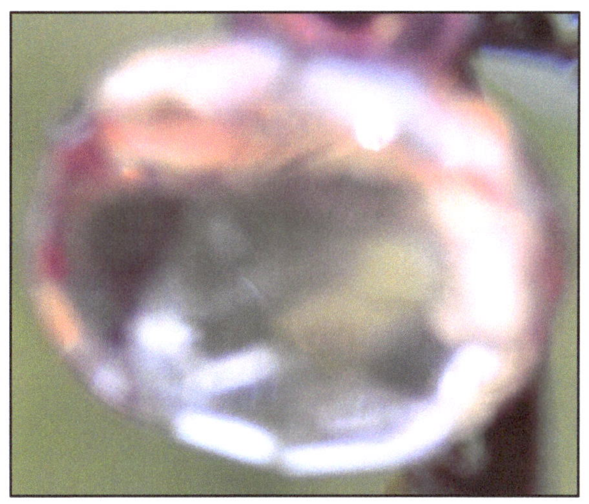

"Amen. Come, Lord Jesus."

"Do not weep! See, the Lion of the tribe of Judah,
the Root of David, has triumphed.
He is able to open the scroll and its seven seals."

Revelation 5:5

11

LION & LAMB

The only One who truly has the right to say, “It is finished,” is the Lord. Months ago, when I thought I had finished this book, I continued to learn new things each day. In addition to the thought of writing two more chapters, I also received a program that can enlarge, or blow up, the images. The process either helps a photo become clear or it makes it fuzzy. Therefore, certain pictures will appear clearer in the revised version.

When I first saw the cover of the book, I suddenly noticed a lion and a lamb on the golden building above the East Gate.

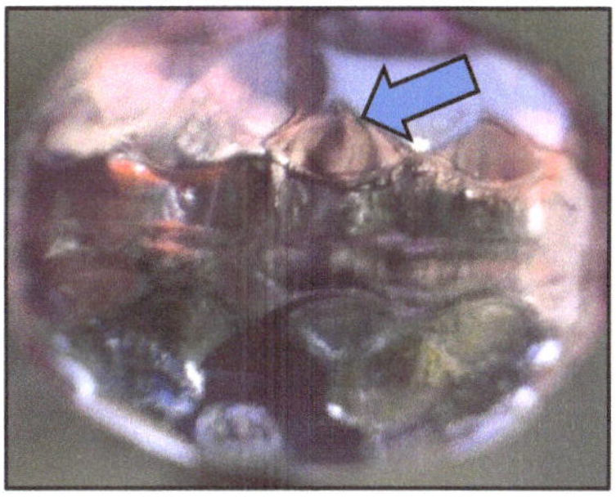

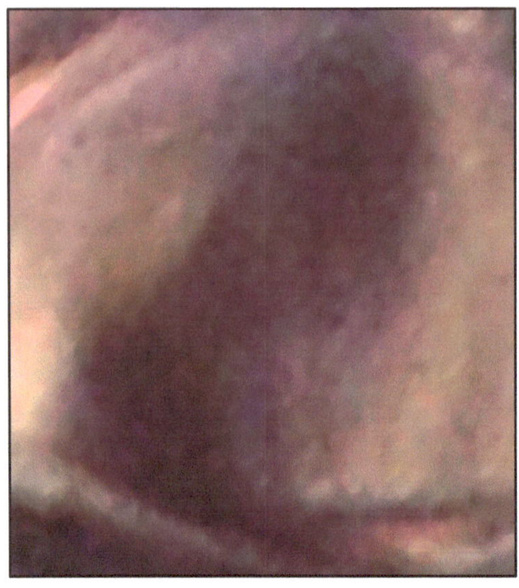

The lion is large.

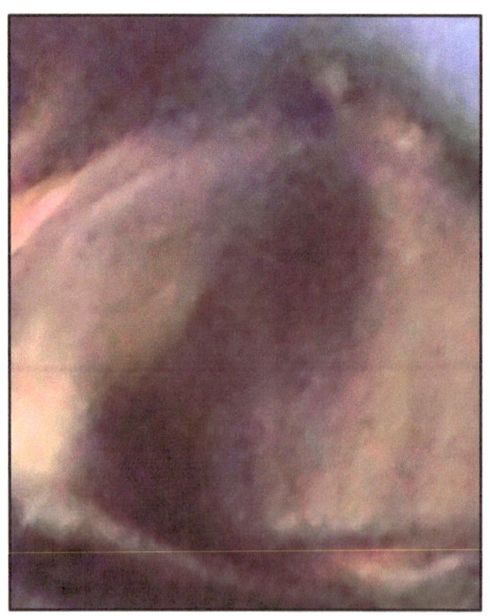

The lamb is above the lion on top of the building.

The lion and the lamb describe different aspects of the Lord's character. First of all, Jesus is the Lion of the tribe of Judah. When Jacob blesses his sons, this is what he has to say about his fourth one: "You are a lion's cub, Judah; you return from the prey, my son. Like a lion he crouches and lies down…" (Genesis 49:9).

As we have already seen, there is a cub near the Lord in the lower right-hand corner.

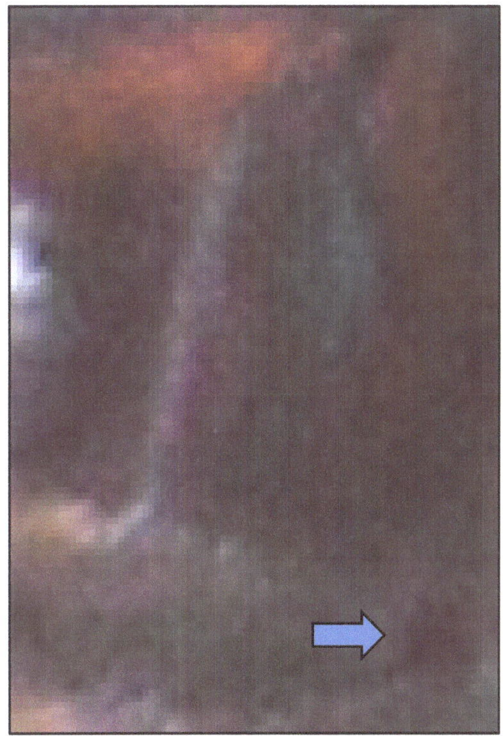

Jacob also tells us that "he will wash his garments in wine, his robes in the blood of grapes" (v. 11). This description goes along very well with the picture.

Jesus fulfills the prophecy of Genesis 49:8-12 in that He is the Messiah who comes from the tribe of Judah. The scepter in verse 10 is a symbol of His lordship and power. David helped fulfill the prophecy when he became king since he descended from the line of Judah. Jesus, of course, is the "root of David," meaning that Jesus descended from this kingly line, and He is the "root" of David's kingly power.

The façade of the Church of All Nations in Jerusalem has a mosaic depicting Jesus as the mediator between God and man. On the rooftop, next to the cross, are two bronze deer. They remind me of the deer (and donkey) in the second picture.

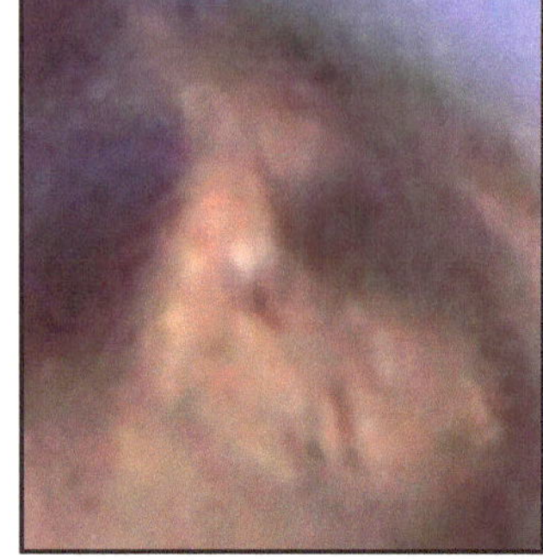

They also remind me of the lamb at the top of the building in the first picture.

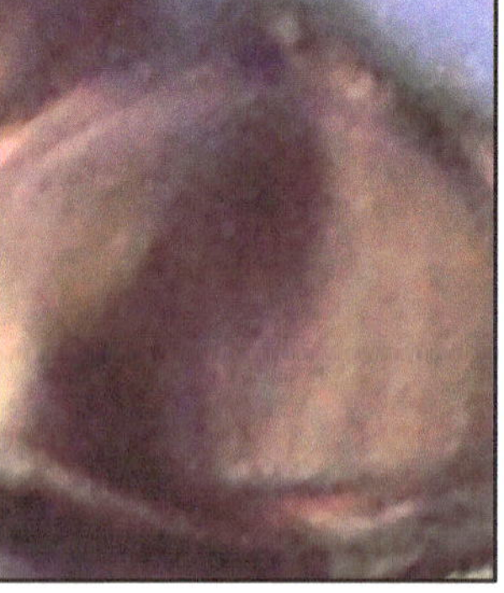

Lamb

When John the Baptist saw Jesus coming toward him, he said, "Behold the Lamb of God, which taketh away the sin of the world" (John 1:29, KJV). Jesus is the perfect sacrifice for our sins, the Passover Lamb who saves us from eternal separation and death.

When the angels, the living creatures, and the elders encircled the throne in Heaven, the beloved disciple, John, heard them say, "Worthy is the Lamb, who was slain, to receive power and wealth and wisdom and strength and honor and glory and praise!" (Revelation 5:11-12).

City of Gold

The first and second pictures are interesting. I often wonder, "How can the images on the buildings look so different from one another? For example, why do we see a lion and a lamb in first picture? Then, in a blink of an eye, in less than a second, we find a deer and a donkey?" The answer, I think, is found in Revelation 21:18. It tells us that "the wall was made of jasper, and the city of pure gold, as pure as glass." When you look at a piece of glass, you can see through it. Therefore, I think the images are in layers. I have discovered layers throughout the pictures. I will show you another example in the next section. It kind of reminds me of a hologram, where you can see different things depending on the light or depending on where you are standing.

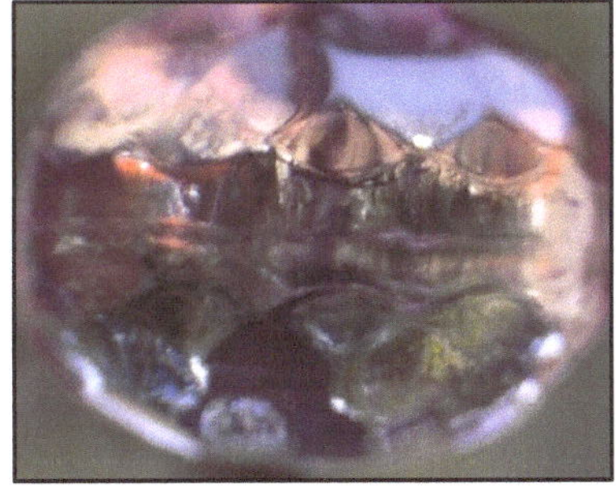

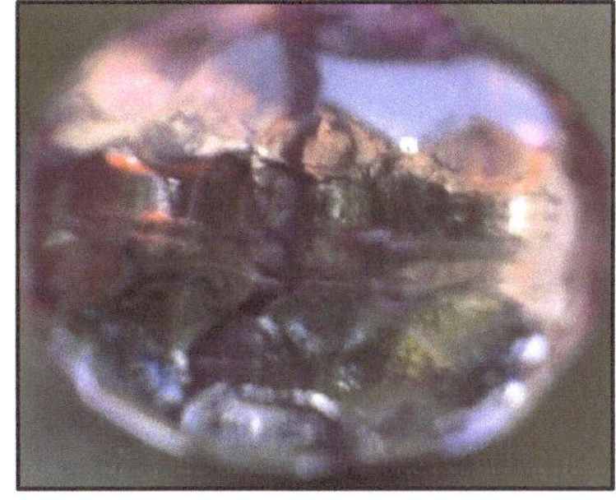

As we walk through the New Jerusalem, I believe we will see reminders of God and His people. It will be like a museum with paintings that depict Bible stories and sculptures of important events.

I discovered a fascinating image of a man in the first photo. He is on the side of the golden building. Perhaps he is a part of the wall. The image is "blown up" on the next page.

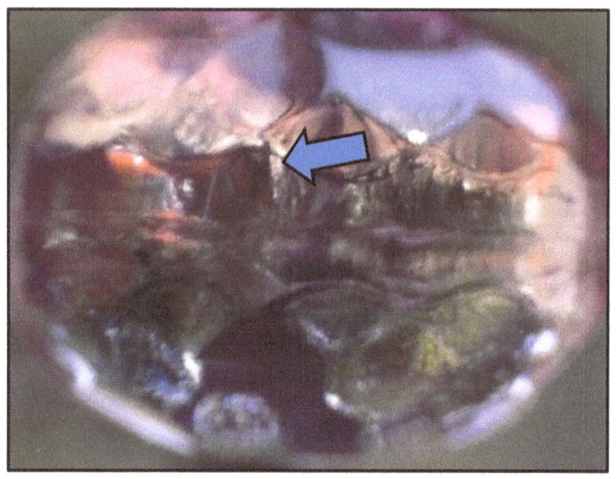

At first I thought he was an angel. I even considered the possibility that it could be the Lord. What stood out the most to me, however, was that the man looked as if he stood in the cleft of the rock. Moses suddenly came to mind.

Exodus 33:7-11 describes the tent of meeting. "Anyone inquiring of the Lord would go to the tent of meeting outside the camp" (v. 7). Whenever Moses went to the tent, the people would stand outside the entrances of their own tents. Then, when Moses went into the tent, a pillar of cloud would come down and stay at the entrance. Verse 11 explains that "the Lord would speak to Moses face to face, as one speaks to a friend."

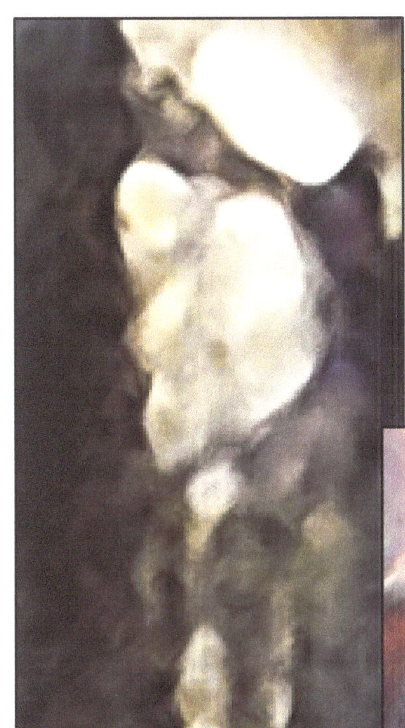

Cleft of the rock

Before the Lord instructs him to chisel out the stone tablets, Moses says, "Now show me your glory" (v. 18). And the Lord said, "I will cause all my goodness to pass in front of you, and I will proclaim my name, The Lord, in your presence. I will have mercy on whom I will have mercy, and I will have compassion on whom I will have compassion. But…you cannot see my face, for no one may see me and live" (vv. 19-20). Of course, we already know that Moses spoke with the Lord face to face. When it comes to His glory, however, he could not survive in the fullness of His presence. It would be too overwhelming.

The Lord told Moses, "There is a place near me where you may stand on a rock. When my glory passes by, I will put you in a cleft in the rock and cover you with my hand…" (vv. 21-22).

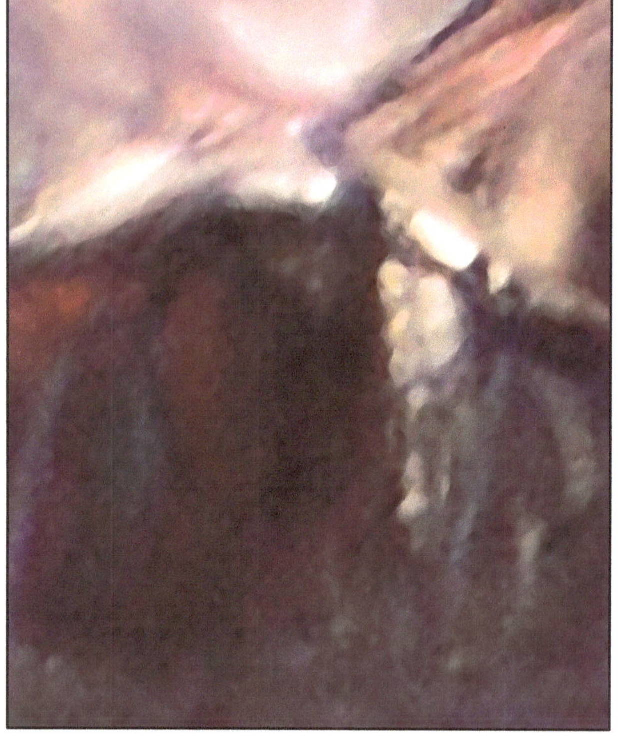

When Moses came down from Mount Sinai with the Ten Commandments, he did not know that his face was radiant. It was radiant because he had spoken with the Lord (34:29).

Please note Moses' head resting against the wall. He is near the East Gate, which could represent the entrance to the tent of meeting. His entire being appears radiant, a reminder of the glory of God. Also, there are two goats near his legs. One goat I thought was a camel, initially. Remember, we could have layers of images. The second goat is white or cream-colored. He is next to him.

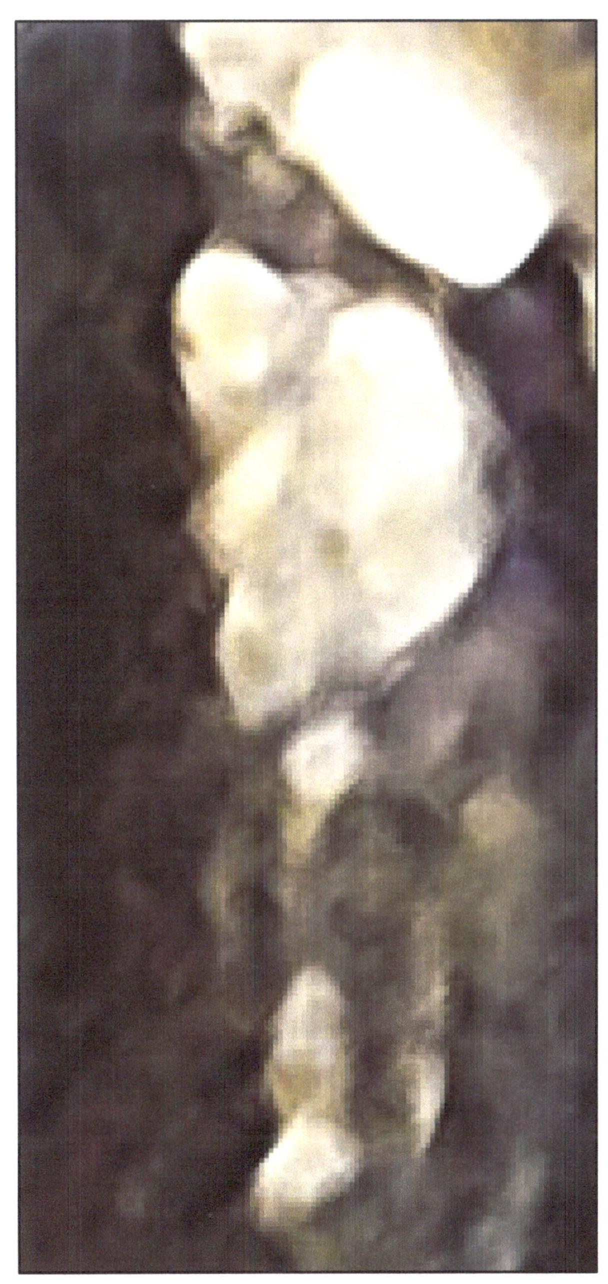

It has been enjoyable to read through parts of the Dead Sea Scrolls translated into English. While in Israel, we visited a museum where they had the scrolls on display. The Isaiah Scroll was the most complete, and, therefore, the most beautiful. We also saw the Qumran Caves from a distance. They didn't allow people to walk through them, although our tour guide told us about the Bedouin shepherd boy who looked for his goat in one of the caves and discovered a scroll in an earthenware jar. What a find!

Throughout history people have lived in caves. In fact, there are details in the Dead Sea Scrolls that give us insight into the living quarters in the New Jerusalem. Column 4 describes marble and jasper. It talks about doors, a staircase, and even gates that open "toward the interior of the blocks of houses." This makes me think of a really ornate cave.

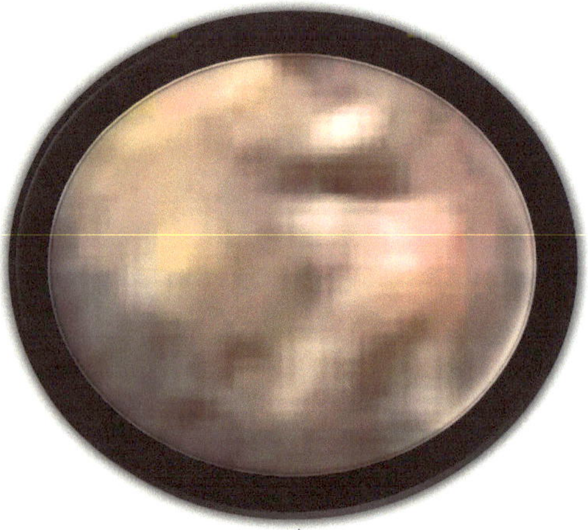

There are buildings above the bull & goat in the first picture.

In the second photo, I noticed several figures of people above the East Gate (and below the donkey). It took a little effort to enlarge the photo.

Second Picture

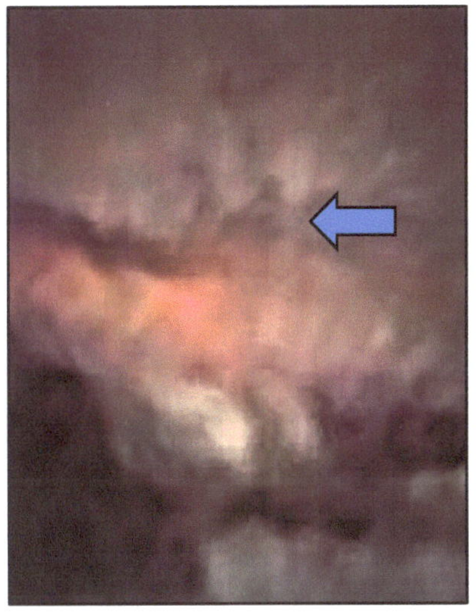

The clearest figure looks like someone is wearing a prayer shawl around his shoulders. He also appears to have something in his hands, perhaps a crown or a bouquet.

Whenever I use the magnifying tool on my computer, I can see walkways and entryways. I even noticed a man and a woman walking arm in arm. I have cropped the cream-colored structure below, which could be a staircase.

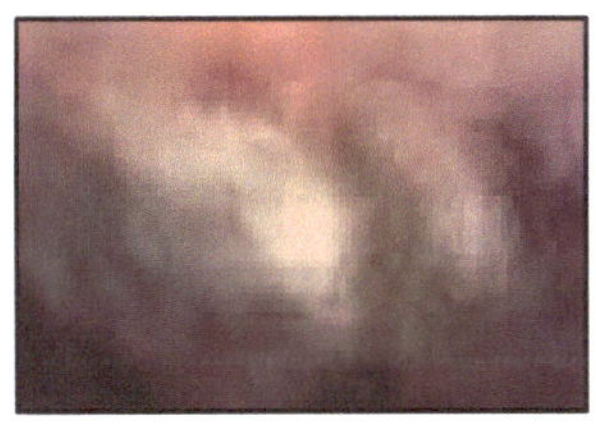

The Dead Sea Scrolls describe two towers, one to the right of each city gate and one to the left. Since the most detailed gate in this collection is of the East Gate, we will use the image below for our study. It looks like a tower is on our right.

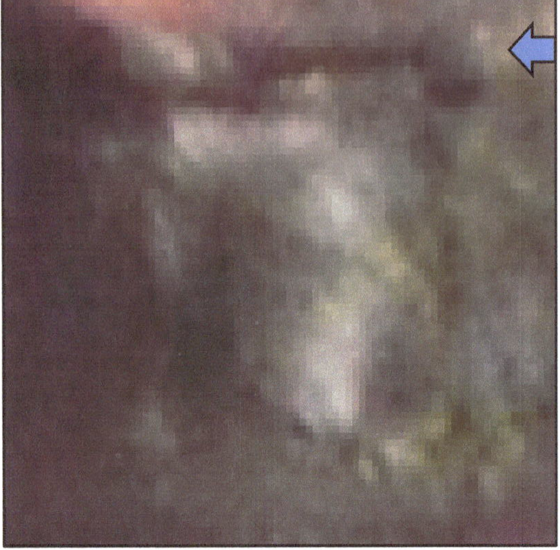

On the left, we have the staircase. Then, just below it, there is a great eagle resting on a rock. I think he could be one of the four living creatures that we read about in Revelation 4:7. The creatures in Revelation are slightly different from the cherubim in Ezekiel. For example, this particular eagle has enormous talons instead of calf feet. Also, Revelation tells us that each creature has six wings (v. 8), while the cherubim in Ezekiel have four.

So, what is the purpose of the eagle in this picture? I think he may serve as a reminder of the cherubim in Genesis 3:24. They guarded the east side of the Garden of Eden. The eagle could also represent the return of God's glory. Do to his placement in the photo, however, we are unable to see a second tower.

As we come to a close on the Dead Sea Scrolls, let's take a moment to look at one last important detail. We actually find a reference to each gate and its particular tribe in the New Jerusalem! According to column 2, the gates on the east side of the New Jerusalem will be the following:

Judah Levi Simeon

Simeon, Levi, and Judah are three of Leah's sons. In fact, they are her second, third, and fourth sons. Levi, of course, is the priestly tribe and Judah represents our King. Hebrews 4:14-16 suddenly comes to mind:

> "Therefore, since we have a great high priest who has ascended into heaven, Jesus the Son of God, let us hold firmly to the faith we profess. For we do not have a high priest who is unable to empathize with our weaknesses, but we have one who has been tempted in every way, just as we are—yet he did not sin. Let us then approach God's throne of grace with confidence, so that we may receive mercy and find grace to help us in our time of need."

Needs

The United States is about two weeks away from electing a new president. During a campaign, the candidates lay out their plan for jobs, the economy, trade, healthcare, food, safety, shelter, and the list goes on and on. We all have needs, even if it's the simple need to voice an opinion. Some leaders, of course, care about the people they govern. As human beings, however, we have limitations with how much sympathy and empathy we can deliver. Even pastors grow weary of their restless flocks at times. When it comes down to it, there is only One who can meet all the needs of all the people. The most basic need is that of love. Politicians may care at times. Pastors may truly love at times. But only Jesus can care and love all the time. In this life, we embrace His love and care through faith. Sometimes it may seem as if our needs are not being met, but God knows what is best for us. "As the heavens are higher than the earth, so are my ways higher than your ways and my thoughts than your thoughts" (Isaiah 55:9).

In the Sermon on the Mount, Jesus says, "Blessed are the poor in spirit, for theirs is the kingdom of heaven" (Matthew 5:3). Oftentimes poor people seem to have the greatest faith. When one has exhausted every other option, when there are no other resources or answers, trusting God becomes everything. One doesn't have to be poor in things, however, to be poor in spirit. It all begins with the idea that we have nothing without God. He is our everything. Understanding this concept makes us blessed.

There is nothing more important than meeting a spiritual need. Jesus, as the Great High Priest, did not enter a sanctuary made with human hands, but rather He entered Heaven itself (Hebrews 9:24). He offered Himself once for all (10:12).

When Abraham took his son to Mount Moriah, Isaac asked him, "Father…the fire and wood are here…but where is the lamb for the burnt offering?" (Genesis 22:2, 7). Abraham told him that God would provide (v. 8).

We see the ultimate fulfillment of God's provision in Jesus. He is both the High Priest as well as the Sacrificial Lamb. Jesus explains, "I am the way and the truth and the life. No one comes to the Father except through me" (John 14:6). In light of this revelation, it makes sense that the name of the tribe of Levi may have a place on the East Gate.

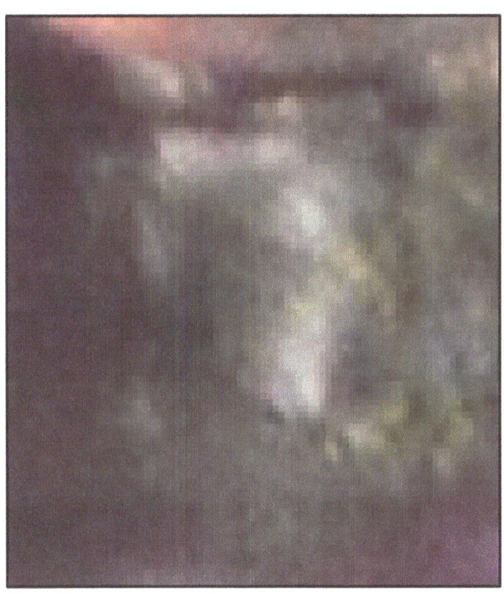

When someone accepts Jesus as Savior and Lord, they should also see Him as their Priest and King. In Levi, we see Jesus as Priest and Lamb. In Judah, He is the ruler of our lives, the Lion-King of the tribe. The lion, of course, is the king of all the wild beasts. And Jesus is the King of the universe. He oversees everything from the complex stars and planets in the sky to our simple daily bread.

I have decided to point out one last image in this particular photo. Next to the face of the lion, there is a faint figure of a man kneeling.

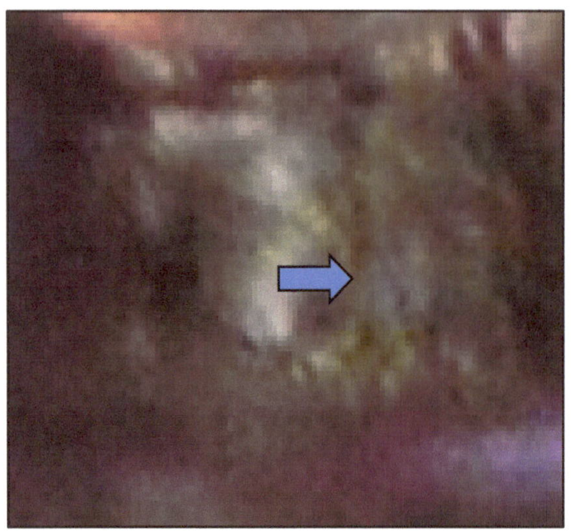

He is wearing a purple sash or vest. He also appears to have a beard.

Two verses suddenly come to mind. First, Isaiah 60:3 tells us that "nations will come to your light, and kings to the brightness of your dawn." The man in the photo looks like he could be a king. Then, in Revelation 4:9-10, John explains how the elders lay their crowns before the throne in Heaven.

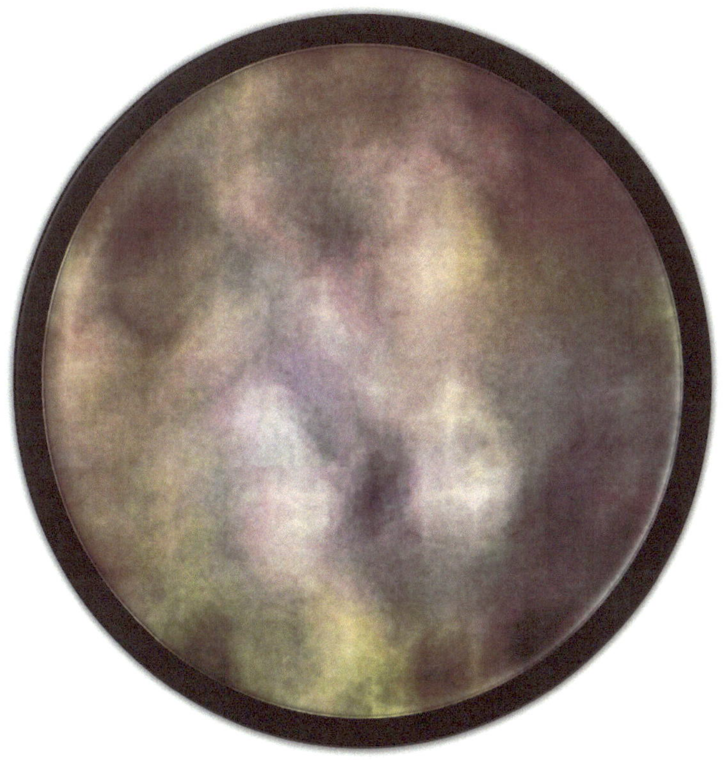

An elder or king presenting a gift to the Lord

"You are worthy, our Lord and God, to receive glory and honor and power, for you created all things…" (Revelation 4:11). Children of Your oppressors will bow before You (Isaiah 60:14). They will bow down at Your feet. They will call you the City of the Lord.

"The wolf will live with the lamb, the leopard will lie down with the goat, the calf and the lion and the yearling together; and a little child will lead them."

Isaiah 11:6

12

THE CITY GOD LOVES

I am a little teary-eyed as we come to the last chapter of our journey. Of course, this is just the beginning of so much more in Scripture.

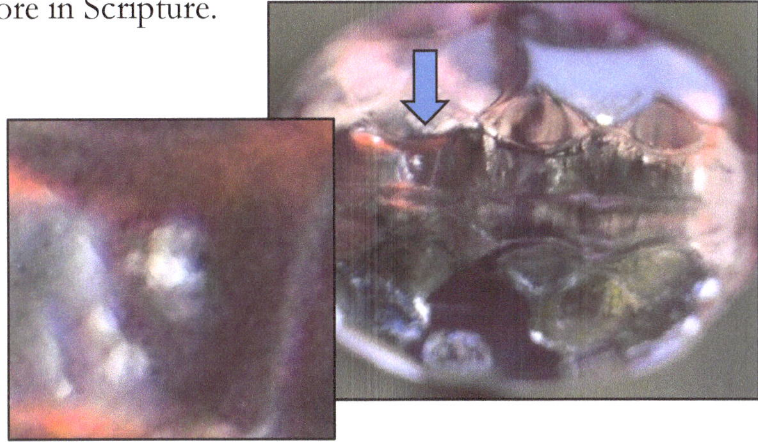

Out of all the images in the photos, I have to say that there is one that has certainly sparked my curiosity. Perhaps you have thought about it too. I have to wonder, who is in the tunnel? There are a couple of figures in the first gate. So, who are they?

It took a little work, but I finally got some answers to my question. The picture has been enlarged and magnified. And inside the tunnel is the most amazing discovery. If you can believe it, there is a little boy holding a puppy! He is sitting on the pearl gate. I never would have dreamed of this in a million years.

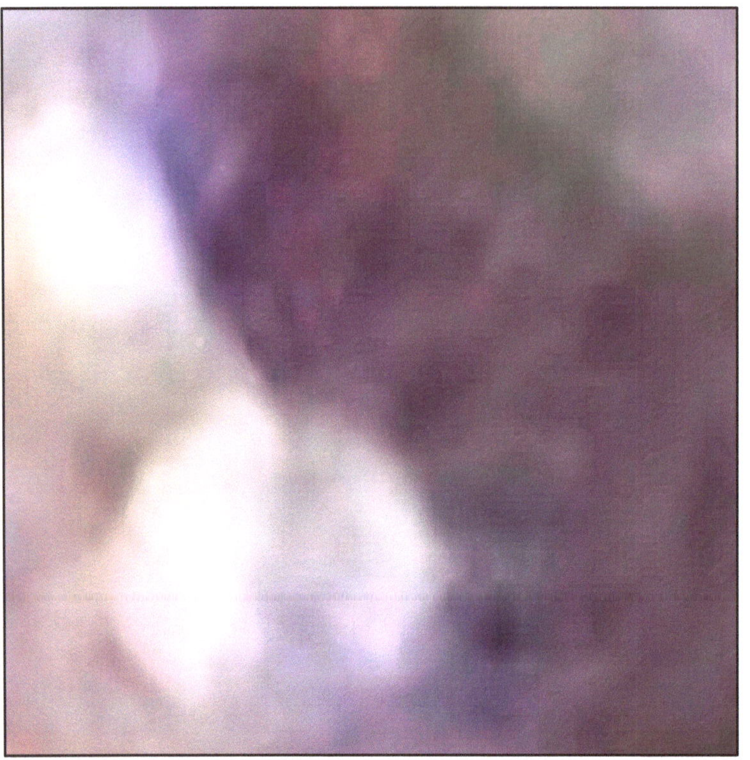

The boy is wearing a hat and a striped shirt. He looks like a toddler. Perhaps he is the little one mentioned in Isaiah 11:6. The pup could even be the wolf from the same verse. And to think that God provides pearl chairs for His loved ones at the pearly gates!

When you look at the life of Jesus, it is remarkable to see His heart for children. In Matthew 18:1-5, His disciples ask, "Who is the greatest in the kingdom of heaven?" If you have read this story before, you will probably remember that Jesus calls a little child. He says to His disciples, "Truly I tell you, unless you change and become like little children, you will never enter the kingdom of heaven. Therefore, whoever takes the lowly position of this child is the greatest in the kingdom of heaven. And whoever welcomes one such child in my name welcomes me."

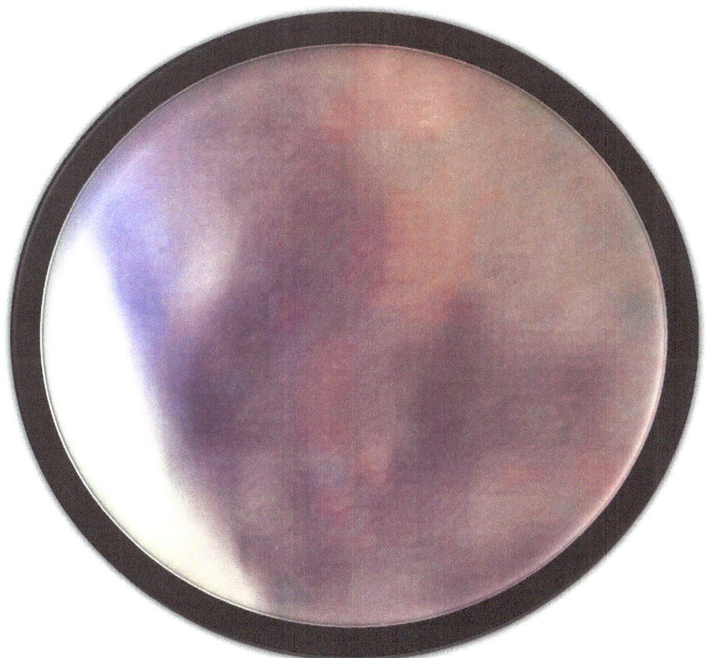

Of course, it takes a place of humility for someone to admit that they need God. When Jesus called the little child, he or she came to Him. The verse doesn't explain whether the child was a little boy or a little girl. I like to think that gender wasn't included so that each one of us, whether male or female, would be able to relate to the child. In order to enter the Kingdom of Heaven, we must become like little children. We must come to God when He calls.

The only story I could find about a son near a gate is in the Book of Deuteronomy. It says, "If someone has a stubborn and rebellious son who does not obey his father and mother and will not listen to them when they discipline him, his father and mother shall take hold of him and bring him to the elders at the gate of his town" (21:18-19).

A couple of sons suddenly come to mind. First of all, due to the violence at the hands of the tribe of Simeon, they were left out of Moses' blessing in Deuteronomy 33. What is wonderful, however, is that Simeon will have a gate in the millennial kingdom as well as the New Jerusalem. God is all about restoration and forgiveness.

There is nothing more important than knowing God loves you. "For God so loved the world that he gave his one and only Son…" (John 3:16). When I think about stories from the Bible that show our Father's love toward a rebellious son, the prodigal son is at the top of the list. The man in the story represents our Heavenly Father. The older son represents the Pharisees and the teachers of the Law, while the younger represents the son who strayed.

The younger son spent everything. He eventually ended up getting a job feeding pigs. As he looked at the pods that the pigs were eating, he wanted some too. He had reached his lowest point. The prodigal son decided he would go back to his father and say to him, "Father, I have sinned against heaven and against you. I am no longer worthy to be called your son; make me like one of your hired servants" (Luke 15:18-19).

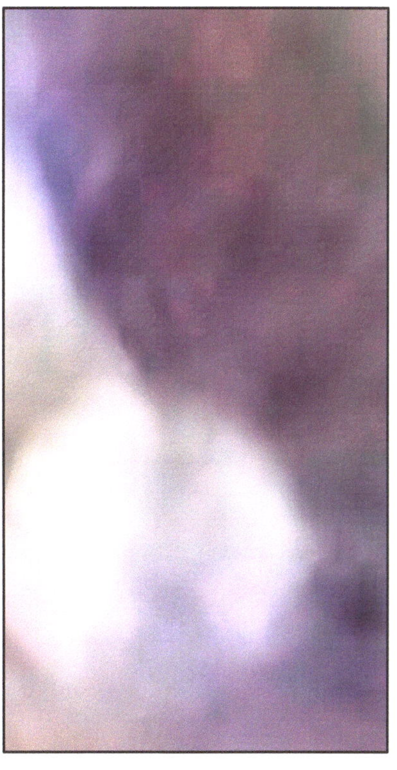

Don't you love how the story ends? His father was waiting for him! He had compassion for his lost son. In fact, he ran to his son, and then he hugged him and kissed him. He loved him. And our Heavenly Father loves us.

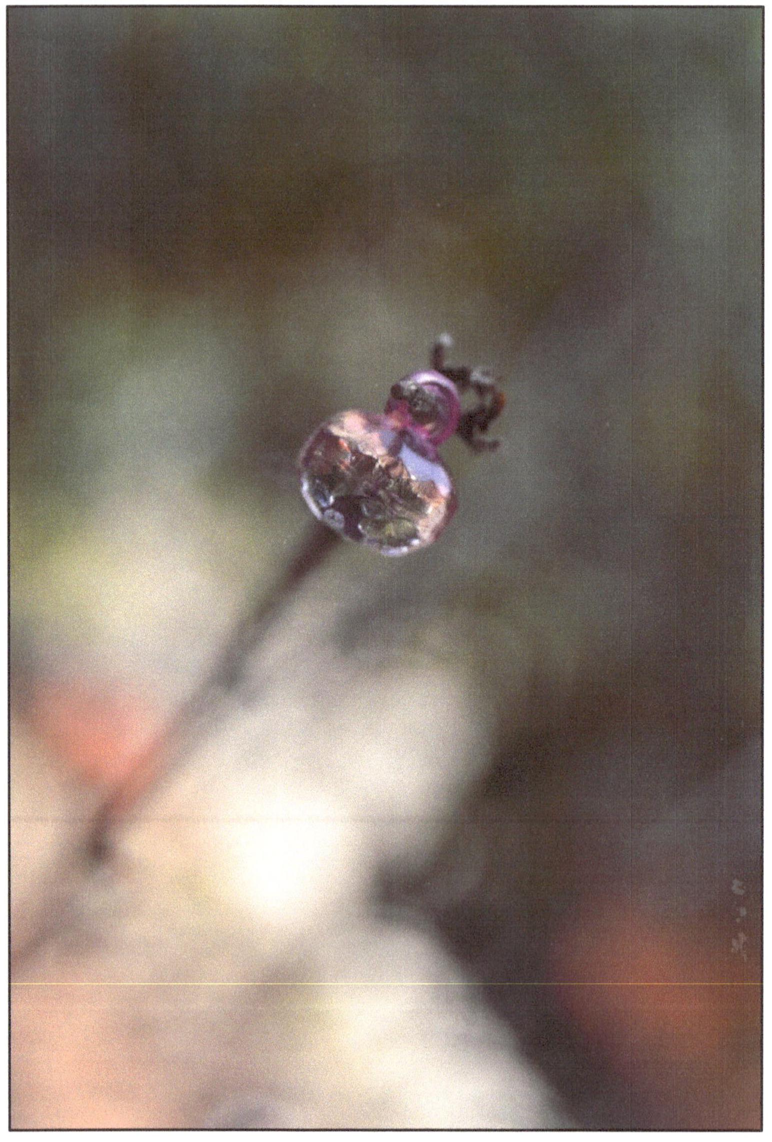

Let's take one last look at the photo that inspired this study. John says, "I saw the Holy City, the new Jerusalem, coming down out of heaven from God, prepared as a bride beautifully dressed for her husband" (Revelation 21:2).

"And he that sat upon the throne said, Behold, I make all things new" (21:5, KJV). According to the Strong's Concordance, the word "behold" means "see."

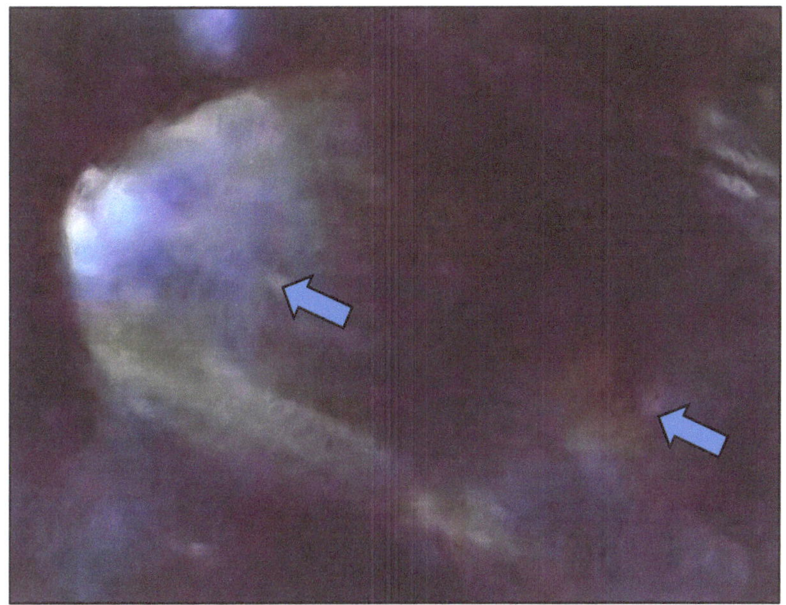

In the photo of the fish, the woman and the child are watching or "seeing" the creation of the New Heaven and Earth. By the expression on her face, we can tell that the woman is amazed.

I have darkened the eye on our right and supplied a temporary nose. The other pictures of the woman, however, have not been touched-up.

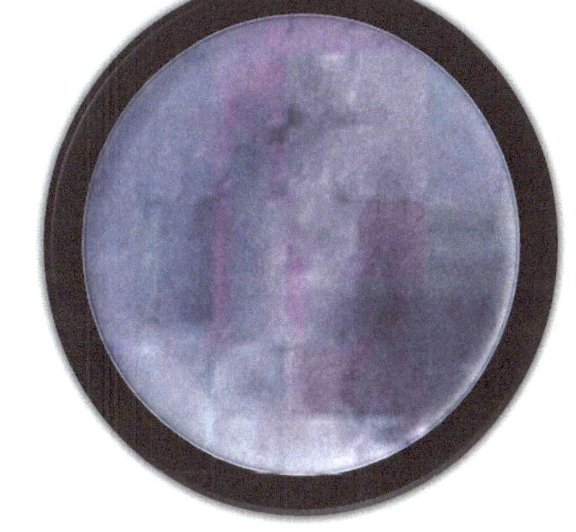

The child's posture tells us that he or she finds the process intriguing. It is not scary or else the child would have a curved back and covered eyes. Instead, it is more like a fascinating television program or planetary show.

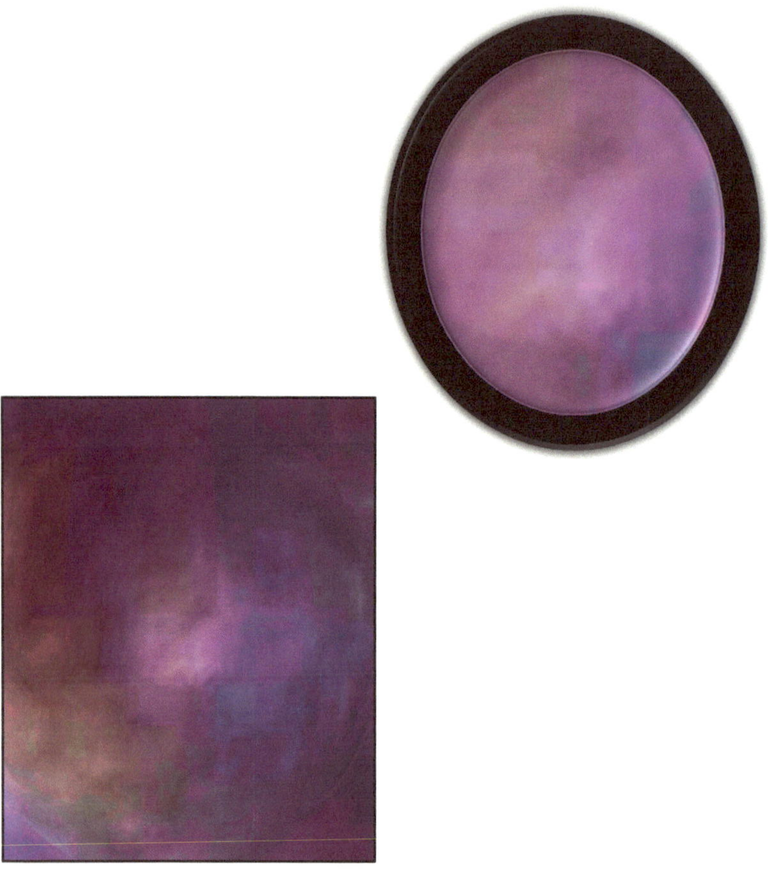

Then John heard the roar of rushing waters and loud peals of thunder (19:6). Servants of God were shouting, "Hallelujah! For our Lord God Almighty reigns. Let us rejoice and be glad and give him glory! For the wedding of the Lamb has come, and his bride has made herself ready. Fine linen, bright and clean, was given her to wear" (vv. 6-8).

The fine linen represents the righteous acts of God's holy people (v. 8). What a blessing it will be to look lovely for the Lovely Lamb at His supper.

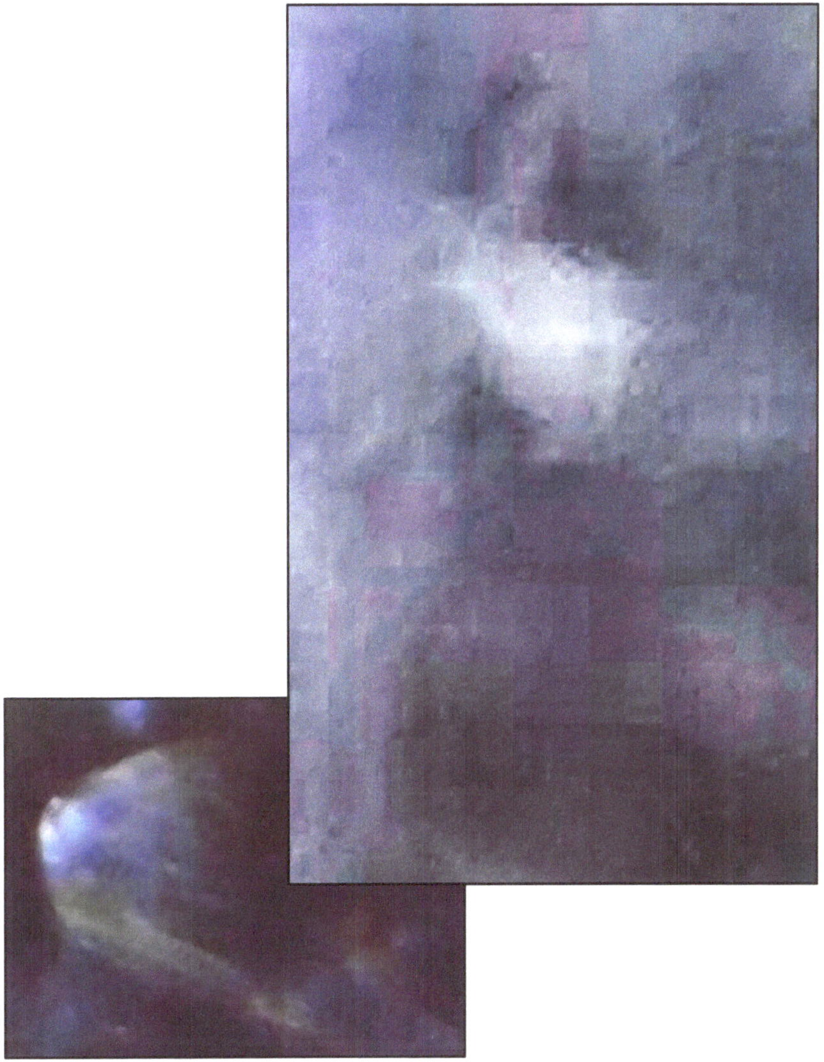

It is important to note that the image of the fish fits into a space that is 1/16 of an inch or less. That means the woman and the child are teeny-tiny specks. The details are truly amazing when you consider their size.

The woman and the child also have tall pillbox hats (or crowns).

The woman's hat seems to shimmer in the light.

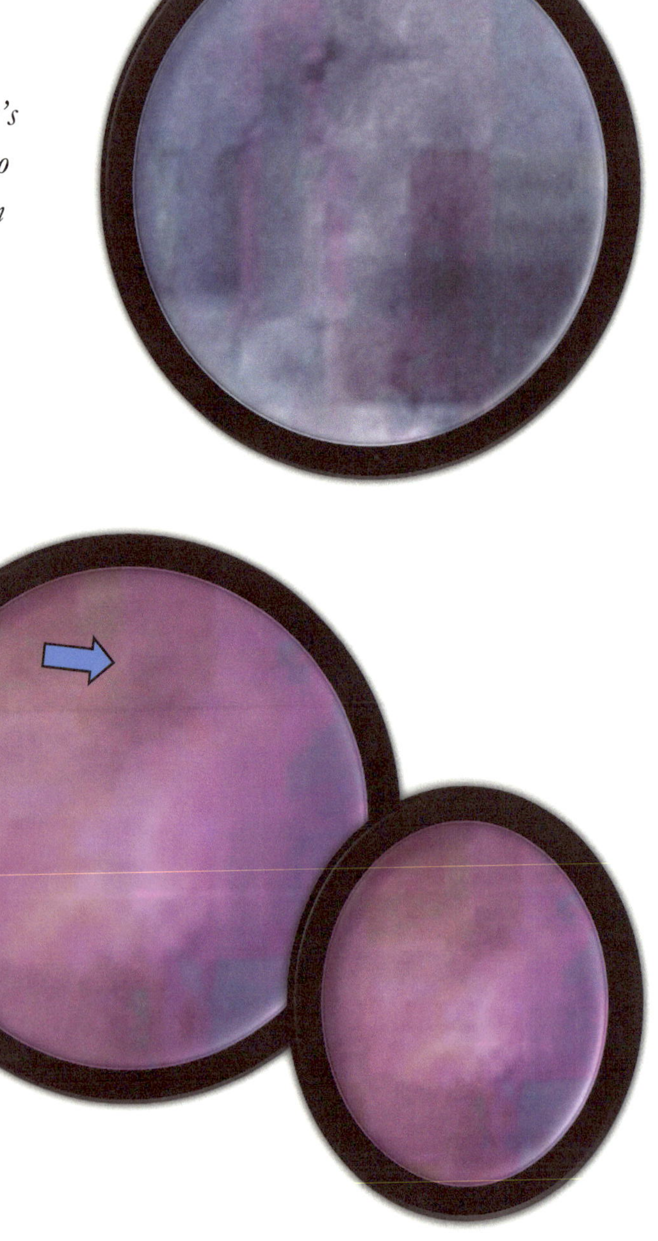

We now return to the floral emblem on John's headpiece.

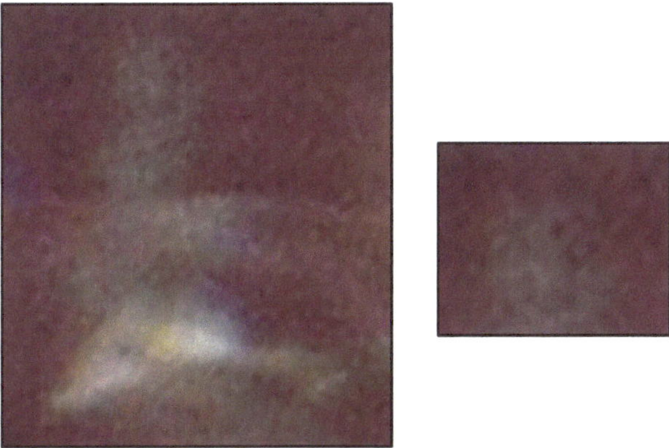

If you can believe it, the woman has a similar design on her wedding dress and hat!

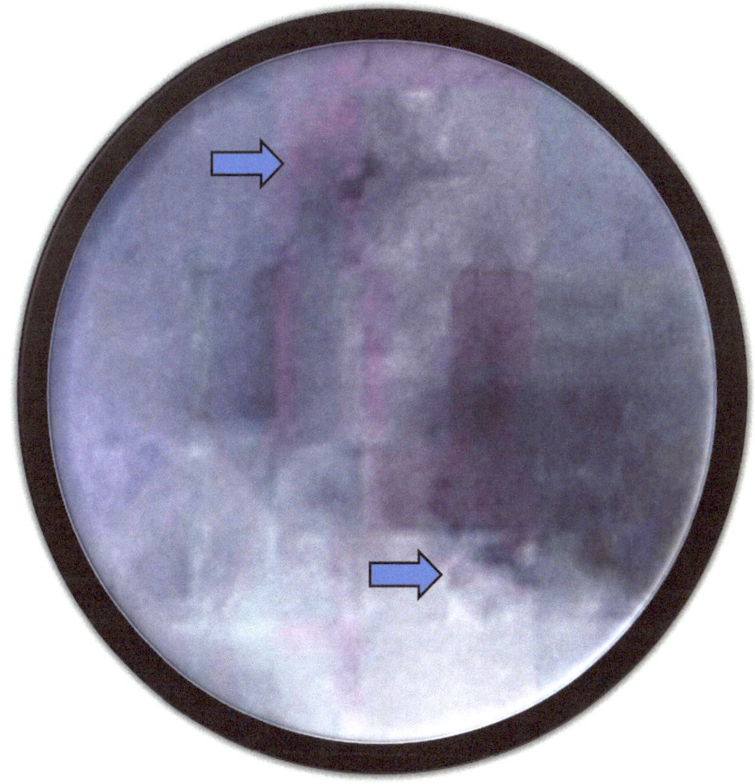

I have placed a square around the design on her hat.

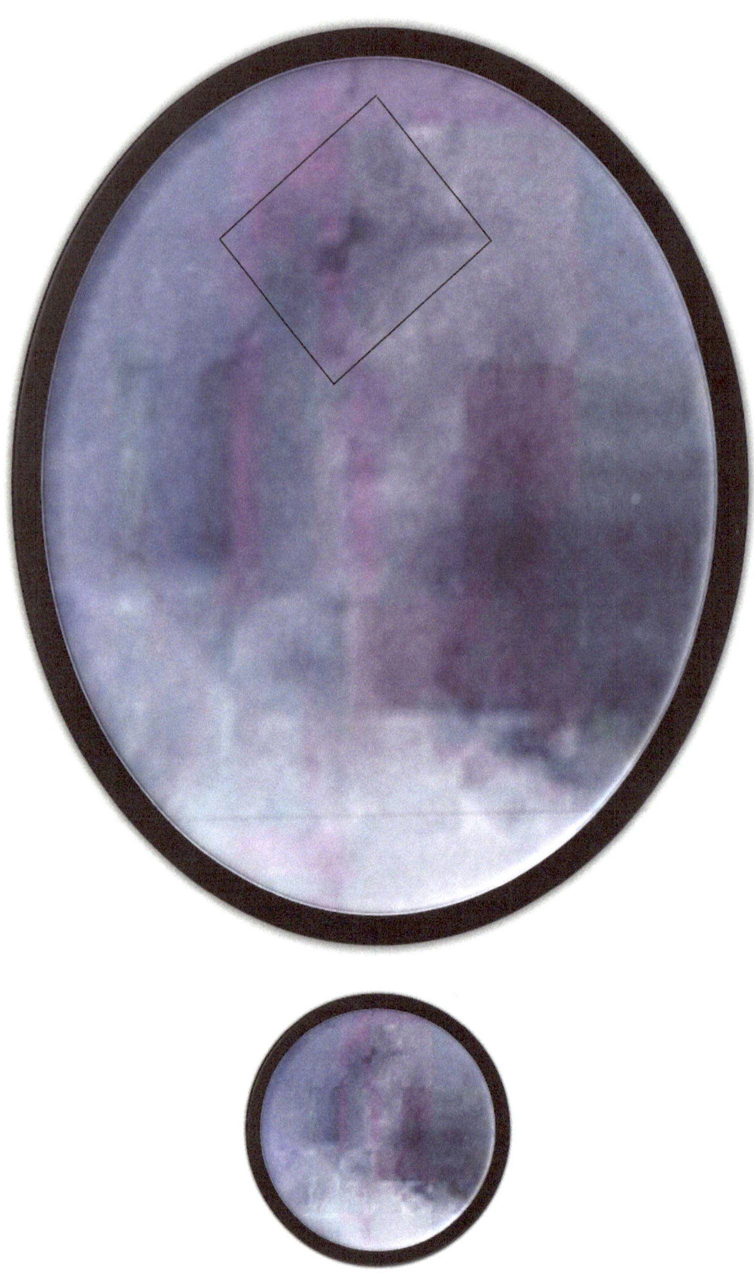

It is faint, so you will have to look carefully.

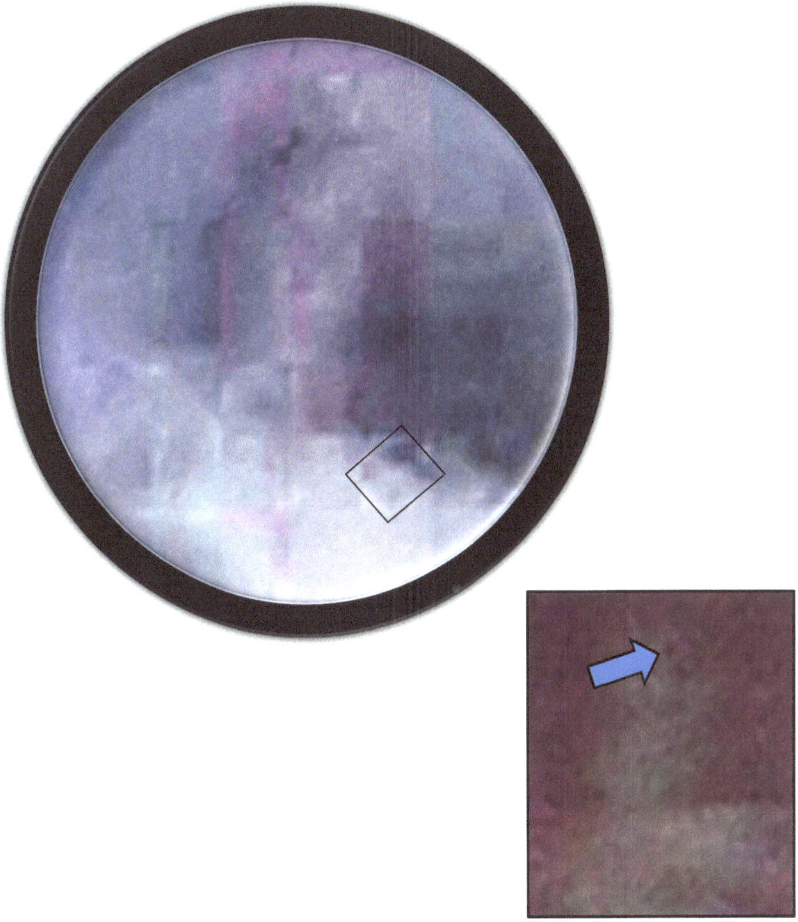

Please note the similar shape and design.

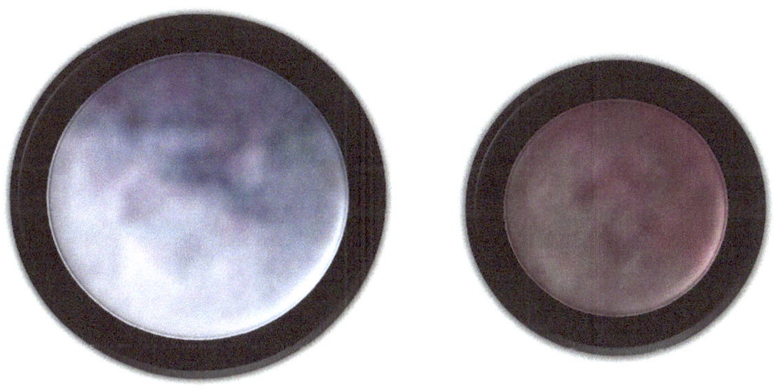

In Revelation 21:16, we read how "the city was laid out like a square, as long as it was wide." Shortly after I first saw the emblem on John's headpiece, I thought it resembled the New Jerusalem. Oftentimes when someone attempts to create a diagram of the Holy City, it comes across as straight and boring. I do think the structure of the city will be a square (or cube). The design, however, will have curves. If you think about it, pearls are sometimes round. As we have seen, the gates in the New Jerusalem will have a curve to them. The wall will have the texture of a gemstone mountain. It will look similar to what we have now, but it will be even more beautiful.

The beloved disciple, John, did not see a temple in the New Jerusalem because "the Lord God Almighty and the Lamb are its temple" (21:22). And His name will be on His servants' foreheads (22:4). Everything in the tabernacle and temple points to Jesus. Even the structure and design, I believe, embrace who He is. It is just a guess, but I think the design of the New Jerusalem contains the Lord's name. Actually, I think the Lord's name is the foundation for the design of the tabernacle, temple, and the New Jerusalem. When John tells us that His name will be on our foreheads, it could look like the emblem on the headpiece and wedding clothes. This, of course, is just my humble opinion. I don't think it will be a tattoo on the forehead. Rather, I think we will have clothing with emblems that represent what is in our hearts and minds.

The President of the United States generally wears an American flag pin on his lapel over his heart on the left. This shows his love and care for America and its citizens. The woman in the picture has the emblem of the New Jerusalem over her heart and her mind. Jesus said that the greatest commandment is to "love the Lord your God with all your heart and with all your soul and with all your mind" (Matthew 22:37).

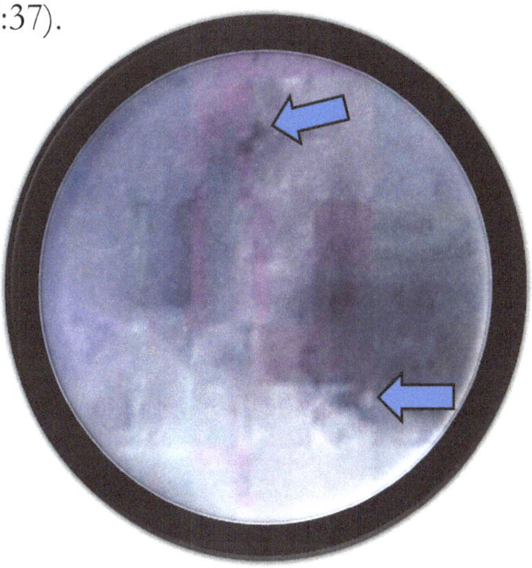

You may have also noticed a flower on the woman's hat and shoulder, each flower arranged on or around the emblem. This could be one of the most interesting discoveries I have made so far. Late last night I was admiring the flower, so I decided to try to learn its kind. First, I have to point out that I know nothing about Israel's flowers. So, I began to look at pictures of all kinds of flowers. I needed to find one that had a raised center and round petals. Since the color of the petals are darker in the picture, I was looking for something purple, magenta, or red. I finally found an anemone.

A few names for the "anemone" are the windflower, poppy anemone, and the lily of the field. When Jesus taught His disciples about worry, He said, "And why take ye thought for raiment? Consider the lilies of the field, how they grow; they toil not, neither do they spin: And yet I say unto you, That even Sol'-o-mon in all his glory was not arrayed like one of these" (Matthew 6:28-29, KJV).

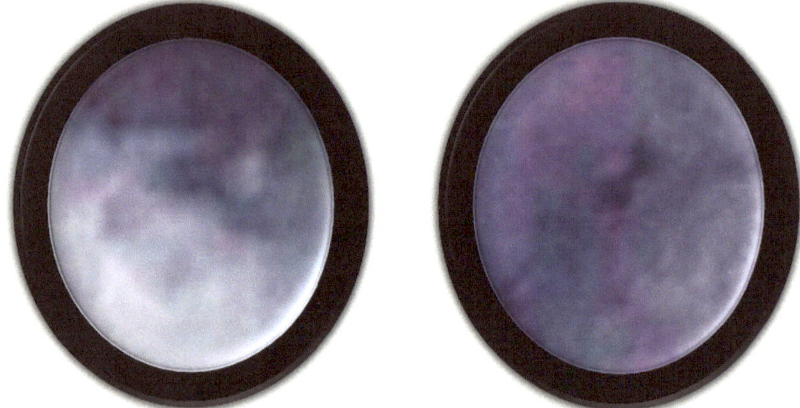

Traditionally, the *anemone coronaria* is known as the lily of the field. In Hebrew, the anemone is *kalanit metzuya* or calanit. It comes from the Hebrew word *kala*, which means "bride." Yes, it means "bride"! How amazing is that! The beauty of the anemone is like a majestic bride on her wedding day. It is the perfect flower for a crown (*coronaria*).

In 2013, the Society for the Protection of Nature conducted a poll where the *anemone coronaria* was elected Israel's national flower. Another name for this flower is the Jerusalem Red. Each spring the bright red flowers cover the southern fields in Israel. It couldn't be a more suitable fit for the bride of the Lamb than to wear this gorgeous national flower.

As you may recall, Jesus also taught His disciples not to worry about food (vv. 25-27). Rather, He told them to seek first the Kingdom of God and His righteousness. Then, all these things would be given to them (v. 33). Interestingly enough, in God's kingdom He will clothe us with fine linen before we attend the wedding supper of the Lamb. Our needs for both clothing and food will be gifts from our Beloved.

This has been a fascinating journey, don't you agree? If you remember back to chapter two, I initially covered up the bubble in the river. It's kind of funny how one often overlooks the important things the Lord is trying to say, especially when it's right in front of one's nose.

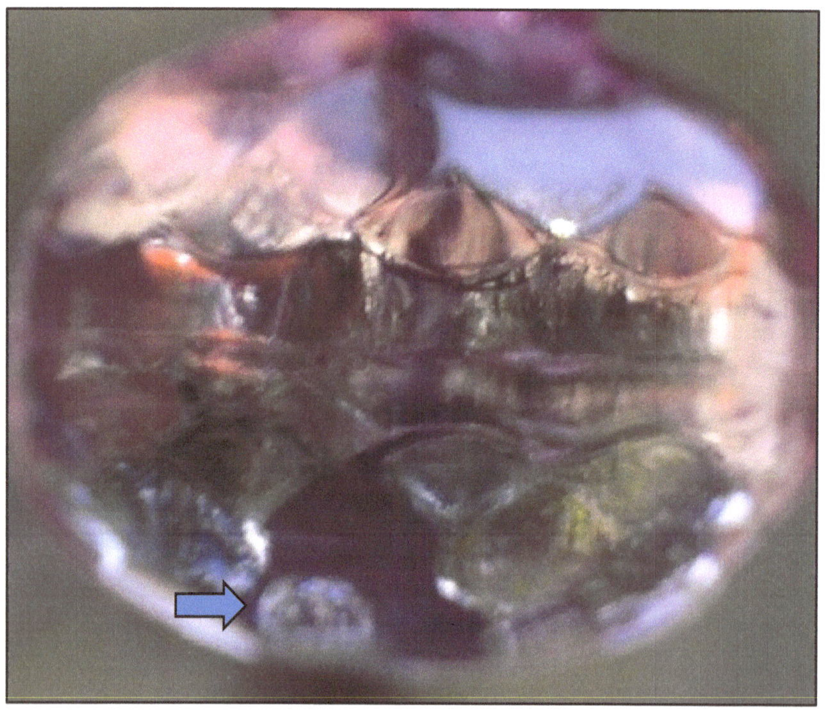

Several months ago, my husband was looking at the first photo on his computer. He suddenly called for me. He said, "Heidi, you have to see this!" There was something inside of the bubble. By this time, I had analyzed most of the pictures, but I had never looked inside of the bubble. I'm glad the thought crossed Kirk's mind because it is the most personal discovery for us both.

Ezekiel 47:9 tells us that "swarms of living creatures will live wherever the river flows." Well, there are several animals inside of the bubble. In fact, two of them are kittens.

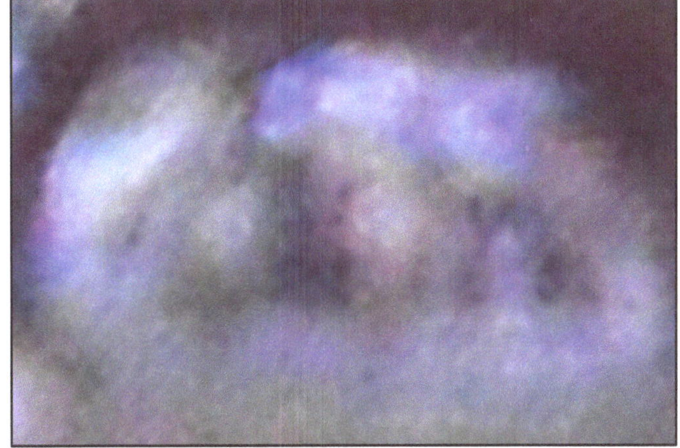

My study of Heaven began in 2008 after one of our cats passed away. My hope was that animals, especially our beloved pets, would go there. Well, I think the Lord has given me a very special answer since the two kittens in the picture are my two cats that passed away. Their names are Concha and Tame. (Tame is short for "Tamar" since I wanted her to have a biblical name.) Only a very loving Heavenly Father would have answered His little girl by putting her "kitties in a bubble." And they are right up front in the photo, a place of honor among the living creatures.

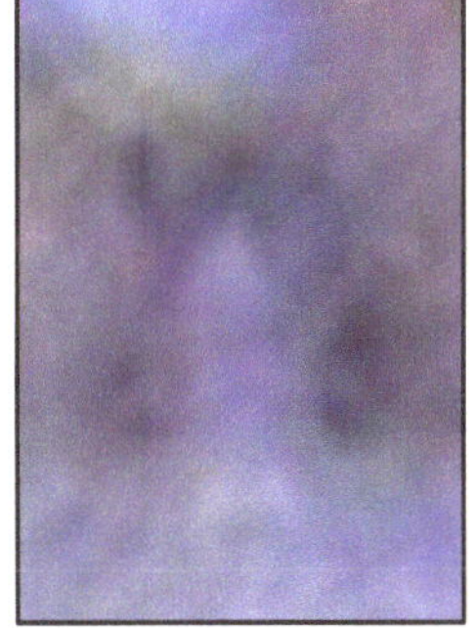

Concha & Tame

Since we are talking about animals, I would like to point out a fawn and a foal above the East Gate. The fawn is a part of its mother's face.

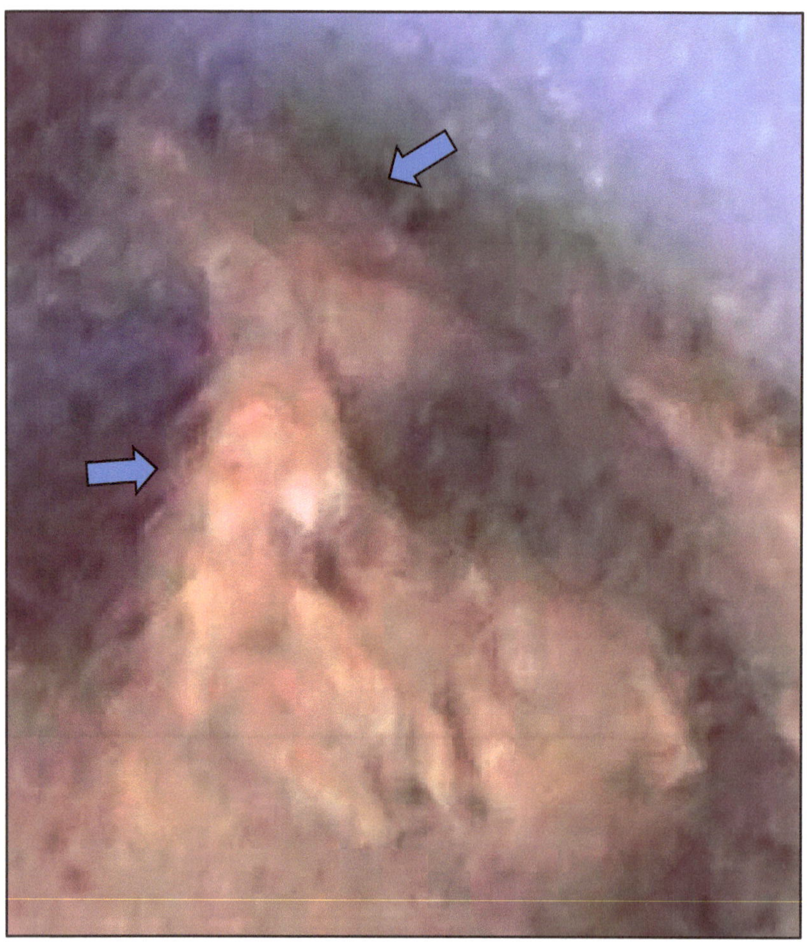

The foal is reaching its head up to its mother, like he is nudging her cheek. Remember, it was a foal and its mother that the Lord rode into Jerusalem (Matthew 21:5-7).

What a blessing to see so many animals in the Lord's kingdom! Why wouldn't they be there? They are, of course, a part of His creation. He loves them too.

It was Albert Einstein who said, "There are only two ways to live your life. One is as though nothing is a miracle. The other is as though everything is a miracle." He understood the intricacies of the universe better than most people. I do agree that life in and of itself is truly a miracle.

When we think of miracles in terms of what it is unusual or out of the ordinary, however, we should use caution. There are false signs, so we need to look at the fruit (Matthew 7:15-16; Galatians 5:22-23). Also, can it be found in Scripture? When I realized the photos were unusual, I considered whether they line up with the Bible. Also, what kind of fruit did they produce in my life? Since everything has been good and sound, I trust that the miracle pictures have come from the Lord.

When I was little, my mom used to sit on the edge of my bed and teach me a line from the Lord's prayer. We would say it together. Better yet, we would pray it together. Perhaps now more than ever the following words speak to my heart: "Our Father which art in heaven, Hallowed by thy name. Thy kingdom come. Thy will be done in earth, as it is in heaven" (Matthew 6:9-10, KJV).

Ever since our pilgrimage to Israel, Psalm 84 has meant so much to me. I especially love the verses that say, "Even the sparrow has found a home, and the swallow a nest for herself, where she may have her young—a place near your altar, Lord Almighty, my King and my God. Blessed are those who dwell in your house; they are ever praising you" (vv. 3-4).

During our button journey, we have had the opportunity to look inside of one of the Lord's gates where we found a little boy and his dog. Now let's walk through the gate (with thanksgiving, of course) and travel to the end of the tunnel. I have often wondered about the bright light.

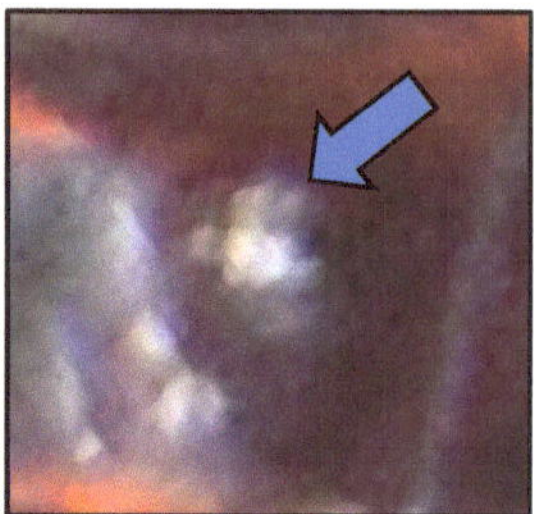

This last week, while enlarging some of the images in the river, I glanced at the end of the tunnel and noticed several distinct figures. As I zoomed in on their spot, which is only about 1/64 of an inch, I discovered angels!

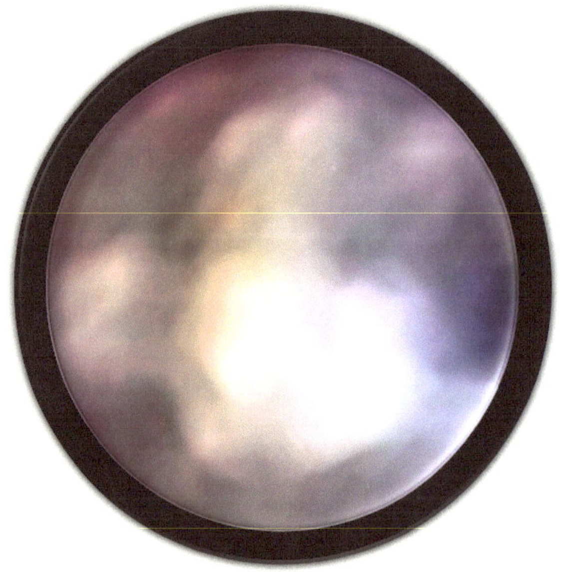

The angel on our right is the most obvious one. It looks like he is kneeling.

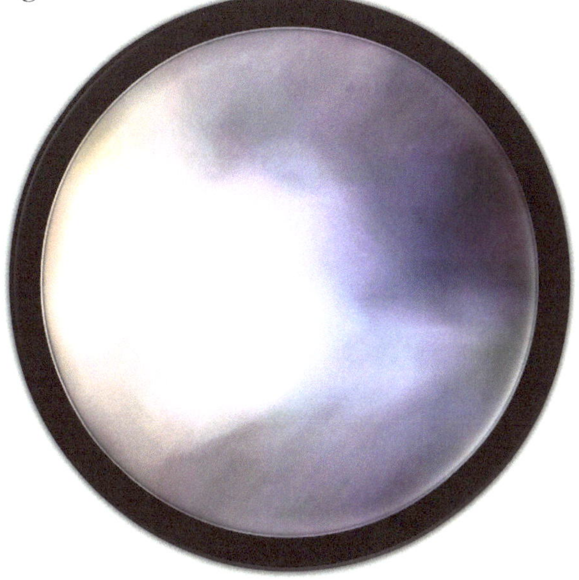

Right away I wondered about the hole in between his shoulder blades. Then I realized that his wings fold back. They form a circle while he is resting.

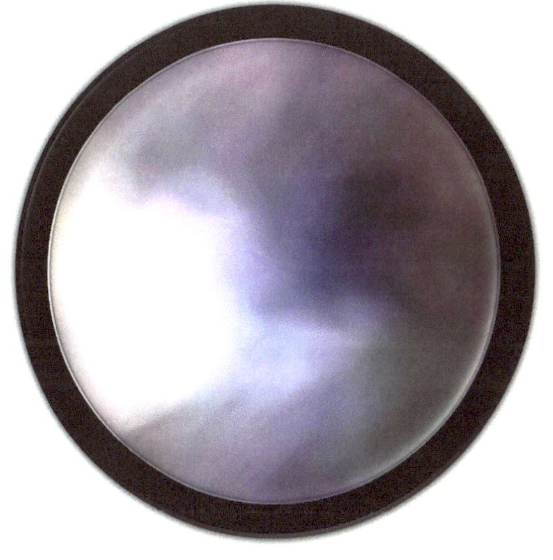

There is also a black lab next to the angel.

It certainly was a surprise to find another puppy! I couldn't figure out why he was there. Sure, God's kingdom has many animals, but why here? Why now?

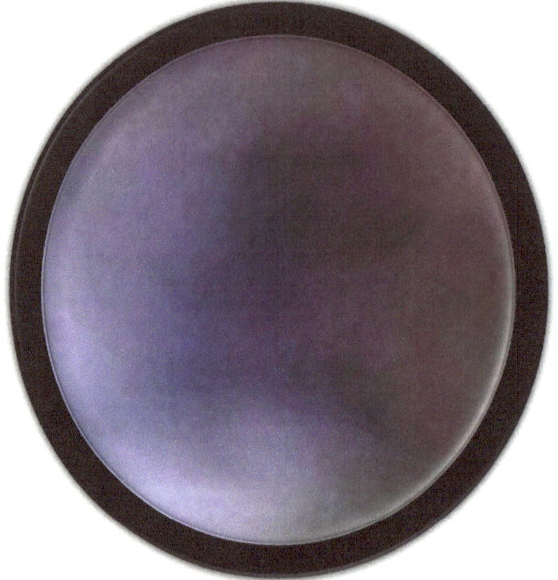

Revelation 7:11 tells us that "all the angels were standing around the throne and around the elders and the four living creatures. They fell down on their faces before the throne and worshiped God." According to the Strong's Concordance, the word "worship" in this verse is the Greek word *proskuneo*. It means "to kiss, like a dog licking his master's hand," "to fawn or crouch," "to prostrate oneself in homage (do reverence to, adore): —worship." Suddenly, the dog made complete sense. He is symbolic of heavenly worship!

I did a little research on Labrador retrievers and discovered that they are one of the most loyal dogs. And God's angels, of course, are loyal in their service to the Lord.

The colors have been saturated in several of the photos. Notice how the rainbow of colors starts on the left and moves across to the right.

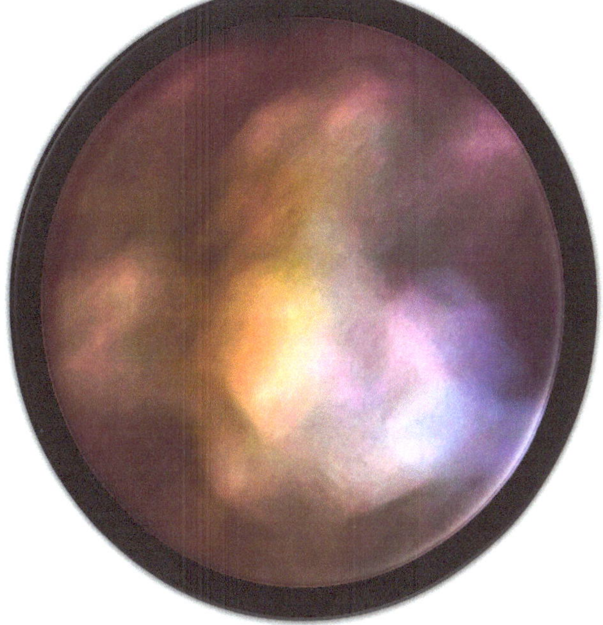

The angel below is looking over his shoulder.

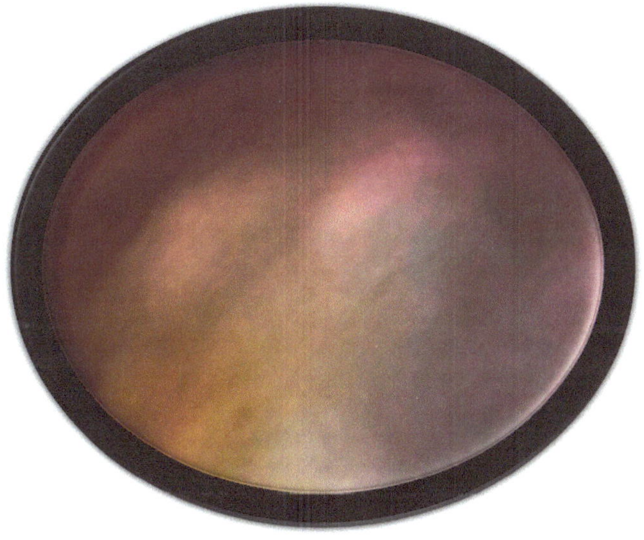

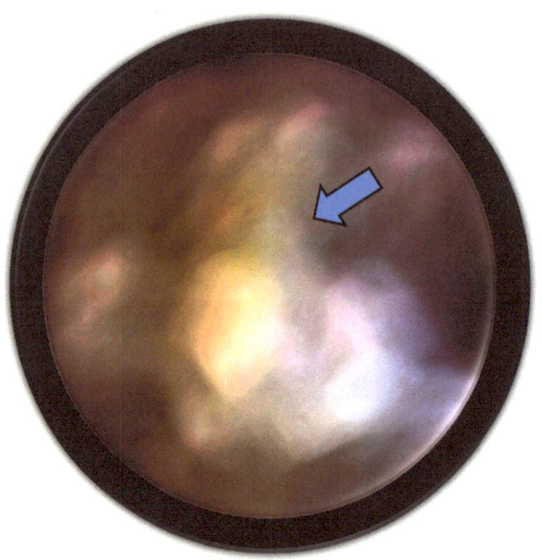

There is also a woman in the center of the photo. I believe she is receiving fine linen for the wedding of the Lamb. Her clothes are clean and white. They are also bright, probably from the glory of the Lord. The two angels on our left look like they are arranging her gown.

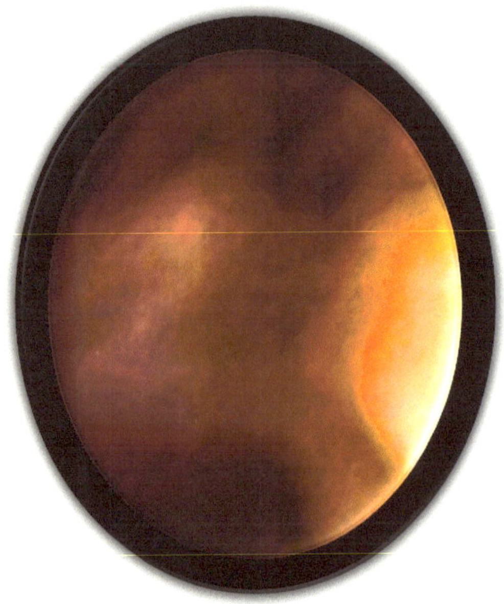

It is also interesting to note the floral image. It is over the woman's heart and mind, but this time it makes up the base of her crown.

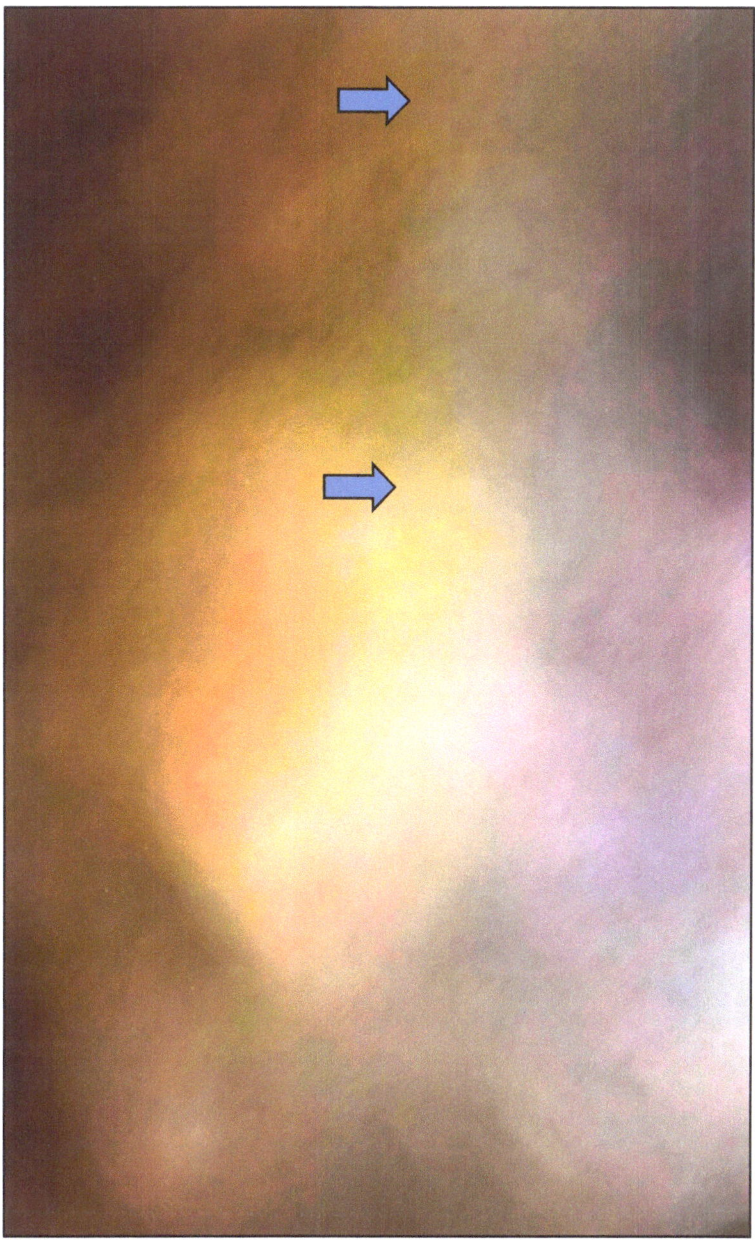

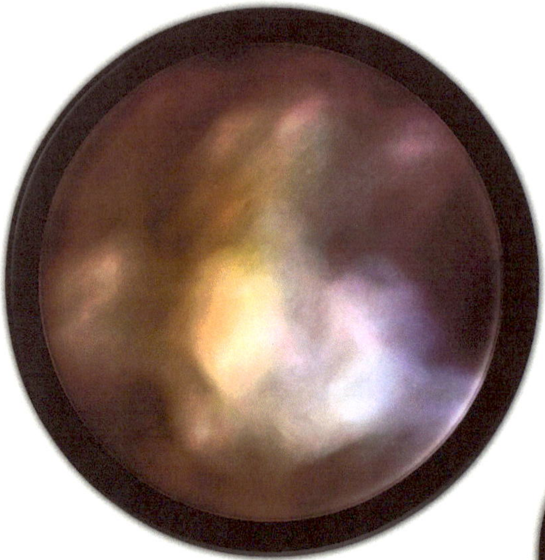

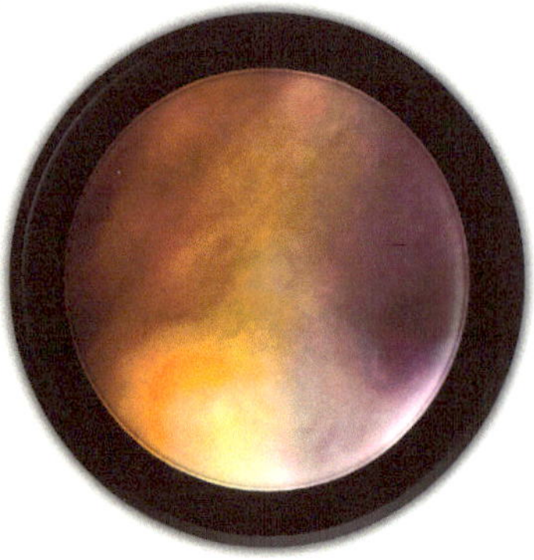

Her crown is enormous, so she must be a very special person.

As a reward, God will give His faithful people at least one of five heavenly crowns: the incorruptible crown, the crown of righteousness, crown of life, crown of glory, or the crown of rejoicing.

A few years ago, we taught a children's lesson on crowns, so I decided to pull out our notes. Let's begin with the incorruptible crown. In order to receive this crown, people will have to make some sacrifices (1 Corinthians 9:24-27). For example, an athlete has to eat right and train. He cannot eat cookies and sit on the couch all day. He has to work out. God will ask us to give up certain things to do His will. Missionaries suddenly come to mind since they choose to give up the comforts of home to serve in a foreign country.

The next crown is the crown of righteousness. We become "righteous" or "right with God" through Jesus. When I was a little girl, the following verse hung on the wall beside my bed. I used to read it every night: "For the ways of the Lord are right; the righteous walk in them" (Hosea 14:9). This crown is given to those who enjoy a close walk with the Lord and look forward to His return. The apostle Paul says, "Now there is in store for me the crown of righteousness, which the Lord, the righteous Judge, will award to me on that day—and not only to me, but also to all who have longed for his appearing" (2 Timothy 4:8).

The third crown is the crown of life. Some people call it the "martyr's crown" or "victor's crown." This will be given to people who suffer severe hardship, testing, tribulation, and even physical death for their faith (James 1:12; Revelation 2:10).

The fourth crown is the crown of glory. This will be given to those who shepherd and teach the flock (1 Peter 5:1-4).

And the last crown is the crown of rejoicing, also known as the "soul winner's crown." People who share the good news of Jesus outside the church will receive this one. "For what is our hope, our joy, or the crown in which we will glory in the presence of our Lord Jesus when he comes? Is it not you? Indeed, you are our glory and joy" (1 Thessalonians 2:19-20).

I came across this image the other night. A couple of weeks ago, I cropped it and labeled it "lady." Finally, two nights ago, I got around to enlarging it…and what a discovery. I quickly called my husband into the room. He said, "It looks like you!" As I look at the picture, I can see a much younger, much lovelier version of myself. Funny enough, there is a faint image of a young man smiling at her, and he resembles Kirk when we were dating. We both laughed. Only God could have placed us in His heavenly picture.

For years I have struggled with my hair. It is naturally very wavy, so I have straightened it and curled it, always trying to figure out an easy day-to-day solution. If this is in fact me, then my wavy hair has finally found a manageable style. This alone makes me very happy!

What is interesting about God's artwork is how He layers the images. Details are often intricately woven. When I first saw the photo, I noticed a woman looking down, her skirt blowing in the wind. Kirk saw something different. He described a woman sitting or kneeling. He saw her back, and there were two long white sleeves of a dress. Instead of looking down, she was looking up. Of course, both interpretations are correct. The images often represent movement or the passing of time. For example, in this photo the woman is in a windstorm. Then, suddenly, she has changed into a white gown and has a joyful countenance. When the Lord returns, I believe it will be very windy. In 1 Corinthians 15:51-52, it says, "Listen, I tell you a mystery: We will not all sleep, but we will all be changed—in a flash, in the twinkling of an eye, at the last trumpet. For the trumpet will sound, the dead will be raised imperishable, and we will be changed."

Her crown is also worth mentioning. It looks like glass. In fact, it reminds me of "the city of pure gold, as pure as glass" (Revelation 21:18). When I first saw the crown I thought it looked kind of small, but then I realized that the points extend across her head. It really is beautiful!

In addition to crowns, God's people will receive white clothing. Revelation 19:8 says that the bride of Christ will "be arrayed in fine linen, clean and white" (KJV).

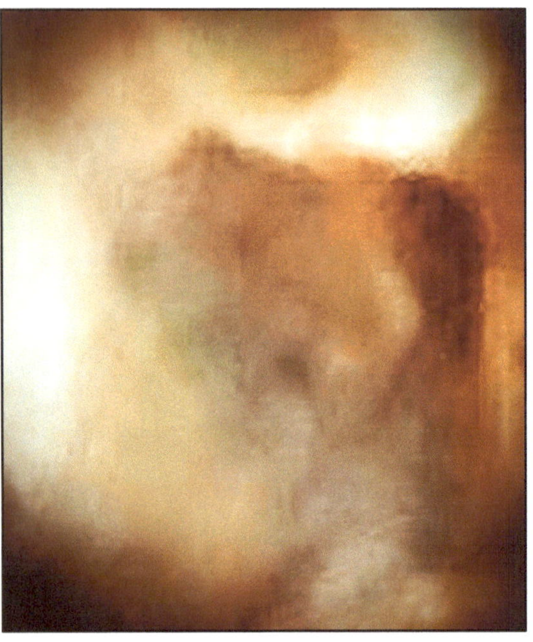

Please note how the sleeves on the woman's dress resemble a robe. In Revelation 7:9, we learn that "a great multitude that no one could count, from every nation, tribe, people and language, [were] standing before the throne and before the Lamb. They were wearing white robes and were holding palm branches in their hands." So, who are these people? Apparently, they died during the tribulation (v. 14). Although the details are not given, it is likely that they died for their faith. Even though death, especially a death of this kind, is a troubling thought, we can find comfort in knowing that "they are before the throne of God and serve him day and night in his temple; and he who sits on the throne will shelter them with his presence" (v. 15).

It seems as though the world has become increasingly unsettled, and yet my heart is at rest. The thought of Heaven brings me peace. King David tells us that "the life of mortals is like grass, they flourish like a flower of the field; the wind blows over it and it is gone, and its place remembers it no more" (Psalm 103:15-16). God's love, however, is everlasting (v. 17). He crowns us with His love and compassion forever (v. 4).

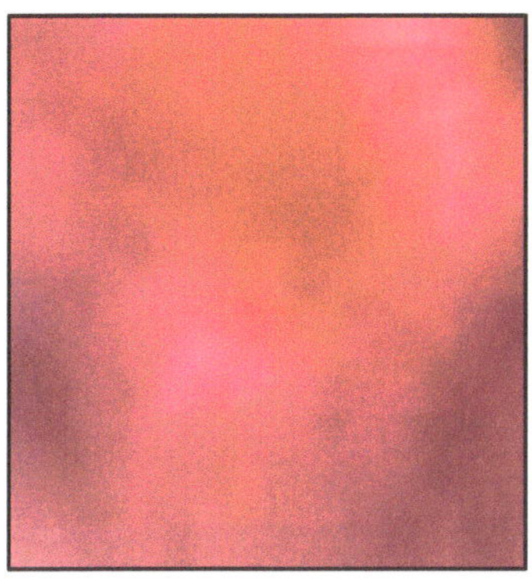

Kitten

Before we say goodbye, I have to mention the little cutie pie in the picture. She is actually sitting on my lap. When I realized she was there, any doubts I had about the person in the photo suddenly melted away. I haven't met this particular kitty yet, but perhaps she will join my family here on earth. If not, I look forward to sharing a seat with her in the New Jerusalem.

"Give thanks to the Lord,
for he is good.
His love endures forever."

Psalm 136:1

I also discovered one more cutie pie.

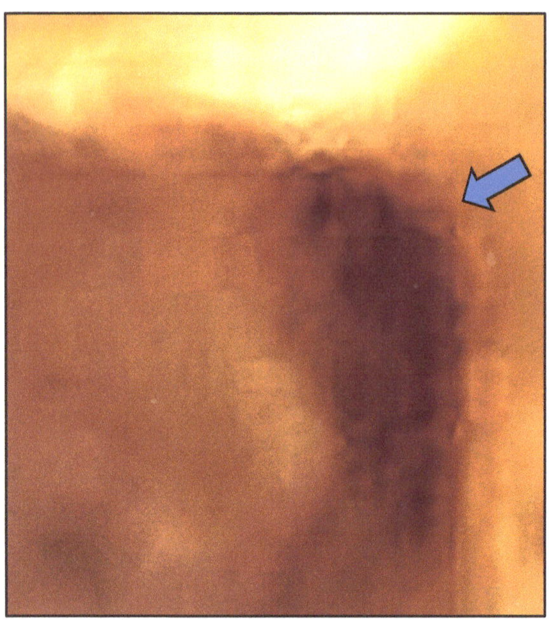

At first I thought it was a raccoon or cat, but then I realized it may have round ears. After giving it some thought, I decided it could be a koala bear in my hair. Actually, he is likely resting on my shoulder. How sweet is that! I do hope to work with God's creatures in His kingdom.

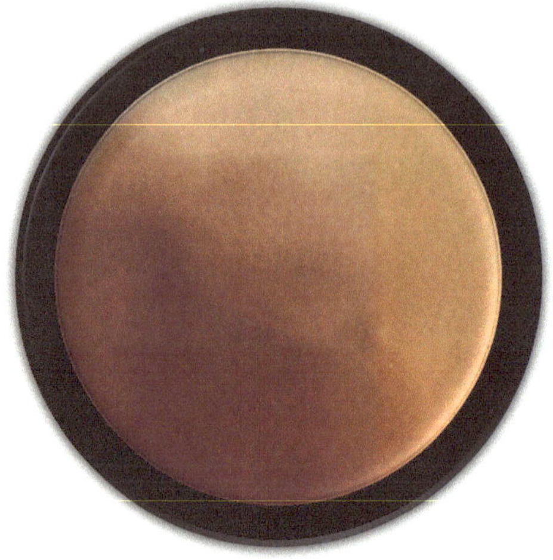

Shortly after I discovered the koala (or cat), I cropped a picture of a dog. Since the setting was dark, I decided to use the bleach filter. Suddenly, a whole city appeared!

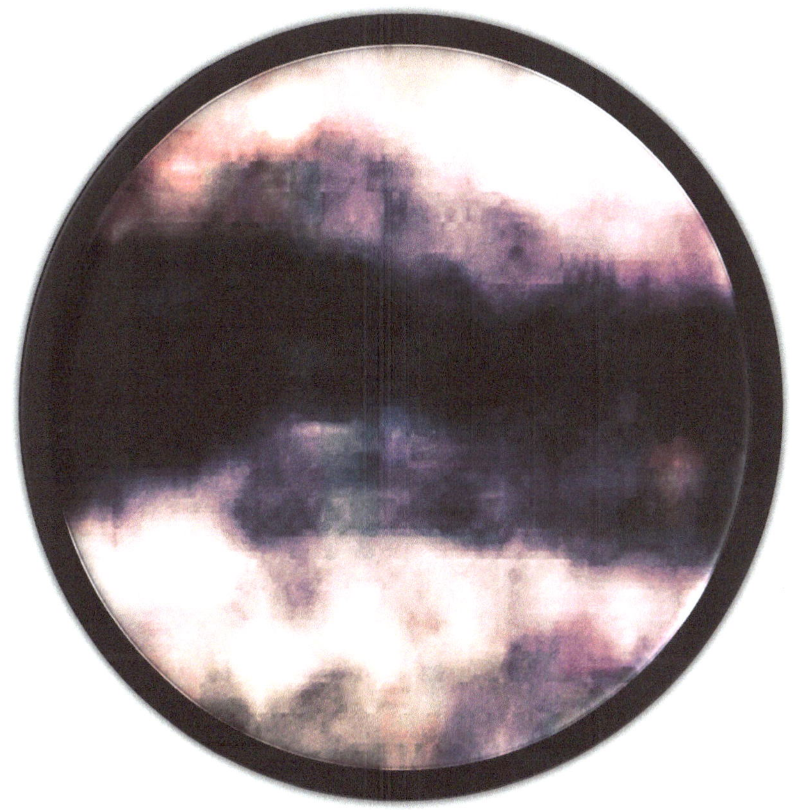

Of course, the Lord tells us that He will resettle towns and rebuild ruins (Ezekiel 36:33). "His kingdom will never end" (Luke 1:33). The cities we see in this photo are outside of the New Jerusalem. In fact, He will rule and reign over the entire Earth. And yet the New Jerusalem will always be dear to Him. It will forever be the city God loves.

Bibliography

Alcorn, Randy. *Heaven.* Carol Streams: Tyndale House Publishers, Inc., 2004.

Boice, James Montgomery. *Psalms, An Expositional Commentary.* Vol. 2. Grand Rapids: Baker Books, 1996.

Eisenman, Robert, & Michael Wise. "The New Jerusalem." Dead Sea Scrolls Uncovered. Bibliotecapleyades.net, 1992.

Graham, Billy. *Angels, God's Secret Agents.* Waco: Word Book, 1986.

Moore, Beth. *A Woman's Heart, God's Dwelling Place.* Nashville: LifeWay Press, 2007.

Shepherd, David R. *Ezekiel.* Nashville: B&H Publishing Group, 1998.

Shepherd, David R. *Isaiah.* Nashville: B&H Publishing Group, 1998.

Shepherd, David R. *Revelation.* Nashville: B&H Publishing Group, 1999.

Strong, James. *Strong's New Exhaustive Concordance of the Bible.* Madison: World Bible Publishers, Inc., 1980.

Young, Edward J. *The Prophecy of Daniel, A Commentary.* Grand Rapids: Wm. B. Eerdmans Publishing Company, 1949.

www.ingramcontent.com/pod-product-compliance
Lightning Source LLC
LaVergne TN
LVHW052250100826
845147LV00001B/5

* 9 7 8 0 9 9 7 2 1 2 1 1 2 *